Koufax Throws
a Curve

Koufax Throws a Curve

The Los Angeles Dodgers
at the End of an Era, 1964–1966

BRIAN M. ENDSLEY

McFarland & Company, Inc., Publishers
Jefferson, North Carolina

All photographs courtesy National Baseball Hall of Fame Library,
Cooperstown, New York.

Library of Congress Cataloguing-in-Publication Data

Names: Endsley, Brian M.
Title: Koufax throws a curve : the Los Angeles Dodgers
at the end of an era, 1964–1966 / Brian M. Endsley.
Description: Jefferson, North Carolina : McFarland & Company, Inc.,
Publishers, 2018. | Includes bibliographical references and index.
Identifiers: LCCN 2018000287 | ISBN 9781476669427
(softcover : acid free paper) ∞
Subjects: LCSH: Koufax, Sandy, 1935– | Baseball players—United
States—Biography. | Pitchers (Baseball)—United States—Biography. |
Los Angeles Dodgers (Baseball team)—History—20th century.
Classification: LCC GV865.K67 E64 2018 | DDC 796.357/640979494—dc23
LC record available at https://lccn.loc.gov/2018000287

British Library cataloguing data are available

ISBN (print) 978-1-4766-6942-7
ISBN (ebook) 978-1-4766-3239-1

Front cover image of Sandy Koufax after his perfect game
of September 9, 1965, at Dodger Stadium—the fourth no-hitter of his career
(National Baseball Hall of Fame Library, Cooperstown, New York)

Printed in the United States of America

*McFarland & Company, Inc., Publishers
Box 611, Jefferson, North Carolina 28640
www.mcfarlandpub.com*

Table of Contents

Preface

This is the third and final book on the history of the Los Angeles Dodgers in the Sandy Koufax era: 1958 to 1966.

Bums No More: The 1959 Los Angeles Dodgers, World Champions of Baseball covered the Dodgers' first two years on the West Coast from their seventh-place finish in 1958 to their remarkable turnaround season of 1959, culminating in a miracle World Championship–the final triumph of the transplanted *Boys of Summer*.

Finding the Left Arm of God: Sandy Koufax and the Los Angeles Dodgers, 1960–1963 told the story of the Dodgers' volatile fortunes during the transformation of Sandy Koufax from a wild, young left-hander with a career losing record to an artist with a baseball. In 1960, the Dodgers plunged back into the baseball wilderness after their 1959 World Championship season. The aging *Boys of Summer* rapidly declined while a new generation of exciting young players such as Frank Howard and the "Davis Boys," Tommy and Willie, arrived on the scene. A 24-year-old Sandy Koufax struggled through his worst—and nearly his last—season. In 1961, the team returned to pennant contention in their last year in the Los Angeles Memorial Coliseum. This year saw the metamorphosis of a *new* Sandy Koufax: from the turning point in spring training when he discovered the art of controlling the baseball; to his emergence as an All-Star; to his breaking of a 52-year-old league record for strikeouts in a season. The Dodgers' first year in Dodger Stadium, 1962 was a year of triumph and tragedy for perhaps the finest Los Angeles Dodgers team with Maury Wills as the new major league stolen base king, Don Drysdale as the Cy Young Award winner, and Tommy Davis as the batting champion and most prolific run producer in the National League since 1937. It was a year that also saw the crippling effect of losing Sandy Koufax to a freak, amputation-threatening finger injury at mid-season that set the team on a collision course to a year-end collapse, culminating in a catastrophic post-season playoff defeat to the San Francisco Giants. The year 1963 saw the dramatic resurrection of the Los Angeles Dodgers from maligned "choke artists" to World Champions again as Sandy Koufax blossomed fully into baseball's greatest pitcher.

The present work completes the story. We travel through the "Lost Year" of 1964 in which the defending World Champion Dodgers disintegrate, beginning with the meltdown of their principal power hitter, Frank Howard, in spring training. This is soon followed by the loss of manager Walter Alston's "money pitcher," Johnny Podres, to an elbow injury. Koufax carries the team until he himself hurts his left elbow in a freak accident sliding into a base in Milwaukee on August 8. It is believed that this blow to the elbow triggered a traumatic arthritis condition that would eventually cut short his career. Koufax, on his way to another Cy Young Award season, is shut down a week later with a 19–5 record. Los Angeles finishes the disastrous 1964 season with its first losing record since 1958.

In 1965, the Dodgers begin the season with the physical condition of Sandy Koufax again the most important question: Will the game's best pitcher be relegated to the status of a "Sunday pitcher" with an arthritic elbow? The trainers come up with an ingenious hot-cold regimen employing a post-game "ice bath" to restore Koufax to an every-fourth-day starter. The result is a year of historic proportions: a 26–8 record, a perfect game, and a major league record 382 strikeouts. Koufax and Drysdale (23–12) will propel the Dodgers to their fourth World Championship. Their combined 49–20 record remains one of the best by a modern 1–2 combination.

The year 1966 begins ominously with the groundbreaking joint holdout by Koufax and Drysdale prior to the season, with an agent demanding a three-year deal for $1 million, to be split evenly. It is a major distraction that lasts until two weeks before Opening Day, when they dismiss the agent and sign individual one-year contracts. The Dodgers' already formidable pitching rotation of Koufax, Drysdale, and Osteen is joined by a 20-year-old, rookie right-hander named Don Sutton. They clinch the pennant on the last day of the season, only to be swept away by the Baltimore Orioles in the World Series. The story ends on November 18, 1966, when Koufax calls a press conference to make a shocking announcement. In Dodgers history, this day will be forever known as Black Friday.

Prologue

Dodger Stadium, October 6, 1963, 3:50 P.M.

Sandy Koufax has just retired Hector Lopez to win Game 4 of 1963 World Series, 2–1, and complete the Dodgers' four-game sweep of the New York Yankees—the first time the mighty Bronx Bombers have been swept. Only a titanic solo home run by Mickey Mantle in the seventh inning prevented a second straight Dodgers shutout. The Dodgers used only four pitchers in the Series: starters Koufax, Johnny Podres, and Don Drysdale; and reliever Ron Perranoski. Against this quartet, the Yankees could manage only four runs, and struck out 37 times in the four games. The Series was a tour de force for Koufax. He won two of the four games and struck out 23 batters—including a Series-record 15 in Game 1 at Yankee Stadium. He was named the Most Valuable Player of the Series.

On October 24, a select committee of the Baseball Writers' Association of America made Sandy Koufax the first unanimous winner of the Cy Young Award. Six days later, the BBWAA also named him the National League's Most Valuable Player. Life was good for the World Champion Dodgers as they headed into what would be a momentous month of November. Several of the players were scheduled to open the Joey Bishop show in Las Vegas beginning December 21—nine days before Koufax would turn twenty-eight.[1] There was talk of a baseball dynasty in Los Angeles.

1

Off with a Bang, and Off a Cliff

I don't like to get off to a bad start.[1]—Walter Alston, April 19, 1964

When the new year of 1964 arrived, America was still in mourning over the assassination of President John F. Kennedy that shook the nation in Dallas on November 22. On that same day, Vice President Lyndon Baines Johnson succeeded him as the 36th President of the United States. On February 7, 1964, an English rock band called *The Beatles* arrived at the newly-named John F. Kennedy Airport in New York City. Two days later, the largest American television audience in history—73 million or 34 percent of the American population—watched the group's first U.S. television performance on *The Ed Sullivan Show*. On February 25, 21-year-old Cassius Clay became boxing's heavyweight champion with a stunning technical knockout of the heavily favored Sonny Liston in Miami.[2] Two days later in Paris, French Foreign Minister Maurice Couve de Murville warned that there was no possibility of a military conclusion to the guerrilla war in Vietnam: "It is difficult to believe that the United States can win with 20,000 men where France failed with 200,000."[3] His warning would go unheeded.

Spring Training—Early Warning Signs

When the World Champion Dodgers officially opened spring training on March 1 at Vero Beach, they were heavily favored to win the 1964 National League pennant. However, there were some early warning signs that this was too optimistic. The first sign was evident that first day: where was their principal power hitter, Frank Howard?

Exile in Green Bay

The 27-year-old Frank Howard was still at home in Green Bay, Wisconsin, with his wife, Carol, and their four children ages 4, 2½, 1½, and seven months. No, he wasn't a holdout. Money was not an issue. After he spent seven months during the season on the road and another seven weeks during the winter in a Dodgers night-club act in Las Vegas, his wife wanted him to give up the game and settle down in her home town of Green Bay. He had written a letter to Buzzie Bavasi asking for a two-week moratorium to deal with some "business and personal problems." On March 2, when asked to comment on rumors that he was contemplating retirement from baseball so that he could spend more

5

time with his family, he reassured the *Los Angeles Times* by telephone, "I want to play and I most certainly expect to—just as soon as I clear up these pressing problems at home."[4]

Ten days later, on March 12, Bavasi received a second letter from Howard. In it he told the Dodgers' general manager, "With deep regret, I am quitting baseball. My mind is made up."[5] A few hours after Bavasi leaked the letter to reporters in Los Angeles, Howard began to hedge in Green Bay: "It was my intention to go down to Vero Beach and talk with Bavasi to get some guidance and advice. Now I don't know what I'm going to do. I may just quit and not see Bavasi."[6] The next day he told the *Associated Press,* "Spring training is well advanced and I'm so far out of shape both mentally and physically that it would be virtually impossible for me to play."[7] By now, shock waves were reverberating through the organization. The Dodgers were depending on Howard to supply much-needed offensive power. They were seventh in the National League in 1963 with 110 home runs. Frank Howard hit 28 of these, though he was still being platooned playing 111 games in the outfield.

The year 1964 was to be the fifth full major league season for Howard. After starring in basketball and baseball at Ohio State, and putting up some jaw-dropping power numbers for two years in the minors, the Dodgers' "Boy Giant" came up to the big club for good in 1960 to win the NL Rookie of the Year Award with 23 home runs in only 117 games. He hit 15 home runs in 92 games in 1961, and 31 home runs with 119 RBI in 141 games in 1962. That he had never played a complete season with the Dodgers was a sore point with him.

The Dodgers' principal power hitter, Frank Howard, threatens to quit baseball before the 1964 season at age 27.

As the days ticked away, financial considerations began to weigh on Howard. He was contemplating going to work full-time with the Green Bay Packaging Corporation, a paper firm that employed him in the off-season. He would be walking away from his $22,000 annual baseball salary that was likely to be increased substantially with a new contract. If he played a fifth season, he would qualify for the major league players' pension. After his employer, George Macklin, of Green Bay Packaging advised him that his best future was in baseball, he began to waiver further on his decision to leave the game. In a March 24 telephone conference, Howard told Bavasi, "I want to play."[8] His four-week retirement was over.

On the evening of March 28, an overweight, 6'7", 255-pound Frank Howard arrived at Vero Beach with two weeks left in spring training. The next day he told reporters, "I had a good year, and

I think I deserve a raise."[9] Fearing that they might lose him to the Milwaukee Braves—their rival that played half of its games 120 miles from Green Bay—the Dodgers presented him with a contract for $30,000, a hefty $8,000 increase. The Dodgers were well aware that Howard expected to get a chance to play every day as the team's regular right fielder. Bavasi quickly diffused the platooning issue, saying, "He's our big offensive threat; we want to play him as much as Frank wants to play."[10] With the Frank Howard meltdown contained, the Dodgers could now prepare in earnest for 1964 season.

On April 9, the Dodgers sold 1959 World Series MVP Larry Sherry to the Detroit Tigers for $10,000 cash. Thrown into the deal was a journeyman minor league outfielder named Lou Johnson. Johnson was immediately optioned to Spokane, his 18th different team since he broke into baseball in 1953.[11]

Genesis of the Podres Elbow Problem

On Sunday, April 12, the Dodgers played their last spring exhibition game against the Angels at Dodger Stadium. Johnny Podres, the 31-year-old, veteran left-hander and key member of Alston's rotation, started for the Dodgers against the Angels' notorious playboy left-hander, Bo Belinsky. From the first pitch of this meaningless game, the Dodgers' pitching picture and pennant hopes changed dramatically. Podres strained his left elbow when he decided to change his delivery to pitch to the Angels' diminutive, 5'7", left-handed-batting leadoff man, Albie Pearson. After facing three more batters, he was forced to leave the game. The Dodgers' team doctor, Robert Kerlan, told reporters that a simple cortisone injection would make Podres ready to start the third game of the regular season.[12] In fact, Podres would not be ready to pitch until the team's 11th game on April 25.

Ominously, the Dodgers finished the spring exhibition season in dead last, with a 9–16 (.360) record.

Off with a Bang on Opening Night

The season opened with the St. Louis Cardinals on Tuesday night, April 14, before a crowd of 50,451 at Dodger Stadium. For the first time since World War II, Stan Musial was not in the starting lineup for St. Louis. Musial, who had retired at the end of the previous season, was on hand as a new Cardinals Vice President.

The Dodgers' starting lineup reflected several changes from the previous year. After Koufax won the Cy Young and Most Valuable Player Awards, Alston rewarded him with his first Opening Day assignment. Ex–USC Trojan John Werhas made his major league debut at third base. It was the eighth consecutive year that the Dodgers opened the season with a new third baseman. Thirty-five-year-old Jim Gilliam, who arrived at Vero Beach in March as a coach, was reactivated as the Dodgers' starting second baseman. Frank Howard, with only two weeks of spring training, started in right field. Ron Fairly moved from the outfield to first base to supplant Bill Skowron, now with the Washington Senators after being sold by the Dodgers for an estimated $25,000 cash in December.[13]

Opening Day Line-Ups

	April 14, 1964		April 9, 1963	
1	Maury Wills	SS	Maury Wills	SS
2	Jim Gilliam	2B	Nate Oliver	2B
3	Willie Davis	CF	Willie Davis	CF
4	Tommy Davis	LF	Tommy Davis	LF
5	Ron Fairly	1B	Bill Skowron	1B
6	Frank Howard	RF	John Roseboro	C
7	John Roseboro	C	Ron Fairly	RF
8	Johnny Werhas	3B	Ken McMullen	3B
9	Sandy Koufax	P	Don Drysdale	P

Koufax continued where he left off the previous October with a six-hit, 4–0 shutout. Only one Cardinal reached second base. Big Frank Howard hit a 400-foot, two-run home run off Cardinals reliever Ron Taylor in the eighth inning to put the game out of reach. All appeared to be well in Dodger Nation.

The next night at Dodger Stadium, things quickly began to go south. What was a tight pitcher's duel between Don Drysdale and Bob Gibson for seven innings was turned into a 6–2 loss when the Cardinals got to Drysdale for five runs in the eighth. Granted, it was only the second game of the season, but for the first time since July 1, 1963, the Dodgers were not in first place. The slide was on. The Dodgers had begun a seven-game losing streak.

After the Opening Night shutout, Koufax lost his next two decisions and then missed his next two subsequent starts due to epicondylitis, a condition caused by tearing a muscle in his forearm in an aborted, one-inning start on April 22 in St. Louis. In the sixth inning of that game, rookie outfielder-first baseman Wes Parker got his first major league hit, a pinch-hit double batting right-handed against Curt Simmons.

The other left-hander

Sandy Koufax is rewarded with the 1964 opening night assignment after leading the Dodgers to a four-game sweep over the Yankees in the 1963 World Series and winning both the Cy Young and Most Valuable Player Awards.

the Dodgers were counting on, Johnny Podres, was finally able to start his first game on April 25 at County Stadium in Milwaukee, facing Warren Spahn. In the third inning, Spahn hit Podres with a fastball in the exact spot he had injured his elbow at the end of spring training. Podres had to be removed and would miss the next 20 games. The Dodgers lost, 5–1. It was the ninth loss in their last ten games. They ended the month of April in ninth place with a 6–10 record, while Gene Mauch's surprising Philadelphia Phillies powerhouse stood atop the heap in the National League.

Sandy Koufax and the Dodgers continued to drift in May. On May 27, Koufax lost, 1–0, in Cincinnati to fall to an even .500 for the season at 4–4. The next night, the Dodgers finished their three-game series at Crosley Field with an inconclusive 17-inning, 2–2 tie to find themselves seven games out in ninth place. On the last day of May, Koufax caught fire and began an 11-game winning streak with a 5–4 victory over the Pirates at Forbes Field. The Dodgers ended May in seventh place with a 21–23 record. They had a team batting average of .236. Tommy Davis, the 1962 and 1963 NL batting champion, was hitting just .258 with 19 runs batted in.

2

The Light Goes Out in August

"I can't say how long it will be before he is sound, but it probably won't be before the season is over.[1]—Dr. Robert Kerlan on Sandy Koufax, August 1964

Twenty-eight-year-old Sandy Koufax would be the lone bright spot in the black hole into which the 1964 Los Angeles Dodgers descended.

The Third Koufax No-Hitter

The defending World Champions were in seventh place when they arrived at Connie Mack Stadium in Philadelphia on June 2 for a three-game series with the league-leading Phillies. The Dodgers lost the first two games, including a tough, 11-inning, 1–0 loss charged to hard-luck Don Drysdale, who pitched 10⅓ innings without giving up an earned run. The club was eight games behind when Sandy Koufax (5–4) took the mound in the June 4 finale against Philadelphia's premier left-hander, Chris Short (3–2), who came into the game with a microscopic 0.64 earned run average—the lowest in baseball.

Warming up before the game, it was evident to Koufax that he would have great stuff that night.[2] In fact, he would come within one pitch of a perfect game. In the bottom of the fourth inning, after falling behind, 3–0, to rookie sensation Richie Allen, he eventually walked him on a close 3–2 call on the seventh pitch, a fastball three inches below the strike zone. But Allen—who would go on to win the NL Rookie of the Year Award—was thrown out by Dodgers backup catcher, and Koufax roommate, Doug Camilli while attempting to steal second base. Koufax thus faced the minimum of 27 batters as he proceeded to retire the next 15 batters in order over the final five innings. Allen was also involved in the nearest thing to a hit. With two outs in the seventh, he hit a high chopper along the third base line—a potential infield single—that Jim Gilliam charged, grabbed on the short-hop, and threw to first to retire the side.[3] The game was a tense, scoreless tie through the first six innings, with Koufax working on a no-hitter and Short pitching a three-hit shutout. Frank Howard—who came to the plate in the top of the seventh with one hit in his previous 29 at bats—put the game out of reach with a mammoth three-run homer that landed on top of the arched pavilion in left-center field.[4]

As the ninth inning began, the Philadelphia crowd was noticeably rooting for Koufax to make history. Leadoff batter Tony Taylor tried to bunt the first pitch, but held up when the ball darted into the dirt. He fouled off the next three pitches but went down swinging on a 2–2 fastball. When Koufax disposed of Ruben Amaro on one pitch—a foul popup caught by first baseman Ron Fairly—the crowd roared in anticipation. Down to his last out, Phillies manager Gene Mauch sent utility man Bobby Wine up to pinch-hit for the pitcher. Wine took the first pitch for a ball—high and out of the strike zone. He fouled the second pitch off the leg of plate umpire Ed Vargo. With Vargo writhing in agony behind the plate, surrounded by his fellow umpires and both trainers, the game had to be delayed for several minutes.[5] One out away from a no-hitter, Koufax was able to maintain his concentration during the delay. When play resumed, he struck out Wine, swinging, on two fastballs to complete his third no-hitter.

Koufax struck out 12 Phillies while employing just two pitches: a cruel, 12-to-6 curve and a rising fastball. Only four balls were hit out of the infield—all fly outs. He was behind in the count on only five batters. It took him 97 pitches to dispose of the league-leading Phillies in one hour and 55 minutes. After the game, Mauch told reporters, "If you're going to have a no-hitter pitched against you, you might as well have it done by the greatest pitcher in the world."[6]

In Sandy Koufax's third no-hitter on June 4, 1964, in Philadelphia, Richie Allen drew a fourth-inning walk to spoil a perfect game. Allen went on to win the NL Rookie of the Year Award.

On Losing Podres

On June 11, Dr. Robert Kerlan removed a marble-sized bone chip from the left elbow of Johnny Podres. Podres had probably functioned with the bone chip for some time. It wasn't until Warren Spahn hit him on April 25 that it started moving around, causing great pain and deterioration to muscles and tendons in the area. In addition to removing the bone chip, Dr. Kerlan had to re-attach muscles higher in the arm to create normal tension.[7] Kerlan was not optimistic, saying it would be "extremely fortunate" if Podres was able to pitch again in 1964.[8] In fact, Podres would be lost for the year after pitching only 2⅔ innings with an 0–2 record and a 16.88 ERA. Though Walter Alston

The loss of Johnny Podres after his June 11, 1964, arm surgery was a devastating blow to the defending world champion Dodgers. Alston's "money pitcher" would last a mere 2⅔ innings with an 0–2 record and a 16.88 ERA for the 1964 Dodgers.

tried to fill the gap by resorting to his "Little Three," consisting of right-handers Joe Moeller and Phil Ortega and left-hander Nick Willhite, the loss of Podres would be a devastating blow for the Dodgers.

On the trade deadline of June 15, 1964, the Cardinals acquired Lou Brock from the Chicago Cubs. Brock would turn their season around.

The Lou Brock Trade

On June 15, the St. Louis Cardinals traded right-handed starter Ernie Broglio to the Cubs for a .251-hitting outfielder named Lou Brock. On this day, the Cardinals were tied with the Dodgers for seventh place. For the remainder of the season Brock would hit .348 and steal 33 bases for St. Louis.

The Lone Bright Spot— Sandy Koufax

Sandy Koufax won five straight decisions in June, including three shutouts. The team finished the month four games below .500 in eighth place, 10½ games off the pace.

	W	L	Pct.	GB
San Francisco	45	28	.616	—
Philadelphia	43	27	.614	½
Pittsburgh	38	32	.543	5½
Cincinnati	38	34	.528	6½
Chicago	35	34	.507	8
Milwaukee	36	37	.493	9
St. Louis	36	38	.486	9½
Los Angeles	34	38	.472	10½
Houston	35	40	.467	11
New York	22	54	.289	24½

On July 1, Sandy Koufax beat the Phillies, 5–2, at Dodger Stadium for his seventh straight win. The next day in the nation's capital, President Johnson signed the Civil Rights Act of 1964 into law.[9] Legend has it that as he put down his pen he told an aide, "We have just lost the South for a generation."

Koufax continued to dominate in the month of July with four more consecutive victories, including two more shutouts. When he shut out the Astros, 1–0, with 12 strikeouts on July 22 at Dodger Stadium, his winning streak had reached 11 straight games and his record was 15–4. Before the game, Don Drysdale suffered a hairline fracture at the base of his right thumb when a bouncing ball struck him[10] during a pre-game workout in the outfield.[11] The thumb was placed in a splint, causing him to miss his start of July 25.

On July 26, Koufax started against the Giants before 49,429 fans at Dodger Stadium to close out an 11-game home stand. He had the Giants shut out through seven innings with nine strikeouts. It looked like he had his 12th straight win wrapped up as he took a 2–0 lead to the eighth inning. The Giants scratched together a run on a sacrifice fly by Orlando Cepeda to make the score 2–1 after eight. The Dodgers' defense let Koufax down in the ninth as errors by Jim Gilliam and Maury Wills allowed the Giants to score four unearned runs and escape town with a 5–2 victory.[12] Sandy Koufax's win streak was ended at 11. He had a record of 15–5 but was now 0–2 against the Giants, the only team he would not beat in 1964.

In 1964, Phillies manager Gene Mauch led the team to their first serious pennant run since 1950.

Although Drysdale shut out the Mets on July 28 after missing only one start, the thumb injury would begin to throw him off in August. Koufax's final July start was a no-decision in the Dodgers' 5–3 win at Shea Stadium. The club finished July with .500 record (50–50), in seventh place, nine games behind the Phillies, who had taken over the lead on July 17.

	W	L	Pct.	GB
Philadelphia	59	41	.590	—
San Francisco	59	44	.573	1½
Cincinnati	56	47	.544	4½
Pittsburgh	53	45	.541	5
Milwaukee	53	48	.525	6½
St. Louis	53	49	.520	7
Los Angeles	50	50	.500	9
Chicago	48	52	.480	11
Houston	45	60	.429	16½
New York	32	72	.308	29

With 16 wins and 12 losses, July was the best month for the 1964 Los Angeles Dodgers.

On August 7, Dodgers were in seventh place, 9½ games behind the league-leading Philadelphia Phillies. On that same day, Congress passed the Gulf of Tonkin Resolution, giving President Johnson approval to take "all necessary measures to repel any armed attack against forces of the United States and to prevent further aggression."[13] The House passed the measure, 416 to 0, and the Senate passed it, 98 to 2. Only Democratic Senators Wayne Morse of Oregon and Ernest Gruening of Alaska voted against the measure, both men skeptical of the reliability of the Defense Department's reports on the so-called "Second Gulf of Tonkin Incident" of August 4.[14]

Jammed Version 2.0—The Onset of Traumatic Arthritis?

The next day, August 8, Sandy Koufax (16–5) started against Tony Cloninger (10–10) and the sixth-place Braves on a Saturday afternoon in Milwaukee. Koufax led off the top of the fifth inning with the Dodgers down, 2–1. Batting only .077, he surprised—and annoyed—Cloninger by lining his first pitch into center field for a single. After Koufax advanced to second on a single by Wills, Cloninger attempted to pick him off. Koufax dove back to the bag, safely evading Braves shortstop Denis Menke's tag, but he jammed his elbow when it landed hard on the County Stadium infield surface.[15] He eventually scored when Ron Fairly cleared the bases with a three-run triple. While the elbow "stung" when Koufax returned to the dugout, the pain subsided, allowing him to stay in the game. He went on to pitch a complete-game, 5–4 victory, his 17th win of the season. With the win, the Dodgers moved up into sixth place. As we have seen in *Finding the Left Arm of God*, the 1962 Dodgers' pennant hopes were dashed when Pirates right-hander Earl Francis jammed Sandy Koufax with an inside fast ball on April 28.[16] An ensuing blood clot caused the Dodgers to lose Koufax for a fatal 66 days after July 17; it almost cost Koufax his index finger. It is likely that the blow to Koufax's elbow in the fifth inning of the August 8, 1964, game caused an "arthritic change"—the beginning of a traumatic arthritis condition that was to cut short his career.

On August 9, Koufax woke up in a hotel in Milwaukee with a lump on his elbow from the joint area filling with liquid.[17] On August 10, the team moved on to Cincinnati. Koufax told the trainer that his arm felt worse, but it loosened up after a throwing workout. The swelling and ache returned on his non-throwing day of August 11.[18]

Warming up before his next start of August 12 in Crosley Field, Koufax's arm loosened up without any problems.[19] He averted a three-game Cincinnati sweep with a complete-game, 4–1 victory over the Reds to improve his record to 18–5. Only a solo homer by Koufax nemesis Deron Johnson in the seventh inning prevented a shutout. A struggling Frank Howard struck out four times, his batting average sinking to .222.[20]

Back at Dodger Stadium on August 16, Koufax shut out the Cardinals, 3–0, in the first game of a Sunday doubleheader. His seventh shutout of the season was a classic case of Koufax domination. He struck out 13 Cardinals, including Lou Brock and Bill White three times each. His record was now 19–5, and his ERA was 1.74. The *Los Angeles Times* proclaimed, "only global atomic warfare, or, perhaps, housemaid's knee can keep Koufax from entering the 25-game winner's circle again."[21] Cardinals left-hander Curt Simmons returned the favor in the second game of the doubleheader by shutting out the Dodgers, 4–0. At the end of play on that day—the day that would turn out to be the last appearance of the season for Sandy Koufax—the Dodgers were at .500 in seventh place, with the Cardinals off the radar in fifth. The Philadelphia Phillies had a 4½ game lead over the field in the National League.

	W	L	Pct.	GB
Philadelphia	70	45	.609	—
San Francisco	67	51	.568	4½
Pittsburgh	63	53	.543	7½
Cincinnati	64	54	.542	7½
St. Louis	62	55	.530	9
Milwaukee	60	56	.517	10½
Los Angeles	58	58	.500	12½
Chicago	55	62	.470	16
Houston	50	69	.420	22
New York	36	82	.305	35½

The Light Goes Out in August

When Koufax woke up on the morning of Monday, August 17, his elbow was so swollen that he couldn't straighten his left arm, which he described as a "waterlogged log."[22] When the arm was just as swollen the next day, preventing Koufax from even working out, Dr. Robert Kerlan took X-rays of the elbow area. The X-rays revealed inflammation of the elbow joint *lining*, a condition known as synovitis. This caused the lining to produce fluid, or "weep." In Koufax's case, it produced enough fluid to blow up his entire arm from the shoulder to the wrist like a balloon. For two days, Dr. Kerlan tried to remove the fluid with a needle and to reduce the inflammation with cortisone injections and oral medication.[23]

It was at this time that Koufax first began taking an anti-inflammation pill called Butazolidin (phenylbutazone alka). Butazolidin, or "Bute," had been used to treat broken down thoroughbred race horses.[24] In addition to upsetting Koufax's stomach, the drug carried the threat of a serious side effect: depletion in white blood cell count. Despite this risk, Koufax was reassured by the fact that Dr. Kerlan, who suffered from rheumatoid arthritis of the spine, was taking the pill himself.[25] Butazolidin would be taken off the market in the mid–1970s.[26] On Thursday morning, August 20, Dodgers fans learned that Koufax had been scratched from his next start, scheduled for that evening against the Braves at Dodger Stadium.[27] He would also miss his August 24 turn against the Giants.

Back on the road, the Dodgers opened a four-game series with the Cardinals at Busch Stadium on Friday, August 28. Before the game, Koufax tested the arm by throwing on the sideline to pitching coach Joe Becker. He threw just three or four pitches before the arm began to swell. Moments later, the session had to be terminated prematurely, forcing him back to the clubhouse to have the elbow packed in ice. There he told reporters, "The elbow felt good when I started to warm up, but the longer I threw, the worse it got. I could feel it grind in there again."[28] Two days later, he was sent home to Los Angeles for more treatments under the care of Dr. Kerlan, who made a grim prognosis: "I can't say how long it will be before he is sound, but it probably won't be before the season is over."[29]

Down three games to none, the Dodgers salvaged the final game of the series at Busch Stadium on August 31 with Don Drysdale's complete-game, 12–3 win. They closed out August in seventh place, three games below .500. The Cardinals, with an 18–10 month, had crept into fourth place.

	W	L	Pct.	GB
Philadelphia	78	51	.605	—
Cincinnati	73	57	.562	5½
San Francisco	73	59	.553	6½
St. Louis	71	59	.546	7½
Pittsburgh	66	64	.508	12½
Milwaukee	66	64	.508	12½
Los Angeles	63	66	.488	15
Chicago	60	70	.462	18½
Houston	57	75	.432	22½
New York	44	86	.338	34½

As September began, the Dodgers were already thinking about making changes for next year. Bavasi told the press, "The time has come to change faces, even if you don't want to," fueling trade rumors about Frank Howard—or even Tommy Davis.[30] Beginning September 17 in Los Angeles, the Dodgers played their final four-game series with the league-leading Phillies. That night the Dodgers were officially eliminated from contention when the Phillies scored four unearned runs off Drysdale to beat him, 4–3, in the opener. In the second game on September 18, Phillies left-hander Chris Short took a 3–0 lead to the bottom of the seventh inning before Howard tied the game with a three-run home run. The Dodgers won the game, 4–3, on Bart Shirley's two-out RBI single in the bottom of the ninth. The Dodgers won the next night, September 19, by an identical 4–3 score in 16 innings. With two out in the bottom of the 16th inning and the fleet Willie Davis on third base, Gene Mauch removed his ace right-handed relief pitcher, Jack Baldschun, and brought in a rookie left-hander named Morrie Steevens. It was risky, since young Steevens—making his first appearance at the major league level in 1964—would be pitching with his back to the runner on third. Davis exploited this advantage by stealing home with the winning run.[31] When the game ended at 2:13 a.m. the next morning, the Phillies' lead was sliced to 5½ games. Criticism of Gene Mauch's over-managing had now reached a fever pitch in the Phillies' clubhouse.

Koufax, the warrior, would not give up on getting another chance for his 20th win. He tried to work out before each of the first three games of the series in hopes of facing Phillies ace Jim Bunning in the series finale on Sunday, September 20. But the swelling persisted and he was unable to go. Bunning beat the Dodgers, 3–2, for his 18th win. The Phillies left Los Angeles with a 6½-game lead and 12 games to play. Sandy Koufax was officially shut down for the year.[32]

3

A Season Ends in Chaos

All this—for nothing. I just wish that I had done my job as well as the players did theirs.[1]—Gene Mauch, October 4, 1964

After the Phillies left Los Angeles on September 20, they went into a free-fall, losing their next ten games. The National League pennant race was thrown into chaos. On September 27, the Phillies were knocked out of first place for the first time since mid–July.

Alston Survives

On September 29, the Los Angeles Dodgers hastily arranged a press conference. With Walter O'Malley standing in the wings, Executive Vice President and General Manager Buzzie Bavasi announced that the Dodgers were rehiring manager Walter Alston for his 12th season in 1965. It was only the second time since the Dodgers moved from Brooklyn that Alston's retention had been announced before the winter meetings. Bavasi told the press, "We decided to do it now because of the unfounded rumors that were making the rounds."[2] Earlier in the day, the Mets announced that Casey Stengel would return as their manager, thereby dispelling a wire service "exclusive" that Alston would take over at Cincinnati with the 74-year-old Stengel taking his place in Los Angeles.

The Final Weekend

Going into the final weekend of the season beginning Friday, October 2, the St. Louis Cardinals, by virtue of an eight-game winning streak, had supplanted the Phillies atop the NL standings. What's more, it was mathematically possible for four teams to win the pennant: St. Louis, Cincinnati, Philadelphia, or San Francisco.

	W	L	Pct.	GB
St. Louis	92	67	.579	—
Cincinnati	92	68	.575	½
Philadelphia	90	70	.563	2½
San Francisco	89	70	.560	3

In the American League, on Saturday, October 3, the New York Yankees clinched their 29th pennant with a come-from-behind, 8–5 win over the Cleveland Indians at

Yankee Stadium.[3] It was a heartbreaking conclusion to the season for the Baltimore Orioles under first-year manager Hank Bauer, a former Yankee. The Orioles occupied first place for 111 days of the season. Their brilliant third baseman, Brooks Robinson, led the league in runs batted in and won the Most Valuable Player Award.They would finish third, behind the White Sox.

By the dawning of the season's final day, Sunday, October 4, the number of National League pennant contenders had been reduced to three: Cincinnati, St. Louis, and Philadelphia. The Giants had been eliminated by the Cubs the day before at Candlestick Park despite two home runs by Willie Mays.

	W	L	Pct.	GB
Cincinnati	92	69	.571	—
St. Louis	92	69	.571	
Philadelphia	91	70	.565	1

The Cardinals had Curt Simmons on the mound at home against the tenth-place Mets. The Phillies, behind Jim Bunning, would play the Reds at Crosley Field in Cincinnati. And the Phillies finally came through. Bunning pitched a masterpiece, a six-hit, 10–0 shutout in which no Reds runner advanced beyond second base. Ritchie Allen drove in four runs with a double and two homers. The Phillies and Reds, now tied for first, sweated out the outcome of the Cardinals-Mets game in St. Louis.

At Busch Stadium, the Mets knocked Curt Simmons out of the game with two runs in the top of the fifth inning to take a 3–2 lead. Johnny Keane had to bring in Bob Gibson from the Cardinals bullpen to get the final two outs. The stage was set for the season to end in an unprecedented three-way tie. But the Cardinals bounced back to score three runs in the bottom of the fifth to take a 5–3 lead. The Cardinals scored six more runs to win the game, 11–5, and a trip to the World Series to meet the Yankees.[4] Gibson pitched four strong innings in relief to pick up his 19th victory.

After spending the previous 50 games in seventh place, the Dodgers ended the season with an 11–1 win over the Astros at Dodger Stadium to finish tied with the Pirates for sixth place with an 80–82 record. It was only their second losing season since 1944.

	W	L	Pct.	GB
St. Louis	93	69	.574	—
Cincinnati	92	70	.568	1
Philadelphia	92	70	.568	1
San Francisco	90	72	.556	3
Milwaukee	88	74	.543	5
Los Angeles	80	82	.494	13
Pittsburgh	80	82	.494	13
Chicago	76	86	.469	17
Houston	66	96	.407	27
New York	53	109	.327	40

The 1964 World Series

The World Series began at Busch Stadium on October 7. The Cardinals came from behind to beat Whitey Ford and the Yankees, 9–5, in Game 1.[5] The next day, the Yankees gained a split in St. Louis as Mel Stottlemyre went all the way to beat Bob Gibson and the Cardinals, 8–3, in Game 2. Stottlemyre was brought up from the minors on August 11 and won nine games for the Yankees down the stretch.[6]

After a travel day, the Series resumed in New York. Buzzie Bavasi, who was there representing the Los Angeles Dodgers, was busy wheeling and dealing from his four-item "shopping list" for next season: 1. An infielder for second or third base; 2. An outfielder with some sock; 3. An established starting pitcher; and 4. A back-up catcher to support John Roseboro.[7] At the same time, the Dodgers delivered a bombshell: they had fired their entire coaching staff, including Leo Durocher, Joe Becker (Koufax's pitching coach since 1955), Greg Mulleavy, and Pete Reiser.[8]

Game 3 was played on October 10 before 67,101 fans at Yankee Stadium. First-year Yankees manager Yogi Berra chose Jim Bouton as his starter; Johnny Keane went with Curt Simmons. Though Bouton—who would write the iconoclastic baseball book, *Ball Four*—was only 25, this was his second World Series start. The 35-year-old Simmons had waited 14 years to make this, his first post-season appearance. After both teams scored a total of 25 runs in the first two games, this one was a pitchers' duel. The Yankees got on the board first when Clete Boyer doubled home Elston Howard with two out in the second inning. Cardinals catcher Tim McCarver led off the top of the fifth with a sharp single and advanced to second base when Mickey Mantle fumbled the ball in right field for an error. With two out, Curt Simmons lined a ball off Clete Boyer's glove at third base to drive in McCarver with the tying run.

The game went to the ninth tied 1–1, with both starters pitching brilliantly, Simmons a four-hitter, Bouton a six-hitter. In the top of the inning, leadoff batter McCarver reached base on an error by Yankees shortstop Phil Linz. Mike Shannon moved him to second with a sacrifice bunt. Bouton walked former Dodger Carl Warwick, pinch-hitting for Dal Maxvill in the eight-hole. With two runners on and down to his last two outs, Keane had no choice but to remove Simmons for a pinch-hitter in the person of Bob Skinner. Skinner flied out to Roger Maris in deep center field, moving McCarver to third. But Curt Flood lined out to Mantle in right, leaving McCarver stranded to end the inning.

Keane's gamble of taking out Simmons had not paid off. The game was still tied, and he now had to bring in knuckleball pitcher Barney Schultz to pitch to Mickey Mantle in the bottom of the ninth. Mantle was tied with Babe Ruth for most career World Series home runs, with 15. Before he came to the plate, Berra told him, "This thing is getting late and serious and you oughta hit a homer. I'm going to stand in the runway to get a head start to the clubhouse when you hit it."[9] Schultz's first pitch to the left-handed-batting Mantle was—predictably—a knuckleball. Only it didn't *knuckle*; it sort of *floated* as it came up to the plate. Mantle took his characteristically vicious lash at the ball. Mantle fans all over the country watching the game on television, including the author, were deflated as the trajectory of the ball appeared to be about 80 degrees as it came off the bat—a sure popup. But the ordinary laws of physics did not apply to "The Mick." The baseball kept soaring and soaring until it landed in the third tier in right field. One pitch, one record-breaking homer, and the Yankees had a two-games-to-one lead in the Series. Slumped on a stool in front of his locker in the visitors' clubhouse after the game, his balding head bowed, Barney Schultz told reporters, "Just think, you throw one pitch—and it's gone."[10] His major league career would be over in less than a year.

The next day, Sunday, October 11, at Yankee Stadium, New York left-hander Al Downing was cruising with a one-hitter and a 3–0 lead through the first five innings before things fell apart. The first two Cardinals batters, pinch-hitter Carl Warwick and Curt Flood, singled to open the sixth. Downing settled down to get Lou Brock to fly out, and then looked for a double play to get out of the inning. Dick Groat, the veteran St.

Louis shortstop with mediocre speed, hit the perfect double play ball, a sharp grounder to the right of Yankees second baseman Bobby Richardson. Richardson fielded the ball, but he couldn't get it out of his glove. By the time he shoveled it to shortstop Phil Linz, just as Flood arrived at second, Linz couldn't handle it. Everyone was safe, the inning was still alive, and NL RBI leader—and eventual Most Valuable Player—Ken Boyer was heading for the batter's box with the bases loaded. Boyer took Downing's first pitch for a ball, then parked the next one—a high change-up—in the left field seats for a grand slam to catapult St. Louis into the lead, 4–3. The Cardinals' ace reliever, Ron Taylor, held the Yankees hitless over the next four innings, and the Series was tied at two games apiece.[11]

Mickey Mantle won Game 3 of the 1964 World Series with a bottom of the ninth, walk-off moon shot off a Barney Schultz knuckleball at Yankee Stadium.

Game 5, on Monday, October 12, the last game of the Series in New York, was another matchup between Mel Stottlemyre and Bob Gibson. A Yankees error helped the Cardinals to score two runs off Stottlemyre in the top of the fifth. Gibson, overpowering through eight innings, allowing just four singles and striking out 11, took the 2–0 lead to the ninth inning. Many of the 65,633 fans were heading for the exits when leadoff batter Mickey Mantle reached first base on an error by Cardinals shortstop Dick Groat. Gibson blew away Elston Howard on three pitches for the first out. Joe Pepitone followed with a line drive that ricocheted off Gibson's backside and rolled toward third base. Ignoring the pain, Gibson chased down the ball and made an off-balance throw to first, nipping Pepitone by an eyelash. This unleashed a violent protest by Yogi Berra and the Yankees, to no avail—they were down to their last out. The call would have a major impact on the outcome of the Series. The umpires allowed Gibson some time to regroup before he had to face Tom Tresh. Tresh hit Gibson's first pitch 400 feet into the right field bleachers to tie the game at 2–2. Had Pepitone been ruled safe, the game would have been over, and the Yankees would have taken a three-games-to-two lead. Instead it moved to the tenth inning.[12]

Yankees reliever Pete Mikkelsen walked Bill White to start the tenth. Ken Boyer, who had not had a sacrifice bunt since 1958, bunted one down to the right of the mound. The ball was placed so perfectly that he was able to beat it out for a hit. Minutes later, Tim McCarver hit a Mikkelsen 3–2 pitch over Mickey Mantle's head and into the right field stands for a three-run home run to make the score 5–2, Cardinals. After Gibson held the Yankees scoreless in the bottom of the inning, it was the Cardinals who had the three-games-to-two lead as they prepared to fly back to St. Louis.

Helped by solo home runs by Roger Maris and Mickey Mantle, and a grand slam by Joe Pepitone, Jim Bouton beat the Cardinals for the second time on October 14 in Busch Stadium. The one-sided, 8–3 Yankees win extended the Series to a seventh game.

The Series would be decided on the same field the next day when Mel Stottlemyre and Bob Gibson—both pitching on two days' rest—locked horns for the third time. Gibson shut out the Yankees for the first five innings. He had a commanding 6–0 lead as he took the mound for the sixth inning. Gibson appeared to be running out of gas as the first two batters, Richardson and Maris, got to him for singles, bringing the ever-dangerous Mantle to the plate. The Mick, who would turn 33 in five days, was having his last great year, with 35 home runs, 111 RBI, and a .303 batting average during the regular season. Mantle cut the lead in half with a three-run homer over the left field wall, his 18th World Series home run. It is still the record.

Johnny Keane decided to stay with Gibson, who made it to the ninth with a 7–3 lead. It was a wobbly Bob

Bob Gibson and Ken Boyer embrace after the final out of Game 7 of the 1964 World Series. Gibson was named Series MVP.

Gibson who gave up solo home runs to Clete Boyer and Phil Linz to put the game within reach for the Yankees at 7–5. But he survived by getting Bobby Richardson—who had a record 13 hits in the Series—to pop out to end the game.[13] The St. Louis Cardinals were World Champions for the first time since 1946. The game and the Series put the 28-year-old Gibson on the map. He struck out 31 batters, and was named Most Valuable Player of the Series. The New York Yankees would not play in another World Series for 13 years.

* * *

On October 27, actor Ronald Reagan launched his political career when his 30-minute campaign address for Republican presidential candidate Barry Goldwater, "A Time for Choosing," was broadcast nationally by NBC. The speech raised $1 million for the foundering Goldwater campaign. The reaction of many Republicans, dispirited over the lack of appeal of the dour Goldwater in black horn-rimmed glasses, must have been, "There's our candidate!" On November 4, Goldwater went down to one of the worst landslide defeats in U.S. history, winning only 52 electoral votes—from his home state of Arizona and five southern states from the Old Confederacy.[14] Two years later, Reagan would be elected Governor of California.

4

Autopsy for a Lost Season

We have to have some hitting—it doesn't matter from what position—to come back next year.[1]—Walter Alston, on being rehired, September 29, 1964

The 1964 Los Angeles Dodgers occupied first place for 24 hours—immediately following Sandy Koufax's Opening Night shutout victory. But they never recovered from the two blows they sustained before the season even started: the near meltdown of Frank Howard and the elbow injury to Johnny Podres. By the first of May they were out of contention. Koufax was their lone bright light that went out after August 16.

Losing Koufax

When Sandy Koufax made his final appearance in game number 117 on August 16, he was on pace to surpass most of his remarkable 1963 statistics.

	G	W	L	IP	SHO	SO	ER	HR	BB	ERA
Actual through August 16	29	19	5	223	7	223	43	13	53	1.74
Projected after August 16	11	7	2	86	3	86	17	5	20	1.74
Projected Full Year	40	26	7	309	10	309	60	18	73	1.74

Losing Podres

The loss of Johnny Podres was a devastating blow. He had averaged nearly 15 wins per year in the Dodgers' first six years in Los Angeles. As we have seen, the Dodgers lost him on May 17—before he had contributed a single victory. Don Drysdale had 18 wins, but no other Dodgers pitcher could contribute more then seven. Ron Perranoski, 16–3 the year before from the Dodgers' bullpen, slipped to 5–7.

Lack of Hitting

The 1964 Dodgers finished eighth in the league in runs scored with 614, and ninth in home runs with 79—their lowest total since 1946. Frank Howard led the team with a modest 24. They were sixth in the league with a .250 team batting average. For the first time since 1948, no Dodger regular hit .300. Willie Davis led the team at .294.

An Unreliable Defense

The Dodgers pitchers had an unreliable defense behind them. The team was third in the league in committing errors and second-worst in turning double plays.

A December Earthquake

On December 4, the last day of the winter meetings, the Dodgers rocked the proceedings by trading Frank Howard, Ken McMullen, Pete Richert, Phil Ortega, and Dick Nen to the Washington Senators for Claude Osteen, John Kennedy, and $100,000 cash.[2] The 28-year-old Howard, who was signed by the Dodgers off the Ohio State campus in 1958 as "the next Babe Ruth," was ready for a change after his batting average slipped to .226. He would finally reach his potential in Washington under the guidance of managers Gil Hodges and Ted Williams. The 25-year-old, left-handed starter Osteen was 15–13 with the ninth-place Senators. He would play a key role for the Dodgers for the next nine seasons.

In December of 1964, the Dodgers traded Frank Howard to the Washington Senators for left-hander Claude Osteen.

Sandy Koufax at 29

Sandy Koufax turned 29 on December 30. A month before, he finished third in the voting for the Cy Young Award despite missing the team's last 47 games. He led the league in shutouts (7), earned run average (1.74), and winning percentage (.792). Now the Dodgers were in the same uncertain position they were in two years before: their chances for the next season depended on whether Koufax could recovery from a physical injury. In 1962 it was the left index finger; now it was the left elbow. And as was his practice, he would not pick up a baseball for the entire winter.

* * *

By the end of the next day, December 31, 1964, the number of U.S. troops in Vietnam had reached an estimated 23,300.[3]

* * *

5

The Spring of Doubt

If Sandy Koufax can only pitch on Sunday the Dodgers are in real trouble.[1]—Leo Durocher, ABC sports

Spring training began for the 1965 Dodgers on February 28 at Vero Beach. The team was in the same position they were in two years before: their chances depended on the uncertain physical condition of Sandy Koufax. In 1963, the question was the condition of his left index finger; now it was his left elbow. Koufax entered camp with a well-rested arm, having not thrown a baseball in six months. Things looked encouraging as they moved through the exhibition season. He threw a complete game against the Tigers on March 26, and another complete game—with ten strikeouts—against the White Sox on March 30. But the morning after that last outing, he woke up with a swollen arm. Twenty-four hours later the season was cast into doubt when Koufax was put on a plane back to Los Angeles for an appointment with prominent orthopedist Dr. Robert Kerlan. On April 2, Kerlan broke the unwelcome news to Buzzie Bavasi over the phone: "Sandy is suffering from a traumatic arthritic condition of the left elbow, which tends to flare up under repeated stress. It is too early to tell what the results of treatment will be and too early to tell when he will be able to pitch."[2]

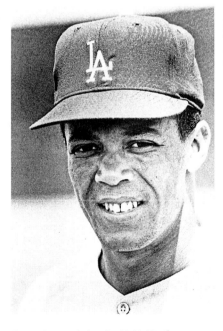

The next day back in Vero Beach, Alston announced to the press that he had named Maury Wills as the team captain. It was an important vote of confidence for Wills since it was the first time since 1959 that he did not get a raise in pay. Wills, now 32, told the press, "I'm going to steal bases this year even if we have a five or six-run lead; our team can't have too many runs."[3] At the time, Wills was tearing up the grapefruit league with a .429 average, with eight runs batted in 15 games from the leadoff spot.

While in Los Angeles, Koufax figured something out on his own. He knew he would throw sidearm pitches to left-handed batters—a pitch that put added stress on his arm. In the game of March 30, the White Sox had two lefties in their lineup. On reflection, this

At spring training in 1965, Dodgers manager Walter Alston named Maury Wills team captain.

was also true of the game that ended his last season, on August 16, against the Cardinals at Dodger Stadium: the large number of sidearm pitches to Cardinals left-handed batters such as Lou Brock and Bill White put a severe strain on his elbow. He therefore stopped throwing that pitch.[4]

In Los Angeles, Dr. Kerlan made a breakthrough with cortisone therapy. He had treated Koufax before with cortisone, and it only gradually reduced the swelling. But now he tried a new technique: injecting it directly into the joint. Miraculously, the elbow was back to normal the next day.[5] On April 6, Koufax returned to the team in Vero Beach. It was at this point that he thought he might have to remove himself from the regular rotation and become just a "Sunday pitcher."[6]

Koufax had already been scratched as the starter of the Dodgers' April 12 opener in New York. But by April 11, his arm felt well enough to pitch three innings in the last spring exhibition game against the Senators in Washington, D.C. He gave up one scratch hit and struck out five of the ten batters he faced. The next morning, the Dodgers got some even more encouraging news when he woke without a trace of swelling in his left arm.[7]

Opening Day

The 1965 season opened on Monday, April 12. A month after the first U.S. combat troops arrived in Vietnam, it was smiles all around as President Lyndon Baines Johnson threw out the first ball before a record crowd of 43,554 at D.C. Stadium with Vice President Hubert Humphrey at his side and Senate Republican minority leader Everett Dirksen looking over his shoulder.[8] Never mind that the Red Sox pounded former Dodgers pitcher Phil Ortega and Gil Hodges' Senators, 7–2; things were looking up.

At the same time, 240 miles to the north, the Dodgers opened their season at Shea Stadium in New York.

	April 12, 1965		April 14, 1964	
1	Maury Wills	SS	Maury Wills	SS
2	Wes Parker	1B	Jim Gilliam	2B
3	Willie Davis	CF	Willie Davis	CF
4	Tommy Davis	LF	Tommy Davis	LF
5	John Roseboro	C	Ron Fairly	1B
6	Jim Lefebvre	2B	Frank Howard	RF
7	Ron Fairly	RF	John Roseboro	C
8	John Kennedy	3B	Johnny Werhas	3B
9	Don Drysdale	P	Sandy Koufax	P

With Koufax scratched due to the recurrence of his elbow problem, Don Drysdale made his sixth Opening Day start in the last eight years. And it was a tour de force for Drysdale. Facing only 29 batters, he pitched a complete-game four-hitter with nine strikeouts. In the fourth inning, he picked up a bat and hit a two-run homer off the Mets' little left-handed starter, Alvin Jackson. The 6–1 victory gave Drysdale a 14–1 career record against Casey Stengel's hapless Mets.[9] Willie Davis went 3-for-3 with a double and a home run. Wills set the tone for his season by stealing two bases. To no one's surprise, the Dodgers opened their ninth consecutive season with a new third baseman. John Kennedy, who had come over from the Senators in the Frank Howard trade in December, batted eighth in the lineup. Kennedy drew a tough 0-for-4 collar as 36-year-old Jim Gilliam watched from the first base coaching box.

Wes Parker, batting second behind Maury Wills, began his role as the Dodgers' regular first baseman that would last for eight years.

Mr. Steady

Born into a wealthy family, Maurice Wesley Parker III began playing baseball at age 11 in the West Los Angeles little league program. He would later say that his Little League coach and long-time mentor, Ned Bowler, was the greatest influence on his becoming a professional baseball player.[10] Parker played high school baseball at the exclusive Harvard School for Boys in Studio City. At a Hollywood party, his well-connected real estate developer father lobbied Dodgers coach Charlie Dressen on his son's behalf. Dressen came out to watch Parker play on his summer American Legion team and invited him to work out regularly at Dodger Stadium.[11] Parker went on to Claremont-Mudd College where, in addition to playing baseball, he was quarterback on the football team for a year. Parker ultimately gave up football after his father advised him that an injury could jeopardize a potential baseball career. He transferred to the University of Southern California and was signed without a bonus by the Dodgers—through his connection to Chuck Dressen—after he graduated in 1963.

Parker began in the Dodgers' farm system at Santa Barbara in the Class-A California League, batting .305 in 92 games. He was promoted to Albuquerque in the Class-AA Texas League, where hit .350 in the last 26 games of the 1963 season. A top bridge player, Parker passed up

Above: Don Drysdale turned in a tour de force performance in the 1965 opener against the Mets at Shea Stadium in New York. *Below:* In 1965, Wes Parker began his eight-year role as the Los Angeles Dodgers' regular first baseman.

an invitation from his father to go to Honolulu as his partner in an international bridge tournament. Instead, he went to the Arizona Instructional League, where he led the league in batting with a .357 average. With Frank Howard's status in doubt the following spring, the Dodgers found a spot for Parker on their Opening Day roster.

Parker appeared in 124 games in a utility role for the 1964 Dodgers, playing first base and all three outfield positions—mostly as a defensive replacement. At Vero Beach in 1965, Walter Alston began looking for a new second-place batter to replace Jim Gilliam, who had been "retired" to the coaching staff. After seeing Parker play several sterling exhibition games at first base, and hearing Ron Fairly tell him that he could better concentrate on his hitting by playing right field, Alston had found a new regular first baseman to bat behind Maury Wills in the order.

Frenchy

Twenty-three-year-old Jim Lefebvre made his major league debut that day as the Dodgers' new second baseman. He had arrived at Vero Beach in February without a big league contract and with the expectation that he would be shipped out to Triple-A Spokane. But he got a chance to show what he could do when Nate Oliver was sidelined with a gashed right hand after being spiked by Milwaukee's Frank Bolling in a pre-season rundown play.[12] Lefebvre seized the opportunity, holding down the second base position and batting .353 for the first nine exhibition games. Toward the end of the exhibition season, he suffered a split nail on an index finger and had to sit out several games. When the team broke camp in Vero Beach and headed north to Jacksonville, Lefebvre had not even been told that any plans were being made for him. Before the Jacksonville game, he walked into Walter Alston's office and audaciously announced, "I think my finger is okay, and I better get in a couple of games before the season starts."[13] Alston, impressed with his confidence, didn't say a word but later penciled his name into the lineup card. Two days later, before the final exhibition series began in Washington, D.C., the weekend of April 10–11, Dodgers Vice President Red Patterson handed Lefebvre a major league contract.

The compact, 6'0", 185-pound Lefebvre was a standout baseball, football, and basketball player at Morningside High School in Inglewood, California. In 1959, 16-year-old Jimmy Lefebvre was the batboy for the visiting teams at the Memorial Coliseum. He learned never to give up by watching that scrappy Dodgers team: "The main thing I learned is when a good ballplayer is

Jim Lefebvre took over the second base position for the Los Angeles Dodgers on Opening Day, 1965.

down, he always bounces back. The idea is to stay with it, don't get discouraged, and keep hustling. Things will start going for you."[14] It paid off. After three years in the minors, where Lefebvre was pegged as a second baseman with limited range and only average speed, Alston placed the switch-hitter in the sixth spot in the batting order on Opening Day. He went hitless at the plate, but he would be the Dodgers' regular second baseman for the rest of the season.

Gomer

Claude Osteen had been a Dodgers fan all his life. As a young boy in Caney Springs, Tennessee, the Brooklyn Dodgers were his favorites. When his parents moved to Reading, Ohio, his high school coach was a Dodgers scout. Osteen probably would have signed with the Dodgers, except he wanted to be on a big league roster, and the Brooklyn Dodgers club was already filled. Consequently, on July 2, 1957, he signed with the Cincinnati Reds for the bonus limit of $4,000. A year later, the limit was removed.

Osteen was shuttled between the Reds' minor league system and the big club for most of his first five years before being traded to the expansion Washington Senators in September 1961. He was a mainline starter with a losing record for the weak-hitting Senators in 1962 and 1963. In 1964, he blossomed into one of the American League's best left-handers. He won 15 games for a hopeless ninth-place team that was shut out in seven games that he pitched, and even finished 30th in the MVP voting. Angels pitching coach Marv Grissom considered Osteen one of the best "stuff" pitchers in either league. When Buzzie Bavasi pulled off the trade for him in the last hour of the Houston winter meetings on December 4, Walter O'Malley left a meeting of baseball executives to congratulate him.

That spring at Vero Beach, Dick Tracewski hung the tag "Gomer" on him because "he looks like that TV guy"[15] (Gomer Pyle). The name stuck. It was there that Johnny Podres, "King of the Changeup," taught him how to throw the pitch. Osteen was a standout from the beginning, leading the team with a 1.67 ERA during the exhibition season. By the time the team broke camp, he was firmly entrenched as the Dodgers' fourth starter—the third left-hander in a four-man rotation along with Podres and, hopefully, Sandy Koufax.

Osteen made a dazzling Dodgers debut in the second game of the season on April 14 with a two-hit, eight-strikeout performance against the Pirates at Forbes

Claude Osteen made a dazzling debut for the Los Angeles Dodgers in the second game of the 1965 season at Forbes Field in Pittsburgh.

Field. He had a one-hit shutout until Bob Bailey hit a solo home run with two outs in the bottom of the ninth inning. The only other hit produced by the Pirates' lineup—that included defending NL batting champion Roberto Clemente—came on a dropped fly ball. He struck out every starter except Willie Stargell, disposing of the Pirates in one hour and 58 minutes. "It was the greatest game I ever pitched,"[16] a jubilant Osteen told reporters after the game. The 3–1 win made the Dodgers 2–0, in an early tie for first place with the Cubs.

Sandy Koufax, Sunday Pitcher

April 18, 1965, was a pivotal day for Sandy Koufax and the Los Angeles Dodgers franchise. Koufax made his first regular season start in eight months against the Phillies at Connie Mack Stadium in Philadelphia. No one, including Koufax, was sure what his future role would be. Was he now just a "Sunday pitcher," or less? Worst case: was his career over at 29? Could the team recover from a dismal sixth-place finish without him? True, he had a satisfactory outing seven days before in an exhibition game against a weak-hitting Senators in Washington, D.C. But the real test would be going up against regular season competition—when the game meant something. Walter Alston had originally planned to start Koufax the day before, but Drysdale was moved into that spot after his turn in the opening game of the series was rained out on Friday night. This meant that Koufax would come into the Sunday afternoon game with six days of rest. In fact, he had pitched only three innings in the previous 18 days.

The first batter Koufax faced on this frigid 49-degree day, Phillies leadoff man Cookie Rojas, greeted him with a ringing line drive single to left field. With two out, he walked power hitter Dick Stuart, who was back in the National League after playing two years in Boston. But he settled down and was able to get Tony Taylor on a pop foul to keep the runners from scoring. After holding the Phillies hitless over the next four innings, he began to wobble in the sixth when Richie Allen singled and Stuart hit a home run deep into the second deck in left field to cut the Dodgers' lead to 3–2. Koufax was laboring at the end with two runners on base in both the eighth and ninth innings. In each situation, Alston came out to the mound with the hook, but decided to leave him in the game. Both times Koufax was able to escape unscathed. He was clearly not sharp from the inactivity. Though he walked five batters and threw a lot of pitches, he managed to complete the game with a six-hit, 6–2 win.[17] The Sunday pitcher had passed his first test. More importantly, his elbow was only "a little puffy" when he woke up the next morning.[18] The only remaining question was: Would Sandy Koufax have to settle for being a Sunday pitcher? That question was rendered moot four days later when he pitched another complete game, a four-hit, 2–1 win against the Mets. Koufax was back in the four-man starting rotation for good.

When the Dodgers ended April, they were on their way to a turnaround season. They had already won the first two games of a four-game series with the Giants at Dodger Stadium and had Johnny Podres and Claude Osteen queued up to go for a sweep over the weekend. Podres had already thrown a shutout in his first start on April 23 against the Phillies. Osteen had a 1.59 ERA. Maury Wills already had nine stolen bases and was hitting .300. At the end of play on April 30, the Dodgers were in first place, a half-game in front of the Cincinnati Reds, the team that then looked like their biggest obstacle.

	W	L	Pct.	GB
Los Angeles	10	5	.667	—
Cincinnati	9	5	.643	½
Houston	10	6	.625	½
Chicago	7	6	.538	2
Milwaukee	6	6	.500	2½
San Francisco	7	9	.438	3½
Philadelphia	6	8	.429	3½
Pittsburgh	6	9	.400	4
St. Louis	5	8	.385	4
New York	6	10	.375	4½

The World Champion St. Louis Cardinals were off to a slow start, and the Giants—at two games under .500—did not look like a threat.

6

Mayday! Mayday!

The 1965 season came to an end for us on May 1.[1]—Sandy Koufax

On May 1, the Dodgers and Giants played the third of their four-game series at Dodger Stadium. The Dodgers, having won the first two games, came into this Saturday night game in first place, a half-game ahead of the Cincinnati Reds. A capacity crowd of 55,312 would see Johnny Podres on the mound for the Dodgers and Gaylord Perry for the Giants. In the bottom of the fourth inning, Dodgers cleanup batter Tommy Davis hit a slow ground ball down the third base line and beat it out for an infield single. When

On May 1, 1965, Tommy Davis fractured and dislocated his right ankle sliding into second base at Dodger Stadium. He was lost for the season and never fully recovered.

Ron Fairly followed with a grounder toward first baseman Orlando Cepeda, Davis broke for second. As he started his slide—premature, indecisive, awkward— his spikes caught in the dirt. He never reached the bag. A hushed silence came over the crowd as he lay face-down in the dirt. When trainer Wayne Anderson reached him, he could see a bone sticking out at a right angle from Davis' right ankle and had to pop it back into place. Moments later, Davis was carried off the field on a stretcher and taken to Daniel Freeman Memorial Hospital, where it was determined that he had a fractured and dislocated ankle.[2]

At the hospital Davis told reporters, "I don't know how it happened. I thought there was going to be a play on me and I came in with a new kind of slide. When I looked down, I thought my ankle was in right field."[3] The Dodgers went on to win the game, 4–2. But on the odds board in Las Vegas, the Dodgers were removed as the favorites to win the National League pennant.

The Nightmare Continues in Left Field

On Sunday, May 2, 35-year-old Wally Moon took over the left field position for the Dodgers as they went for a sweep of the Giants with Claude Osteen on the mound. Osteen was cruising with a two-hit, 1-0 shutout until Willie McCovey rocked him with a two-run homer in the seventh inning. But McCovey was not done. He won the game in the tenth inning with another home run—this one off reliever Bob Miller. Moon went hitless in the game. In five months, the Dodgers would give him his unconditional release, thus ending his career.

Twenty-five-year-old Al "The Bull" Ferrara became the Dodgers' third left fielder on May 4 in Cincinnati.

Thirty-five-year-old Wally Moon briefly took over the left field position after the loss of Tommy Davis.

The Bull

Alfred John Ferrara grew up in an Italian immigrant family in Brooklyn. As a child, Ferrara's maternal grandmother pushed him to study classical piano. While the young Ferrara showed great promise as a pianist, his dream was to play baseball for the Brooklyn Dodgers. He made a deal with his grandmother: if he could accomplish the goal of becoming his teacher's number one student, he could give up the piano and play baseball. When he was 16, he gave a showcase recital at Carnegie Hall as the number one student. He never touched the piano again.

Ferrara graduated from Lafayette High School in 1957, the same school that produced Sandy Koufax and the Aspromonte brothers. A 4-for-48 batting slump at the end of his senior year caused major league scouts to pass on him. His first day working on a dead-end assembly line job, he was told about a tryout to be held by the Brooklyn Dodgers at Ebbets Field for a traveling team called the Dodger Rookies. He made the team and played well enough for them as they toured the Atlantic seaboard that Dodgers scout Buck Lai—who was also the athletic director at Long Island University—got him a baseball scholarship at the school. After one year at LIU, he signed with the Los Angeles Dodgers for a $9,000 bonus before the opening of the 1959 season.

Ferrara spent five years in the Dodgers' farm system before being called up at the end of 1963 to appear in 21 games—mainly as a pinch-hitter. He did not make the World Series roster and was returned to Triple-A Spokane for the 1964 season, where he hit a respectable .280 with 24 home runs. He finally made the Dodgers' Opening Day roster in April 1965.[4]

On May 4 at Crosley Field, in his first at-bat as the Dodgers' left fielder, Ferrara singled home two runs off Reds starter Joey Jay. The Dodgers went on to win the game and moved into a tie for first place with Cincinnati. The next night, Ferrara found himself batting in the cleanup spot in the lineup. He struck out twice, then came through with an RBI single in the top of the seventh inning. In the bottom of the eighth, he badly misplayed a line drive off the bat of Vada Pinson and broke a bone at the base of his little finger when he crashed into the left field box seats. Ferrara was charged with an error, and Sandy Koufax—who survived to record his third win—allowed an unearned run when Pinson eventually scored. But more importantly, Ferrara was unable to remain in the game. In the ninth inning, 31-year-old journeyman outfielder Lou Johnson quietly replaced him in left field.

Twenty-one-year-old Derrell Griffith, from Anadarko, Oklahoma, took over the left field position on May 6 for the series finale in Cincinnati. He got off to a promising start with a single and a home run. But by May 12, his average had plunged to .190.

Sweet Lou

Back on May 3, Lou Johnson was stunned when Peter O'Malley, the 28-year-old general manager of the Spokane Indians, called to tell him the Dodgers had purchased his contract and that he was to join the big club the next day in Cincinnati.

Louis Brown Johnson was born September 22, 1934, to an impoverished black family in Lexington, Kentucky. He lettered in track, football, and basketball—but not baseball—at Dunbar High School in Lexington, because the school didn't have a baseball team.[5] Though only 5'11" tall, he was an All-State and High School All-America basketball player. He played some sandlot softball, but it wasn't until his sophomore year at Kentucky State

University, where he was already a star basketball player, that he became serious about baseball as a career. He learned the game rapidly and was signed by the Yankees as an amateur free agent in the spring of 1953. A friend had to help pay his train fare to his first destination, Olean, New York, in the Class D PONY League.[6] Johnson was buried in the minors for the next 13 years playing for 18 different teams, with brief call-ups to the majors with the Cubs in 1960, the Angels in 1961, and the Braves in 1962. In 1964 with Spokane, he led the Pacific Coast League in batting until the last game of the season, finishing at .328.

On May 10, Lou Johnson got his big chance to start for the Dodgers in left field against the Houston Astros at Dodger Stadium. In the final game of that series, on May 13, he homered off big Astros righthander Bob Bruce in his first at-bat. As a batter, the tenacious Johnson hung over the plate, daring pitchers to move him off. As a consequence, he was often the league leader in

Journeyman outfielder Lou Johnson stepped up to fill the void left by Tommy Davis in left field for the Dodgers.

being hit by pitch. He had been beaned several times. In the sixth inning, Bruce came inside with a high fastball. The pitch got away and struck Johnson in the front of his batting helmet, a mere inches above his left eye.[7] The sickening crack of the impact of the baseball as it broke through the fiber shell of the helmet could be heard all over the ballpark. After several minutes lying unconscious on the ground, Johnson left the field on his own accord and was taken to Daniel Freeman Hospital for observation.[8] It was there that team doctor Robert Woods told reporters that the plastic batting helmet might have saved his life. The helmet was a frightening sight when it was later displayed in the press box with a grotesque imprint of the seams of the baseball above the "LA" initials.

With both Ferrara and Johnson sidelined, the only option left for Alston was to platoon Griffith and Moon in left. On May 15, the Dodgers and Cubs were locked in a pitchers' duel between left-handers Claude Osteen and Dick Ellsworth at Dodger Stadium. Ellsworth took a no-hitter into the bottom of the eighth inning, leading 1–0. The first two Dodgers reached base, Torborg on an error and Tracewski on a fielder's choice. John Kennedy moved the runners to second and third with a sacrifice bunt. His bench depleted, Alston was ready to let Drysdale, batting .300, pinch-hit for the pitcher. Before the game, Ferrara, with a sponge rubber pad and a golf glove on his left hand to protect his broken finger, had asked Alston to play. To Alston it was out of the question since the doctors had advised that the finger needed several more days to heal.[9] But when Ferrara took off his sponge rubber pad and began swinging a bat in the dugout, Alston relented and let him hit instead of Drysdale. With first base open, the Cubs decided to pitch to him instead of the pesky Maury Wills—a hard man to double up—with the bases loaded. On the third pitch, Ellsworth threw Ferrara a sinker that didn't sink. Ferrara launched a moon shot high and deep down the left field line. The only question was whether the curving ball would go foul. When it landed in the left field seats inches inside the foul pole, the no-hitter—and the lead—were gone. The Dodgers mobbed Ferrara when he returned to the dugout.[10] Jim Brewer came in to retire the Cubs in order in the ninth for a seemingly impossible 3–1 win. Ferrara's home run was their only hit in the game.

On May 16, the Dodgers completed their four-game series with the Cubs and their home stand with a Sunday doubleheader. After going hitless in the first game, a ten-inning, 5–3 loss, left fielder Derrell Griffith's average had plummeted to .133. Drysdale salvaged a split in the series with a complete-game, six-hit win in the second game with the ageless Moon in left field. The irrepressible Lou Johnson, who was not even supposed to be in uniform, ended up playing in both games as a late-inning substitute. The next day, on the road in Houston, the Dodgers' nightmare in left field ended when Johnson took over the position for good.

Drysdale-Gibson Masterpiece

On May 25, Don Drysdale and Bob Gibson squared off in a night game at Dodger Stadium. World Series MVP Gibson came into the game with a perfect 8–0 record with three shutouts. In the first inning, St. Louis leadoff batter Curt Flood hit a ground ball back to the mound that glanced off Drysdale's bare hand and continued into center field for a single. It would be the only Cardinals hit of the game. Drysdale retired every remaining batter except Dick Groat, who reached base on an error by Dick Tracewski in the fifth inning. The game was a scoreless tie as it moved to the bottom of the eighth. Drysdale led off with a single to raise his season average to .333. He eventually scored on a two-out, two-run double by Ron Fairly. With a 2–0 lead, Drysdale mowed down the last three hitters in order in the ninth for a one-hitter that took him only an hour and 41 minutes to complete. Though Gibson gave up only six hits, he was handed his first loss of the year. The win enabled the Dodgers to remain in first place, one game ahead of Cincinnati. Drysdale improved his record to 7–3. Earlier that day, the Dodgers activated first base coach Jim Gilliam to serve in a limited role as a pinch-hitter.

The next night, Sandy Koufax lost a tough 2–1 game to Curt Simmons and the Cardinals in the rubber game of the three-game series. The game was a 1–1 tie until the 36-year-old Simmons—0-for-18 for the year—singled with two outs in the seventh inning, prolonging the rally. Julian Javier then singled home Cardinals catcher Bob Uecker with the winning run.[11]

On May 29, Drysdale pitched the third and deciding game against Bobby Bragan's Milwaukee Braves. Lou Johnson hit a solo home run in the fourth inning and then broke a 2–2 tie with a three-run homer in the bottom of the eighth. Johnson clapped his hands with joy as he circled the bases.[12] Drysdale went on to win his eighth game, a 5–3 complete game with 12 strikeouts—including the great Hank Aaron three times. Lou Johnson was now batting .344 to lead the team.

The Dodgers' perceived principal threat, the Cincinnati Reds, came in next for a three-game series to close out the home stand and the month of May. On Memorial Day, May 30, Koufax pitched a complete game with 13 strikeouts to win the opener, 12–5. The series concluded with a doubleheader on May 31. The Dodgers beat Jim Maloney, 5–3, in the first game, but they lost third baseman Dick Tracewski when a Maloney fastball struck him on the right hand. Trusty Jim Gilliam took over the position for the remainder of the twin-bill. "Coach" Gilliam would end up playing in 111 games and hit a solid .280 in 1965. Joey Jay beat Claude Osteen, 6–1, in the second game to gain a split for the Reds. The Dodgers started the game with baseball's first all-switch-hitting infield: Parker (1B), Lefebvre (2B), Wills (SS), and Gilliam (3B). The Dodgers left town in first place with a four-game lead over the Reds and a three-game lead over the surging Giants, in second place after winning five games in a row.

	W	L	Pct.	GB
Los Angeles	29	17	.630	—
San Francisco	26	20	.565	3
Cincinnati	24	20	.545	4

Lou Johnson and great pitching by Koufax and Drysdale helped the Dodgers survive the disastrous loss of Tommy Davis to produce a 19–12 record in May. Johnson survived a near-fatal beaning, hit .306 and drove in ten runs with four doubles and three home runs, and played an errorless left field. Koufax and Drysdale each won five games, setting the tone for one of the greatest left-right combination seasons in league history.

7

Survival Summer

Whatever happens, I am more proud of this team than any I've ever managed.[1]—Walter Alston, after losing three straight to the Mets, August 26, 1965

Alston's scrappy 1965 Dodgers began June with a 14-game road trip. It proved to be a rocky one. They swept a two-game series in St. Louis, then dropped three out of four to the Braves in Milwaukee. The series at County Stadium concluded with a Sunday doubleheader on June 6. The Dodgers were temporarily buoyed when Drysdale became the major leagues' first ten-game winner with a brilliant six-hit shutout in the first game, only to have old nemeses Gene Oliver bury them with two home runs in the nightcap. The Braves had leapfrogged over the Reds and Giants into second place, two games behind the Dodgers. It was now a four-team pennant race.

On June 8, Major League Baseball conducted its first amateur draft at the Commodore Hotel in New York City. The Kansas City Athletics made Rick Monday, a 19-year-old sophomore outfielder from Arizona State, the first number one pick. For their first pick, the Dodgers chose 17-year-old shortstop John Wyatt from Bakersfield High School.[2] Wyatt would never make it higher than Class A ball. In the tenth round, they drafted a 20-year-old pitcher from USC named Tom Seaver. They would never offer him a contract. The draft ended the era of furious bidding wars for the game's top prospects characterized by extravagant handouts for "Bonus Babies" from 1947 through 1965.[3]

That same day in Washington, D.C., the State Department announced that the authority to order American ground forces into combat in Vietnam had been delegated by President Johnson to General William C. Westmoreland, head of the U.S. assistance command in South Vietnam. While U.S. combat forces would be deployed only "if their assistance is requested by the South Vietnamese Army," this marked a major step in the move from a passive to a more active combat role by the American military in Vietnam.[4]

After splitting a four-game series with the eighth place Phillies that concluded on June 10 at Connie Mack Stadium, the Dodgers were an even 5–5 since leaving Dodger Stadium. The good news was that they would end the road trip with four games with the cellar-dwelling Mets at in New York.

Losing Lou

In the June 11 opener before 55,023 fans at Shea Stadium, Drysdale beat a 44-year-old Warren Spahn and the Mets, 2–1, with a complete-game four-hitter. Drysdale won the game in the eighth inning with a solo home run off Spahn—his third of the year.

The following night, Koufax shut out the Mets, 5–0, on five hits. But Koufax's performance was overshadowed by what happened to Lou Johnson in the top of fifth inning. Johnson, who came into the game as the Dodgers' leading hitter at .319, was struck on the right hand by an Al Jackson fastball. Just 30 days after he suffered a near-fatal beaning, Johnson was removed for a pinch-runner and sent to the hospital.

The Dodgers concluded their road trip on June 13 with a Sunday doubleheader sweep before a record Shea Stadium crowd of 57,175. They headed for home after winning four straight in New York in first place, with a 3½ game lead over Milwaukee. They also got some bad news: Lou Johnson had a broken right thumb and would not be able to swing a bat for a minimum of two weeks.[5]

On June 24 at Dodger Stadium, Willie Stargell bludgeoned the Dodgers with three home runs (including two off Drysdale) and drove in six runs in a 13–3 Pirates route. The next night, Lou Johnson returned to the starting lineup with a small splint on his thumb after a 13-day absence. Surprisingly, the team lost no ground without their leading hitter during that period. The reason: great pitching. Claude Osteen won two games, including a one-hit shutout of the Giants on June 17. Four days later, he narrowly lost another one-hitter in the ninth inning at Dodger Stadium when the Mets beat him, 1–0, on a home run by Billy Cowan. Koufax won three straight complete games, allowing only two runs.

Ice Baths, Frostbite and Record Numbers

Sandy Koufax was a perfect 6–0 for the month of June. He was throwing between starts again and had not needed a cortisone injection since spring training. Instead, Koufax and the trainers came up with an alternative: hot-and-cold treatments. Before a start, the trainers would give him a rubdown with the red-hot ointment, Capsolin. While it burned the skin to the point of blistering, it increased the blood circulation in his arm. After the game, he would take an ice bath. This involved soaking his arm in a plastic tub filled with crushed ice and water. Ice was constantly added to keep the temperature of the water-ice mixture at around 35 degrees for the 35 to 40 minutes that his arm was submerged.[6] At first, the treatment severely dried and cracked his skin—what actually amounted to frostbite. But a creative trainer, Bill Buhler, improvised a solution to protect the skin by cutting a full-length "sleeve" from the inner tube of an automobile tire.

It was clear that the new regimen was working. By the end of June, Koufax was 13–3 for the season. With 169 strikeouts in 146⅓ innings, he was on pace to smash his own single-season strikeout record of 306 set in 1963. So every four days, Koufax would perform his otherworldly magic on the mound and then take an ice bath in his inner tube sleeve. The success of the ice bath treatments made it possible for him to control his usage of Butazolidin. Koufax and Buhler began adjusting the dosage downward to the minimal amount that would be helpful on days when he experienced a more than usual amount of soreness.[7] But questions remained. Wasn't it only ten months earlier that his season had to be shut down abruptly? Was this treatment of a human arm really sustainable? And for how long?

At this point in the season, rookie second baseman Jim Lefebvre had not had a day off. With a .183 month of June, his batting average had plummeted to .223.

The Arrival of the 31-Year-Old Belgian Rookie

Don Everett Lejohn was born May 13, 1934, to Belgium immigrant parents in Daisytown, Pennsylvania. After the Brooklyn Dodgers signed him as an amateur free agent before the 1954 season, LeJohn spent the next 12½ years in the minor leagues. He was batting a robust .395 as the third baseman of the Double-A Albuquerque Dukes in the Texas League when his manager, Roy Hartsfield, told him he was to report to the big club the next day in Chicago. On June 30, the 31-year-old LeJohn made his major league debut in the second game of a doubleheader at Wrigley Field. He drove in a run with a single in his first at-bat and scored the game's deciding run after singling in his next at-bat.[8] At the time, LeJohn was believed to be the only player of Belgian origin in the major leagues.[9] The addition of LeJohn enabled the Dodgers to move Jim Gilliam from third base to second and give Lefebvre a much-needed rest.

With Sandy Koufax once again tearing up the league, the Dodgers were in first place by two games at the end of play on June 30.

	W	L	Pct.	GB
Los Angeles	46	31	.597	—
Cincinnati	43	32	.573	2
San Francisco	40	33	.548	4
Milwaukee	37	33	.529	5½
Philadelphia	38	34	.528	5½
Pittsburgh	39	35	.527	5½

Struggling Through a Flat July

Going into the game of July 5 in Cincinnati, the Dodgers had been in sole possession of first place for two months. This night at Crosley Field, they blew a three-run lead to lose the game—and first place by two percentage points—to the Reds. The loss set off Walter Alston's annual volcanic eruption. In the clubhouse after the game, he went ballistic, ejecting a reporter traveling with the team and berating the players for their sloppy play.[10]

The team closed out a 16-game road trip with a Sunday doubleheader in Pittsburgh on July 11, the final date before the All-Star Game break. Koufax won the first game, 4–2, with a complete-game, ten-strikeout performance for his 15th victory of the year. They needed a sweep to maintain their first-place lead over Cincinnati. But pesky Pirates outfielder—and future Dodgers pinch-hitter extraordinaire—Manny Mota beat them with a walk-off home run in the tenth inning. At the All-Star Game break, Koufax was 15–3, Drysdale was 13–8, and Maury Wills had 55 stolen bases—20 games ahead of his record pace of 1962. But after a 7–9 road trip, the Dodgers still trailed the Cincinnati Reds by percentage points.

	W	L	Pct.	GB
Cincinnati	49	36	.576	—
Los Angeles	51	38	.573	—
San Francisco	45	38	.542	3
Philadelphia	45	39	.536	3½

Minnesota catcher Earl Battey was one of six Twins at the July 13, 1965, All-Star Game at Metropolitan Stadium in Minneapolis.

The All-Star Game was played on July 13 before a crowd of 46,706 at Metropolitan Stadium in Minneapolis, home of the Minnesota Twins. Sam Mele's surprising Twins, who went into the break with a five-game lead over the Baltimore Orioles, were represented by six players: starting first baseman Harmon Killebrew, starting catcher Earl Battey, outfielder Jimmie Hall, outfielder Tony Oliva, shortstop Zoilo Versalles, and pitcher Jim "Mudcat" Grant. The Dodgers were represented by starting shortstop, Maury Wills; with pitchers, Drysdale and Koufax. With home runs by Willie Mays, Joe Torre, and Willie Stargell, the National League won a seesaw game, 6–5. The Americans rocked Cincinnati's Jim Maloney in the fifth inning with home runs by Killebrew and Dick McAuliffe. Koufax pitched a shaky sixth inning with two walks, but was credited with the win when Ron Santo singled home Mays with the winning run in the top of the seventh. The overflow crowd even filled the upper deck of the left-field bleachers that were completed only four days before.[11] The club would be doubly glad they added the new section come October.

After the All-Star break, the Dodgers returned to Los Angeles for a 14-game home stand. By July 20, they had won the first six games in a row as Koufax beat the Astros, 3–2. It was his 11th consecutive victory and improved his record to 17–3. Despite his .097 career batting average, Alston let him hit with two outs in the bottom of the ninth with the score tied 2–2 and the winning run on second base. Koufax came through with a walk-off base hit. The Dodgers' first-place lead was now 3½ games over Cincinnati. That lead shrank to one game after they lost four of their next five to the Braves and Cardinals, setting up a big three-game series with the Reds to close out the home stand.

On July 25, Bob Dylan played the Newport Folk Festival in Newport, Rhode Island. Dylan had appeared there five times before, as a solo artist playing an acoustic guitar—sometimes with a harmonica rack. But on this day he set off a firestorm by walking out on stage with a five-piece electric band. The folk purists sat in stunned silence as Dylan, dressed in a garish orange shirt with large white Polka dots and black leather pants, launched into a deafening version of "Maggie's Farm" played through an overwhelmed sound system. By the time he was into "Like a Rolling Stone," the crowd was booing and hurling angry epithets at him: "Sell out!" "This is a folk festival!"[12] An apoplectic Pete

Seeger threatened to take things into his own hands and personally rip out the wires to the sound system. After only three songs, Dylan and his band fled the stage under a storm of boos. There would be no acoustic set. Newport '65 was a tectonic event in American popular music.

In the series opener on July 26, the Dodgers got off to a 5–1 lead after two innings and hung on to beat the Reds, 5–4. Johnny Podres, who had not pitched in 17 days, struggled through the first five innings to get his fourth victory. Podres would never pitch another complete game for the Dodgers. Jim Gilliam and Maury Wills led the team to a 9–7 win the next night at Dodger Stadium. Wills stole two bases and had two hits to run his batting streak to 20 straight games. During the streak, Wills boosted his batting average from .256 to .302. Now with 71 stolen bases, he was 29 games ahead of his record 1962 pace. Gilliam was a perfect 3-for-3 with a double, a home run, and four runs batted in.

The next day, July 28, at a press conference in Washington, D.C., President Johnson announced that the then-current U.S. military presence of 75,000 men in South Vietnam would be increased to 125,000 "almost immediately." Monthly draft calls would be gradually increased from 17,000 to 35,000.[13] When asked by a reporter if the sending of the additional troops implied a change in the policy of relying on South Vietnamese troops and using American troops as an emergency backup, Johnson answered, "It does not imply any change in policy whatever."[14] In reality, it was the beginning of an entirely new policy: what was the South Vietnamese war would become primarily an American war.[15]

That night at Dodger Stadium, the Dodgers had a chance to sweep the series and increase their lead to four games with Sandy Koufax on the mound for the series finale before a season-high crowd of 53,604. But from the start, Koufax had trouble getting loose. He took massage treatments on the bench and disappeared into the clubhouse several times between innings.[16] By the end of the fourth inning, he was already behind, 4–0, and Reds right-hander Sammy Ellis had blown away seven Dodgers on strikes. Ellis went on to pitch a four-hit complete game with 12 strikeouts to beat Koufax and the Dodgers, 4–1. Koufax's 11-game winning streak was ended, as was Maury Wills' 20-game hitting streak. The Dodgers' lead had been reduced to two games over Cincinnati as rumors about a Koufax "elbow flare-up" began to circulate in the press.[17]

On July 30, President Johnson flew to Independence, Missouri to sign the Medicare Bill, expanding Social Security to provide medical care for Americans over the age of 65. The ceremony was held at the Harry S. Truman Library with the 81-year-old Truman at the side of LBJ. In 1945, Truman had asked Congress to enact similar legislation, only to see it founder when the American Medical Association attacked it as it "socialized medicine."[18]

The Dodgers ended the month of July with a tough 4–3 loss to Bob Gibson and the Cardinals in St. Louis. Don Drysdale had to leave the game in the seventh inning with a 3–2 lead when his left knee buckled during a pitch to Tim McCarver. It was a recurrence of an old high school injury; the cartilage in his knee popped out, causing the joint to collapse.[19] Ron Perranoski took over and managed to preserve the lead until the Cardinals loaded the bases with three straight infield singles in the bottom of the ninth. Lou Brock ended the game with a two-run, walk-off single.

At the end of play on July 31, the Dodgers' lead was back to a single game. And there were now serious doubts about whether Koufax and Drysdale could hold up physically with 57 games left in the season.

	W	L	Pct.	GB
Los Angeles	61	44	.581	—
Cincinnati	59	44	.573	1
San Francisco	55	43	.561	2½
Milwaukee	54	45	.545	4

The Wars of August

On August 1, Sandy Koufax calmed the Dodgers organization's fears about his "elbow flare-up" causing another truncated season when he made his regularly scheduled start at Busch Stadium in St. Louis. He beat the Cardinals, 5–2, for his 18th victory, a five-hit complete game with no walks and 11 strikeouts. For good measure, he drove in the deciding run with a sacrifice fly in the seventh inning.[20]

Drysdale was also able to make his next regularly scheduled start on August 4 in the first game of a twilight-night doubleheader in Milwaukee. He went the distance without his knee popping out, but lost a close 4–3 game to the Braves thanks to early solo home runs by Henry Aaron and that man, Gene Oliver. The Dodgers got a split when Osteen won the second game, 3–2, despite a double and another home run by the great Aaron. Koufax beat the Braves, 6–3, the next night with a complete-game, 12-strikeout performance at County Stadium to win the series. Koufax was now 19–4 with 253 strikeouts. The Dodgers left Milwaukee in first place by three games over the Reds and Giants, and 3½ games over the Braves.

On August 6 in Washington, D.C., President Johnson signed the Voting Rights Act of 1965 into law. The signing took place in the President's Room of the Capital Building, just off the Senate chamber. In the same room in 1861, President Lincoln signed a bill freeing the slaves who were impressed into the service of the Confederacy.[21]

That night in Cincinnati, the Dodgers opened a big three-game weekend series at Crosley Field. The Reds shelled Johnny Podres with four solo home runs in the first five innings. After the Dodgers' bullpen held them scoreless over the next five innings, Jimmie Coker, the Reds' third-string catcher with a .161 batting average, broke a 4–4 tie with a pinch-hit single off Ron Perranoski to win the game, 5–4, in the 11th inning.[22] Howie Reed and Perranoski combined to beat the Reds, 5–3, the next night, allowing the Dodgers to maintain a two-game lead over the surging Giants. Don Drysdale and Jim Maloney matched up for the rubber game of the series on Sunday, August 8. It was a disaster for the Dodgers. Drysdale departed after only two innings, down 6–0. Before it was over, the Reds had pounded the Dodgers' bullpen for 12 more runs in an 18–0 route on 20 hits. Everyone in the Cincinnati lineup—except the pitcher—had at least two hits.[23] It is still the worst shutout loss in team history. For his part, Maloney contributed a single and pitched a four-hit shutout. Drysdale's record was 15–10 after being charged with the loss. He had now made five consecutive starts without a win. The Dodgers split the ten-game road trip and headed home to Los Angeles clinging to first place by one game over the Giants and two games over the Reds and Braves.

When they arrived home on August 9, the players read quotes in the newspapers by Reds manager Dick Sisler saying the Dodgers would be the first team to fall out of pennant contention because Drysdale and Koufax were beginning to show the strain of having to pitch every fourth day to carry the team.[24] The taunts backfired. On August 10, Koufax struck out 14 Mets for his 20th victory. The next night at Dodger Stadium, Drysdale shut them out, 1–0, on five singles for his first win in 23 days. After the game, a feisty Drysdale told reporters, "Maybe Sisler will have to eat his words."[25]

On the same hot August night, 13 miles south of Dodger Stadium in the black community of Watts, racial tensions boiled over when a routine drunk driving arrest erupted into a riot. Blacks at the scene complained of police brutality but could provide few specific details.[26] The "Watts Riots" would last for six days, killing 35 people and injuring 1,032–90 percent blacks.[27]

By August 13, Watts was an outright conflagration with buildings and overturned vehicles burning out of control. Two thousand National Guardsmen in military vehicles armed with rifles, bayonets, machine guns, and tear gas moved in to support a beleaguered contingent of 900 policemen and deputy sheriffs. "It's going to be like Vietnam," one Guardsman told reporters.[28] That night in Chavez Ravine, the smoke that drifted in from the war zone hung like a pall over Dodger Stadium. A subdued Friday the 13th crowd of 32,551 watched Claude Osteen beat the Pirates, 3–1.[29]

On Saturday, August 14, another 18,000 National Guardsmen troops were called up to deal with the rapidly deteriorating situation in Watts. California Lieutenant Governor Glenn Anderson, serving as acting Governor while Governor Edmund G. Brown was en route to LAX from an interrupted European vacation, proclaimed a curfew from 8:00 p.m. to sunrise in the 35-square-mile area where the rioting was centered.[30]

Saturday night—Ladies Night at Dodger Stadium—should have been an automatic turn-away sellout with Sandy Koufax on the mound. But a crowd of only 29,237 turned out to watch Koufax pitch against the Pirates on the evening of August 14. Officials estimated that the gravity of the local situation depressed attendance by at least 25,000. Koufax and Pirates starter Don Cardwell both had shutouts until the game entered the bottom of the tenth inning. Cardwell retired the first two Dodgers, then walked Koufax and Wes Parker. Jim Gilliam battled Cardwell to a full count before connecting on a sinking line drive toward Roberto Clemente in right field. The great Clemente only had to take a few steps to get into position to catch the ball. But at the last split-second, he lost sight of the ball in the lights, and it popped out of his glove for a rare error. Koufax scored easily from second base to win the game, 1–0.[31] The ten-inning, five-hit shutout with 12 strikeouts was his 21st victory of the year. With a probable 11 additional starts, there was talk of a 30-win season—the first since Dizzy Dean in 1934.

Just getting home that night was a challenge. When the Dodgers' black outfielder, Willie Crawford, parked his car in front of his house, he looked down the barrels of rifles held by three National Guardsmen. "I didn't say a word and neither did they; I just raised my hands over my head and walked into my house." said Crawford. While Johnny Podres was driving back to his hotel, the car next to his was struck on the hood by a sniper's bullet.[32]

On Sunday, August 15, the fifth day of the crisis in Los Angeles, the Dodgers had a chance to sweep the series from the Pirates with Don Drysdale on the mound. On his way to Dodger Stadium, Wes Parker's sports car died on the Santa Monica Freeway. He walked off the freeway to a phone booth to call for a cab, but no cab driver was willing to enter the rioting area. The Dodgers batboy had to pick up Parker and deliver him to the park less than an hour before game time. A game that would have drawn 40,000+ under ordinary circumstances drew only 25,175. Alston moved Drysdale, batting .300 with five home runs, up to the seventh spot in the batting order. But he lasted only six innings and struck out both times he came up to bat. With two perfect squeeze plays and a sacrifice fly, Harry Walker's Pirates beat Drysdale and the Dodgers, 4–2. The Dodgers' lead was reduced to 1½ games over the Braves and 2½ games over the Giants.

The next night, August 16, the Dodgers began a three-game series with the Phillies to close out the home stand. Though calm was returning to Los Angeles,[33] only 22,611 people were willing to navigate the freeways to see left-handers Johnny Podres and Chris Short at Dodger Stadium. Short threw a complete-game six-hitter to dispose of the Dodgers, 6–1. Only a ninth-inning home run by Jim Lefebvre prevented a shutout. Podres, his career rapidly fading, lasted only two innings. It was his 12th consecutive start without a complete game.[34]

On August 17, the Dodgers, behind the pitching of Clause Osteen and Ron Perranoski, came from behind to beat the Phillies, 4–2, and preserve a razor-thin half-game lead over the Braves.

The series, and first place, would be decided by the August 18 battle of aces between Sandy Koufax and Jim Bunning. Neither man could complete the game: Bunning went 6⅓ innings and Koufax seven. The game moved into extra innings as a 3–3 tie. With two out in the top of the 12th inning and two Philadelphia runners on, Maury Wills fumbled Richie Allen's ground ball to load the bases. Dick Stuart followed with a bloop double down the right field line to score all three runners.[35] The devastating 6–3 loss, completed after midnight on August 19, knocked the Dodgers out of first place for the first time in five weeks. They were now a half-game behind the Braves. There would be no day off for travel. They had 12 hours to get ready for a showdown with the Giants in San Francisco.

The Dodgers checked into the Sheraton Palace Hotel in San Francisco at 4:00 a.m. that morning.[36] There would be little opportunity for sleep. At 1:00 p.m., Don Drysdale was scheduled to meet 44-year-old Warren Spahn at Candlestick Park. Spahn had been given his unconditional release by the Mets back on July 17 after losing eight games in a row, and was signed by the Giants as a free agent the next day. Drysdale got off to a rocky start in the first inning by giving up a two-run home run to Willie Mays. By that time, the scoreboard reflected the Cardinals' win over the Braves in St. Louis. A Giants victory would vault them over Milwaukee into the NL lead for the first time that season—albeit by a .001 margin—with the Dodgers dropping into third.[37] But after getting past the first, Drysdale was able to settle into a rhythm. He hit his own home run in the sixth inning and came within one out of his 17th victory in the bottom of the ninth. With two out and a runner on second base, Giants catcher Tom Haller lined Drysdale's first pitch over the right field fence to tie the game at 5–5 and send it into extra innings. Drysdale soldiered on for two more innings before coming out for a pinch-hitter in the 12th. The game went to the 15th, still tied 5–5. At that point, Gaylord Perry, who had pitched six scoreless innings in relief, ran out of steam. Perry was rocked for a deciding two-run home run by Lou Johnson, followed by three straight singles resulting in the Dodgers' eighth run. When Perranoski pitched his fourth consecutive scoreless inning to close out the Giants in the bottom of the 15th, they had a four-hour, 11-minute, 8–5 win and had regained a narrow half-game hold on first place.

	W	L	Pct.	GB
Los Angeles	71	51	.582	—
Milwaukee	69	50	.580	½
San Francisco	67	50	.573	1½

The second game of the series was played on a frigid Friday night, August 20, before a crowd of 41,858. Bob Shaw, with 13 wins, started for the Giants against the Dodgers' spot starter, Howie Reed.

Several hours before the 8:00 start, Giants groundskeeper Matty Schwab, who had conspired with Alvin Dark in 1962 to turn the Giants infield into a quagmire, covered the home plate area with several inches of loose peat moss. When the Dodgers arrived at Candlestick Park, they immediately lodged a protest, maintaining that the intent was to prevent their speedsters—primarily Maury Wills with his 79 stolen bases—from obtaining quick getaways out of the batter's box. Crew chief umpire Shag Crawford saw right through it and ordered Schwab to remove the offending material and re-roll the area before the game began.[38]

The night was so cold that the fans wore overcoats and brought blankets to wrap around their legs. Some of the Dodgers wore long underwear.[39] The Giants hitters roughed up Howie Reed early. Willie Mays tagged him for a long, two-run homer to right-center field in the third inning. By the end of the fourth, Reed and the Dodgers were down, 4–1.

Tensions between the two clubs began to reach a boiling point in the fifth inning. Wills, already annoyed by the Giants' attempt to sabotage the field, squared around to bunt, then pulled the bat back intentionally to strike Giants' catcher Tom Haller's glove. The ploy worked. Plate umpire Al Forman awarded Wills first base on catcher interference. Giants manager Herman Franks retaliated by instructing Matty Alou to employ the same gamesmanship against Dodgers catcher John Roseboro in the bottom of the inning. When Alou tried it, he was not able to elicit an interference call. But he managed to enrage Roseboro, who, when distracted by the maneuver, was hit in the chest protector by the baseball. He threatened to "get" Alou if he ever tried it again. Juan Marichal, yelling from the Giants' bench, in turn threatened Roseboro.[40] Thus the tone was set for the remainder of the series. Marichal was due to pitch in two days in the series finale.

Jim Ray Hart led off the sixth inning with a home run to knock Reed out of the game before he could get anyone out. Bob Shaw cruised to an easy, 5–1, complete-game win. The loss dropped the Dodgers back into second place for the second time in 48 hours.[41]

	W	L	Pct.	GB
Milwaukee	70	50	.583	—
Los Angeles	71	52	.577	½
San Francisco	68	50	.576	1

On Saturday afternoon, August 21, 42,583 fans turned out to watch Claude Osteen and the Giants' right-handed fireballer, Bobby Bolin, at Candlestick Park. Osteen threw five scoreless innings before Willie McCovey's two-run homer tied the game, 2–2. In the top of the seventh, Johnny Roseboro finished off Bolin with a two-run homer that put the Dodgers back in front, 4–3. The incendiary Willie Mays hit a solo home run in the bottom of the eighth that re-tied the game at 4–4. It was his third home run of the series and his fifth in the last five games. With two out in the bottom of the ninth, Ron Perranoski got Willie McCovey to hit a ground ball to Wes Parker at first base, who flipped the ball to Perranoski covering the bag to send the game to extra innings. In the process, Perranoski pulled a hamstring muscle. He would be out for the next ten games.[42]

With two out in the top of the 11th and Willie Crawford on third base, Wes Parker tried a squeeze bunt on the first pitch thrown to him by Giants reliever Frank Linzy, but fouled if off. He swung away on the second pitch and connected, sending a high fly ball into the jet stream blowing out to right field. Giants right-fielder Matty Alou made a desperate leap for the ball, but could not reach it as it passed over the chain-link fence and disappeared into the crowd for a two-run homer to give the Dodgers the lead, 6–4. The forgotten man, Johnny Podres, who came in from the bullpen to retire the Giants in order in the tenth, did it again in the bottom of the 11th to close out the game and get his fifth win.

Earlier in the day, the Pirates' Bob Friend shut out the Braves, 3–0, in Pittsburgh. Consequently, the Dodgers' win prevented the Giants from moving into first place for the first time since July 1964.[43] Instead, the Dodgers jumped back into the lead by a half-game.

	W	L	Pct.	GB
Los Angeles	72	52	.581	—
Milwaukee	70	51	.579	½
San Francisco	68	51	.571	1½

Mayhem on the Baseball Field

On a hot Sunday afternoon, August 22, 42,807 fans packed Candlestick Park for the series finale and to see the National League's top two pitchers collide: Sandy Koufax (21–4) and Juan Marichal (19–9). There was a lot at stake. With a win, the Dodgers could take the series three games to one and put the Giants 2½ games behind.

Maury Wills opened the game with a bunt single down the third base line. Two batters later, Ron Fairly drove him in with a double into the left field corner to give the Dodgers a 1–0 lead.[44] Marichal didn't like hitters who bunted, and Wills had already gotten under his skin.

In top of the second inning, John Roseboro added fuel to the fire with a run-scoring single off Marichal to make it 2–0, Dodgers. Before the inning was over, Wills, who now had eight hits in the series, was knocked down by Marichal. In the bottom of the inning, Koufax retaliated by sending a fastball high over Willie Mays' head to the screen behind home plate. Mays went halfway down, but stayed on his feet. Koufax would later say that he intended to throw the pitch much closer—to flatten Mays.[45]

In the top of the third, Fairly, who had doubled off Marichal his first time up, was

Johnny Roseboro was fortunate to escape serious injury when Juan Marichal split his head open with a bat on August 22, 1965, at Candlestick Park.

knocked down. An incensed group of players in the Dodgers dugout—and Roseboro in particular—were now yelling at Marichal.[46] At this point, both benches were warned.

It was an uneasy crowd that watched Sandy Koufax, with a 2–1 lead, warm up for the bottom of the third inning, knowing that Juan Marichal would be the first batter he would face. Koufax, who thought the matter was over after he dutifully buzzed Mays, didn't think he had to throw inside to Marichal. But the matter was clearly not over between Roseboro and Marichal. Roseboro was still angry that Marichal had thrown at Wills, his friend and roommate.

Marichal took the first pitch for a strike. The second pitch was low and inside. Roseboro dropped the ball, picked it up, and fired it back to Koufax provocatively close to Marichal's ear. Marichal would claim that the ball actually nicked his ear.[47] Marichal yelled a warning at

The great Juan Marichal, San Francisco Giants, was suspended for eight games after the August 22, 1965, bat incident.

Roseboro: "You better not hit me with that ball!"[48] Roseboro in turn cursed Marichal's mother. Roseboro took off his mask and came toward Marichal. That was the point of no return. All hell broke loose. A threatened Marichal went berserk, striking Roseboro over the head—at least twice—with his bat.[49] After Koufax caught Roseboro's return throw, he had turned his back to home plate and walked back behind the rubber. He heard no crowd reaction. When he turned around to get the sign for the next pitch, he was shocked to see Marichal splitting Roseboro's head open with his bat. Koufax rushed in toward the plate and tried in vain to grab the bat from Marichal.[50] Both benches and bullpens emptied to form a moving mob. While plate umpire Shag Crawford horse-collared Marichal, Giants rookie shortstop Tito Fuentes, the on-deck batter, held a bat over his head cocked at Roseboro, but was bounced out of the epicenter before he could deliver a blow. Lou Johnson, who had sprinted in from left field, was throwing wild punches at anyone in a white San Francisco uniform.[51]

It was 15 minutes before the umpires and stadium security could stop the fists from flying and the spikes from slashing. What was left was a horrific scene. Roseboro was bleeding profusely from a gash on the top of his head. His left eye was filled with blood, leading Walter Alston and others to believe that the eye was out of its socket. Peacemaker Willie Mays finally managed to restrain Roseboro and escort him to the Dodgers' dugout, surrounded by nine Dodgers. Once there, he tenderly wiped blood from Roseboro's forehead and eye.[52] To everyone's relief, the left eye was still in its socket.

Koufax appeared shaken when the game resumed. He managed to strike out pinchhitter Bob Schroder, who completed Marichal's at bat. Tito Fuentes teed off on an errant pitch, but Lou Johnson ran the ball down in deep left field for the second out. Koufax

Willie Mays played the dual role of peacemaker and destroyer in the August 22, 1965, Marichal-Roseboro bat incident. He hit a career-high 52 home runs and was voted the MVP of the National League.

then walked the next two batters, Jim Davenport and Willie McCovey, to set the stage for Willie Mays. Once in the batter's box, Mays was transformed from peacemaker to a shark that smelled blood in the water. He hit Koufax's first pitch over the left-center field fence for a devastating three-run homer. Mays' fourth home run of the series turned the Dodgers' 2–1 lead into a 4–2 deficit from which they would not recover.

Koufax settled down after the third inning and gave up only one more hit—a single to Mr. Mays in the eighth—but went down to a 4–3 defeat. After the game, Willie Mays, peacemaker and destroyer, went to the visitors' clubhouse to pay a visit to Roseboro, whose head had been shaved on the left side, where a white bandage covered the wound inflicted by Marichal. In a strange twist, Roseboro was wearing a Giants baseball cap given to him "as protection" by the San Francisco doctor who attended to him. He would be placed in a taxi and given a police escort out of Candlestick Park.[53] The four-game series ended in a split, with the Dodgers clinging to a half-game lead over the Giants and Braves, in a virtual tie for second.

	W	L	Pct.	GB
Los Angeles	72	53	.576	—
San Francisco	69	51	.575	½
Milwaukee	70	52	.574	½

The day after the brawl, National League president Warren Giles suspended Marichal for eight playing dates through August 31 and fined him $1,750. The suspension would likely cost Marichal two starts. In a strongly worded telegram to Marichal, Giles intimated that the pitcher's "repugnant actions" may have been mitigated by "underlying currents caused by others throughout the series."[54] The editorial board of *The Sporting News* ripped Giles, calling Marichal's behavior a "vicious attack" with a "deadly weapon" that deserved a suspension of at least 30 days.[55] The Dodgers were outraged by the light nature of the penalty. "The penalties inflicted on Marichal were a joke. Giles is gutless," said Wills.[56] Koufax, who had exposed himself to serious injury attempting to wrest the weapon from Marichal, had a problem with the length of the suspension: "Marichal was fined pretty good, but he wasn't set down long enough."[57] A disgusted Walter Alston told reporters, "you wouldn't want to print what I personally think about the suspension and the fine."[58] The mildest reaction came from Roseboro: "I have no reaction to Giles' ruling. I don't carry grudges, and I'm not going looking for Marichal the next time our teams play."[59] The two teams were scheduled to meet at Dodger Stadium September 6–7 in their final series of the season. At the end of the suspension period, Giles would ban Marichal from the series for security reasons.[60]

On the day of the Giles ruling, the Dodgers arrived in New York for a four-game series with the Mets. They appeared to be consumed by it. That night they committed four errors but pulled out an 8–4 win behind Drysdale, who gave them 7⅔ workmanlike innings for his 17th win. They then proceeded to lose the next three games to the tenth-place Mets. Even Koufax—with a career 13–0 record against the Amazin' Mets—couldn't stop them. In the series finale on August 26, 20-year-old rookie left-hander Tug McGraw beat Koufax and the Dodgers, 5–2, before 45,950 fans at Shea Stadium.[61] For the only time in 1965, Koufax had lost two games in a row.

On August 29, Claude Osteen and the Dodgers ended the month by absorbing a 13–3 thumping at the hands of the Phillies in Philadelphia. Alston took Osteen out of the game in the third inning after he had been pounded for six runs and eight hits, including two home runs. The loss lowered his record to 11–13 for the season. The Dodgers, who won the weekend series two games to one, left Philadelphia with a 1½-game lead over the Giants.

	W	L	Pct.	GB
Los Angeles	75	57	.568	—
San Francisco	71	56	.559	1½
Cincinnati	72	57	.558	1½
Milwaukee	71	58	.550	2½

On August 30, Bob Dylan released his groundbreaking album, *Highway 61 Revisited*, that he recorded with an electric rock band. The opening track, "Like a Rolling Stone," already had been at the top of the charts for 12 weeks as a single, albeit at an unheard-of six minutes and 13 seconds long.

The Right Leg of Maury Wills

The 1965 season began with Alston and Bavasi obsessing over the left arm of Sandy Koufax. As the team headed into September, their concern was the right leg of Maury Wills. By the end of August Wills, the Dodgers' catalyst, had 83 stolen bases—12 games ahead of his record-breaking pace of 1962. But a new single-season stolen base record, which looked like a certainty at the All-Star break, was now in doubt. His right leg—the one that hit the dirt first when he slid—was so severely bruised and swollen that he was waking up in the middle of the night from the pain.[62] It would cause him to curtail his base stealing for the next three weeks.

8

September of Colliding Streaks

He tried to throw the ball right past us; and he did.[1]—Ernie Banks, Dodger Stadium, September 9, 1965

On the first day of September, the Dodgers opened the stretch drive by throwing Koufax and Drysdale at the Pirates in a day-night doubleheader at Forbes Field in Pittsburgh. Both aces went down to narrow one-run defeats at the hands of a red-hot Pirates team that had now won 12 out of their last 14 games. Despite striking out ten batters to break his own NL single-season strikeout record, Koufax was beaten, 3–2, by Pirates catcher Jim Pagliaroni's walk-off double with two out in the 11th inning of the day game. Drysdale lost the second game, 2–1, when Maury Wills booted a double play ball to allow the winning run to score in the eighth inning.[2] In Cincinnati, the Reds swept a doubleheader from the Braves to knock the Dodgers out of first place by a single percentage point. Earlier that day, John Roseboro filed a lawsuit in Los Angeles Superior Court against the San Francisco Giants and Juan Marichal, asking for $10,000 in general damages and $100,000 in punitive damages.[3]

The next night, Claude Osteen beat Bob Veale and the Pirates, 7–1, to salvage the series finale and enable the Dodgers to climb back into first place by one game over the Giants and Reds, tied for second in the topsy-turvy NL pennant race.[4] Three hundred miles to the east, at Connie Mack Stadium in Philadelphia, Juan Marichal was greeted with a tumultuous flood of boos on his return to action after a nine-day suspension. Marichal was not sharp due to the layoff, and the Phillies beat him, 4–3, in the first game of a twi-night doubleheader. The Giants rebounded to win the second game, 5–2.[5]

In Houston, the last leg of a 17-game road trip, the Dodgers swept a three-game weekend series. Six different Dodgers pitchers combined to shut out the ninth-place Astros over the first two games. Ron Perranoski saved both games after missing ten days due to the hamstring injury he sustained in San Francisco. In the finale on Sunday, September 5, at the Astrodome, they came from behind on a clutch two-run pinch-hit triple by old pro Jim Gilliam with two out in the ninth inning to pull out a 4–2 win.[6] Gilliam was due to turn 37 in October. The plan had been to give him Sundays off—unless, of course, they needed him. Howie Reed, who pitched the last two innings in relief of Koufax, was the winning pitcher. The Dodgers were in first place by one game over the Reds as they headed back to Los Angeles for a two-game showdown with the Giants, the final meeting of the year between the two clubs.

Rematch at Dodger Stadium

It was raining in Los Angeles the morning of Monday, September 6, when the Giants arrived at LAX—sans Juan Marichal. The day before at Wrigley Field in Chicago, Marichal had beaten the Cubs, 4–2, for his 20th win before flying straight home to San Francisco to comply with an order from the National League office.[7] Because of the threatening phone calls the Giants were receiving following the brawl in San Francisco, they were given a police escort from the airport to Dodger Stadium.[8] The condition of the field was so soggy that the Giants and Dodgers skipped batting and infield practice before the 1 p.m. Labor Day start. It would be Don Drysdale (18–12) for the Dodgers against Warren Spahn (6–16) for the Giants. There was so much interest in this much-anticipated rematch that NBC broadcast the game to a national audience. It was a complete sellout of 53,581.

The Dodgers knocked Spahn out of the game in the second inning to jump out to an early 4–0 lead. From there it turned into a seesaw thriller. A marginally effective Drysdale was cuffed around for nine hits, including two home runs, and threw two wild pitches. He lasted until the top of the ninth inning, when Tom Haller hit his first pitch over the right field fence to tie the game, 6–6, and send it into extra innings.

Ron Perranoski took over for Drysdale and held the Giants scoreless through the 11th inning. The Dodgers pinch-hit for Perranoski with a runner on second base in the bottom of the inning, but could not score. Howie Reed came in to pitch the top of the 12th. Giants reliever Frank Linzy led off with a single to left field. After Reed struck out Dick Schofield, Matty Alou hit a perfect double play ball to Wes Parker at first base. Parker threw to Maury Wills to force Linzy at second, and Wills threw back to Reed covering the bag at first in time for what appeared to be an inning-ending double play. But first base umpire Bill Williams ruled that Reed's foot missed the bag, setting off a heated rhubarb. The Dodgers spent the next few minutes in a futile attempt to change his ruling. Alston wanted no part of Mays and ordered Reed to walk him intentionally and pitch to Jim Davenport instead. The plan backfired when Davenport, batting .247, looped a single into left-center field to score Alou with the winning run.

Aside from Don Drysdale brushing back Orlando Cepeda twice, there were no hit batters, no incendiary incidents.[9] Lawsuit plaintiff and catcher John Roseboro hit a single, a double, and a home run. A hobbled Maury Wills was thrown out both times he attempted to steal second base. Juan Marichal watched the game on his television set at home. The Giants moved to within one game of the Dodgers.

	W	L	Pct.	GB
Los Angeles	79	60	.568	—
San Francisco	76	59	.563	1
Milwaukee	77	61	.558	1½
Cincinnati	77	61	.558	1½

The concluding game of the series, and the final meeting of the year between the two teams, was played on Tuesday night, September 7. Another large Dodger Stadium crowd of 48, 576 turned out to see a matchup between Dodgers left-hander Claude Osteen (12–13) and Giants right-hander Bob Shaw (14–8).

Willie Mays, on his way to an MVP season, was the hitter the Dodgers feared most. But it was Jim Ray Hart, runner-up to Richie Allen in the 1964 Rookie of the Year Award voting, who was a one-man team for the Giants. Hart put the Giants ahead, 1–0, when he topped a bouncer down the third base line for an infield single to score Jesus Alou in the first inning.[10] The Dodgers tied the game, 1–1, in the third on back-to-back doubles by Wes Parker and John Roseboro.

Osteen held the Giants scoreless in the second through fourth innings. In the top of the fifth, he walked the dangerous Mays, who had already singled and doubled off him, to set the stage for Hart. The 5'11", barrel-chested Hart had strengthened his arms, wrists, and hands chopping cotton as a boy in Hookerton, North Carolina.[11] Hart hit Osteen's high and outside fastball over the 410-foot sign in center field for a crushing two-run home run to put the Giants in front, 3–1. The red-hot Hart had now hit seven home runs and driven in 20 runs in the last 13 games.

That was the end of the scoring. Shaw, with help from the Giants' left-handed Japanese reliever, Masanori Murakami, shut out the Dodgers the rest of the way. It was a devastating loss for the Dodgers. San Francisco swept the series to take over first place for the first time since July 15, 1964—albeit by only two percentage points.

	W	L	Pct.	GB
San Francisco	77	59	.566	—
Los Angeles	79	61	.564	—
Cincinnati	78	61	.561	½
Milwaukee	77	61	.558	1

After the downcast crowd filed out of Dodger Stadium, stoic Walter Alston told reporters in the clubhouse, "We've got Koufax going against the Cubs on Thursday night, and I can't think of a better man to straighten us out."[12] But nervous Dodger fans were well aware that Koufax had now made five consecutive unsuccessful tries for his 22nd win. In fact, Koufax and Drysdale had both hit a lull, with a combined 2–5 record with four no-decisions since August 15.

How to Cure a Five-Game Winless Streak: Don't Let Anyone Reach First Base

On Thursday, September 9, the Chicago Cubs were in town for an unusual one-game stop at Dodger Stadium. The Cubs started left-hander Bob Hendley, from Macon, Georgia. Hendley, who came over with Harvey Kuenn and Ed Bailey from San Francisco in a trade for Dick Bertell and Len Gabrielson at the end of May, had just been recalled after a brief demotion to Triple-A Salt Lake City. By the luck of the draw, the Cubs would have to face Sandy Koufax that night.

Koufax would later recall that he had "just average" stuff at the beginning of the game, relying mostly on his curveball.[13] His battery mate was 23-year-old catcher Jeff Torborg, two years out of Rutgers University. John Roseboro had the night off. The second batter Koufax pitched to, Cubs second baseman Glenn Beckert, hit a bullet down the left field line that landed foul by inches; he struck out looking on the next pitch. In the second inning, Cubs rookie left fielder Byron Browne—playing in his first major league game— hit a line drive, but right at center fielder Willie Davis for the third out. It would be the last hard-hit ball off Koufax. By now the Cubs had already violated one of baseball's cardinal rules: when facing a great pitcher, you had better get to him early.

When the game moved to the bottom of the fifth—the mid-point of the game—

both pitchers had retired every batter in order: Hendley 12 up and 12 down; Koufax 15 up and 15 down. Hendley's perfect run ended when he walked leadoff batter Lou Johnson. Ron Fairly promptly sacrificed him to second with a bunt back to the mound.[14] On Hendley's next pitch, Johnson took off for third base. He slid in safely with a steal and scored when a hurried throw by Cubs rookie catcher Chris Krug sailed over Ron Santo's head and into left field.[15] Krug was charged with a throwing error. After five innings, the Dodgers were up, 1–0, on an unearned run.

Koufax mowed down the Cubs in order in both the sixth and seventh innings. Hendley was behind, 1–0, but still had his own no-hitter going when he started the bottom of the seventh. He got the first two batters, Jim Gilliam and Willie Davis, to ground out before having to deal with the pesky Lou Johnson again. Hendley's first pitch to Johnson was a fastball out of the strike zone. Hendley then threw an off-speed "slip pitch"[16] that Johnson hit off the end of his bat for a bloop double

Chicago Cubs left-hander Bob Hendley pitched a brilliant one-hitter on September 9, 1965, at Dodger Stadium. Unfortunately his opponent, Sandy Koufax, pitched a perfect game.

that landed near the right field foul line. Remarkably, it would be the only hit of the game. Hendley escaped the seventh by getting Ron Fairly to ground out on a 3–1 pitch, leaving Johnson stranded at second.

Koufax was getting stronger by the inning. His fastball had come alive. He would recall that in the last half of the game, it was as good as he had all year.[17] In the eighth inning, it took him 11 pitches to strike out Cubs captain Ron Santo, Ernie Banks, and rookie Browne in order.

The crowd of 29,139 was on its feet as Koufax walked out to the mound to pitch the ninth inning. The voice of Dodgers broadcaster Vin Scully reverberated through the stadium, amplified by a multitude of little transistor radios. The first batter was the Cubs' big, right-handed-batting catcher, Chris Krug. Krug stayed alive for six pitches before striking out, swinging, on a 2–2 fastball. Vin Scully told the radio audience, "You can almost taste the pressure now."[18] Joe Amalfatano came up to pinch-hit for shortstop Don Kessinger. Like Koufax, Amalfatano was one of the original "Bonus Babies," having signed with the New York Giants in 1954. It took Koufax three pitches to dispose of Amalfatano, who barely managed to tap a 1–0 curveball foul before being blown away by a fastball on the third pitch. Down to his last out, Cubs "Head Coach" Lou Klein sent veteran Harvey Kuenn up to pinch-hit for Bob Hendley. By now the tension was almost unbearable at Dodger Stadium. For the second time, Harvey Kuenn stood between Sandy Koufax and history. On May 11, 1963, Kuenn, wearing a Giants uniform, made the last out in Koufax's second no-hitter. Now Koufax would throw him nothing but fastballs. Kuenn took the

first one for a strike. Koufax was so amped up that he lost his cap when he reared back and nearly threw the second pitch over catcher Torborg's head for ball one. After the third pitch again sailed high and out of the strike zone, Koufax blew a fastball by Kuenn to even the count at 2–2. The fifth pitch would be critical, as he did not want to pitch to the former AL batting champion with a full count. Koufax toed the rubber, went into his windup, and sent another blazing fastball toward home plate. Harvey Kuenn took a vicious swing at the ball but missed it by a mile. It was over, a perfect game for Sandy Koufax, who had just struck out the last six batters in a row. The scoreboard clock read 9:46 p.m. above a mass of zeroes.

The game, which took only one hour and 43 minutes, was historic on many levels. Koufax's fourth no-hitter broke the major league record set by Bob Feller, who had thrown no-hitters in 1940, 1946, and 1951. It is still the only game in major league history in which there was only one hit. And it came within an off-field bloop double of being a double no-hitter.

Koufax struck out 14 Cubs that night to reach 332 for the year, and come within 14 of Bob Feller's major league record of 348 set in 1946. He was in com-

Top: Sandy Koufax losing his cap while pitching to Harvey Kuenn in the ninth inning of his perfect game on September 9, 1965, at Dodger Stadium. *Bottom:* Sandy Koufax after his perfect game of September 9, 1965, at Dodger Stadium—the fourth no-hitter of his career.

plete command, throwing 70 percent of his 113 pitches for strikes. He threw his best pitch, "strike one," to 20 of the 27 batters he faced, and fell behind in the count on only five. It took a perfect game for him finally to reach his 22nd win on the sixth try. When Dodgers owner Walter O'Malley sent a post-game bottle of champagne to the clubhouse, the modest Koufax put it in the ice box and asked for a glass of beer instead.[19]

The hard-luck Cubs had to move on to San Francisco to play the next night against the surging Giants, who were midway through a 14-game winning streak. Despite the excitement of Koufax's perfect game, the Dodgers ended the night in a second-place tie with the Reds, one-half game behind the Giants.

With wins by Drysdale and Osteen, the Dodgers took two out of three from the Astros to close out their brief, six-game home stand on Sunday, September 12. The problem continued to be the Giants; they refused to lose. They swept a doubleheader from the Cubs that day in San Francisco for their tenth win in a row. In the second game, Willie Mays hit his 46th home run and the ageless Warren Spahn pitched a complete game for the final win of his career. As the Dodgers prepared to fly to Chicago, they were in second place, two games behind the Giants.

	W	L	Pct.	GB
San Francisco	83	59	.585	—
Los Angeles	82	62	.569	2
Cincinnati	81	62	.566	2½

It's All Over in Chicago ... Or Is It?

On September 14, five days after the perfect game, Sandy Koufax and Bob Hendley had a rematch at Wrigley Field. The eighth-place Cubs came into the game with an 8-game losing streak. Through the first five innings, the left-handers were again locked in a tight pitchers' duel, both with shutouts. In the bottom of the sixth, Koufax came up against Chicago's best hitter, Billy Williams, with one out and a runner on first base. On the first pitch, Koufax made what he described as "good pitch, low and outside."[20] But Williams went out and got it, driving the ball into the left-center field bleachers for a two-run home run to break the scoreless tie. Don Drysdale pinch-hit for Koufax with two out in the seventh inning and singled home Wes Parker to cut the Cubs' lead to one run.

Maury Wills led off the eighth inning with a bunt single. Wills, now wearing heavy, improvised pads in lieu of standard sliding pads to protect his hemorrhaging right leg, was promptly picked off first base.[21] The base running blunder extinguished the Dodgers' last scoring opportunity, as Hendley, using an assortment of fastballs, curves, sliders, and his "slip pitch," went all the way to beat Koufax, 2–1.[22] Wills had now gone eight games without a stolen base.

The next day, Don Drysdale, staked to a 3–0 lead in the first inning, was hit in the right foot by a vicious line drive off the bat of Ernie Banks in the bottom of the second. The impact of the ball could be heard all through the park. Drysdale had to be removed from the game and taken to the hospital for X-rays.[23] The game soon degenerated into a chaotic affair in which the Dodgers used seven pitchers, six pinch-hitters, and hit into four double plays. The result was a tough, 8–6 loss.[24] For the first time since the first week of the season, they were in third place, 4½ games behind the red-hot Giants. The only good news that day came from Wesley Memorial Hospital, where the X-rays determined that Drysdale only had a bruise under his right ankle. He had come within perhaps an inch of a season-ending injury when his shoe absorbed the shock of the baseball.

Just 550 people showed up at Wrigley Field on the grey, drizzly afternoon of September 16 to watch Claude Osteen and the Cubs' flakey, side-arming right-hander, Bill Faul, match up in the final game of the series. Faul, who bit off the heads of live parakeets and swallowed live toads "to put an extra hop on his fastball,"[25] lasted only an inning and two-thirds. The former University of Cincinnati All–American had to be removed after his two-out walk to Willie Davis with the bases loaded in the second inning gave the Dodgers a 2–0 lead.

Osteen cruised through the first eight innings with a 2–0 shutout. However, after he walked the dangerous Billy Williams to start the ninth, Alston did not hesitate to bring in Koufax from the bullpen to pitch to Ron Santo. It looked like Santo had tied the game when he connected on Koufax's second pitch, launching it high and deep toward the left field bleachers. The wind, blowing out to Lake Michigan, nearly blew the ball over Lou Johnson's head. But Johnson was able to haul it in with his back against the ivy. Koufax retired the next two batters, Ernie Banks and Harvey Kuenn, to save the game for Osteen.

September 16 in Chicago was a pivotal day in the season. Koufax's third save of the year not only stopped a three-game Dodgers losing streak, it marked the start of a winning streak that would eventually reach 13.

The Final Two Weeks on the K&D Express

Friday, September 17—In Milwaukee the Braves ended the Giants' 14-game winning streak as Hank Aaron rocked Juan Marichal for two home runs in a 9–1 pounding.

Marichal, who had won his last three starts, would not win another game that year. In St. Louis, Drysdale, pitching with a swollen and discolored right ankle, won his 20th game by beating Curt Simmons and the Cardinals, 3–2. Drysdale knocked in the first two runs of the game with a bases-loaded single in the second inning, but would only last five innings. After Bill White led off the sixth with a home run, Ron Perranoski came in from the bullpen and pitched four no-hit innings to save it.[26] The win cut the Giants' lead to 3½ games over the Dodgers and Reds, tied for second.

The great Henry Aaron in the Braves' last year in Milwaukee. On September 17, 1965, he rocked Juan Marichal for two home runs at County Stadium to snap the Giants' 14-game winning streak.

Saturday, September 18—Sandy Koufax pitched a 1–0 shutout on a humid, 86-degree day at Busch Stadium. The Cardinals managed only four singles off Koufax, who notched his 23rd win. Wes Parker's game-winning, two-out single in the sixth inning was one of only three hits for the Dodgers.[27] Koufax had now won three games since August 10, all by 1–0 scores.[28] With solo home runs by Tom Haller and Willie McCovey, the Giants beat the Braves, 2–0, at County Stadium to maintain their lead of 3½ games.

Sunday, September 19—On September 19, Claude Osteen volunteered to pitch the final game of the series on two days' rest.[29] Osteen—with help from Perranoski in the ninth inning—shut out the Cardinals, 5–0, to sweep the series.[30] The light-hitting Dodgers hit two solo home runs off the great Bob Gibson: Lefebvre in the second and Parker in the eighth. Dodger pitching shut out the defending World Champion Cardinals for the second straight day, and allowed only one earned run in the series. In Milwaukee, the Giants held onto to their three-and-one-half-game lead by beating the Braves, 4–2. The Braves were now eight games off the pace and effectively out of contention.

	W	L	Pct.	GB
San Francisco	89	60	.597	—
Los Angeles	86	64	.573	3½
Cincinnati	85	65	.567	4½

Monday, September 20—The next day was a travel day for the Dodgers as they moved into Milwaukee for a two-game series, with Drysdale and Koufax scheduled to face the Braves. The Giants beat the Reds in Cincinnati to increase their lead to four games. The Giants had now won 17 of their last 18 games. If they split their last dozen games, the Dodgers would have to win 10 of their last 12 to catch them.[31]

Tuesday, September 21—Drysdale beat the Braves, 3–1, in the opener for his 21st victory. He pitched a complete-game six-hitter and knocked in the winning run with a single off Braves starter Denny Lemaster in the second inning. If not for an unearned run in the fourth, the Dodgers would have had their third consecutive shutout. The Dodgers' fifth straight win, coupled with the Giants' 7–4 loss in Cincinnati, cut the San Francisco lead to three games.[32]

Wednesday, September 22—Sandy Koufax came into the last game ever played by the Milwaukee Braves at County Stadium with a 23–8 record. He was opposed by a 21-year-old left-hander named Wade Blasingame. As Koufax later recalled, he "had nothing"[33] that night. Braves second baseman Frank Bolling rocked him for a grand slam in the second inning. He could get no one out in the third. After center fielder Mack Jones led off with a home run and Henry Aaron followed with a ringing single, Alston removed Koufax and brought in Howie Reed. Reed got Joe Torre to ground into a double play, but gave up an inside-the-park home run to inescapable Gene Oliver to put the Braves up, 6–1, after three innings. It looked like the Dodgers' five-game winning streak was over, but they scratched and clawed their way back to tie the game, 6–6, and send it into extra innings. Ron Perranoski, who took over for Reed in the fifth, shut out the Braves for six innings. The Dodgers won it in the 11th when Lou Johnson singled home Maury Wills to make it 7–6, Dodgers. Maury Wills, taped and padded from above his knee to his right ankle, had attempted only six steals and was thrown out four times in his previous 19 games. He was finally able to take off the wraps on this night in Milwaukee.[34] Wills stole three bases and scored each time. Koufax, who was pounded for five earned runs on six hits—including the two home runs—managed to get off the hook with a no-decision.

After the game, the remnants of the crowd of 12,577 stuck around to rip up the pitcher's rubber, home plate, and any other souvenirs that weren't nailed down.[35]

At Crosley Field in Cincinnati, the Giants lost another game off their lead as the Reds hit three home runs off Juan Marichal in a 7–1 thumping. The Dodgers returned to Los Angeles, two games back with ten games to play.

	W	L	Pct.	GB
San Francisco	90	62	.592	—
Los Angeles	88	64	.579	2
Cincinnati	87	66	.569	3½

Friday, September 24—The Dodgers came from behind with two runs in the bottom of the eighth inning to beat Bob Gibson and the Cardinals, 4–3. The decisive blow was Jim Lefebvre's bases-loaded single that scored Willie Davis and Ron Fairly.[36] Claude Osteen started the game and gave Alston seven innings. Perranoski shut out the Cardinals over the final two innings. The Dodgers' winning streak was now seven.

In San Francisco, Milwaukee's Tony Cloninger beat the Giants, 8–2, for his 23rd win. The Giants' fourth straight loss reduced their lead to one game.

Saturday, September 25—Sandy Koufax shut out the Cardinals, 2–0, on five hits with 12 strikeouts to give the Dodgers their eighth consecutive win. Jim Lefebvre broke a scoreless tie with a two-out, run-scoring single in the sixth inning off 22-year-old Cardinals starter Nelson Briles. That was all Koufax needed, as he mowed down eleven of the last 12 batters to nail down his 24th victory. When Koufax struck out Mike Shannon in the third inning he reportedly broke Bob Feller's single-season record with his 349th strikeout.[37] The game was halted for more than a minute as the afternoon crowd of 31,532 gave him a standing ovation.[38] It has been subsequently established that Rube Waddell was the record holder with his 349 strikeouts for the Philadelphia Athletics in 1904. Thus, Koufax actually set the new record when he struck out the next batter, Nelson Briles.

At Candlestick Park, Willie Mays's 50th home run enabled the Giants to hang on to their one-game lead with a 7–5 win over the Braves.

Sunday, September 26—Don Drysdale shut out the Cardinals, 1–0, on five hits for his 22nd win. The resurgent Maury Wills had three hits, stole two bases, and scored the only run of the game in the first inning. Wills beat out an unplayable bunt to lead off the inning. St. Louis starter Ray Washburn had him picked off but first baseman Bill White's throw sailed into left field, allowing Wills to advance to third. Clutch veteran Jim Gilliam lined a single to right field to score him.[39] With their ninth straight win, the Dodgers pulled into a flat-footed tie with the Giants as they went into the final week of the season.

Moments after Drysdale shut out the Cardinals, the Braves beat Juan Marichal and the Giants, 3–2, in San Francisco. Braves' first baseman Gene Oliver was a non-partisan assassin. His sixth inning solo home run over the left field fence off Marichal turned out to be the deciding blow. The Giants had now lost four of their last five.[40]

	W	L	Pct.	GB
San Francisco	91	64	.587	—
Los Angeles	91	64	.587	—
Cincinnati	88	67	.568	3

In Washington, D.C., Jim Kaat beat Pete Richert and the Senators, 2–1, to clinch the American League pennant for the Minnesota Twins. The Twins had been in first place since the 4th of July. It was the first pennant for the franchise since 1933, when they were the Washington Senators.

Monday, September 27—The Giants beat the Cardinals, 8–4, in a matinee game at Candlestick Park. Warren Spahn, in the last start of his career, went 4⅓ innings for the Giants before turning it over to the bullpen, with Frank Linzy picking up the win.

That night at Dodger Stadium, Johnny Podres made his last start in a Dodgers uniform against 21-game winner Sammy Ellis of the Reds. Podres gave Alston five good innings, allowing one run and five hits. The Dodgers knocked Ellis out of the game in the third inning. Willie Davis hit two home runs and drove in three runs to pace the Dodgers to a 6–1 win. Maury Wills sole his 91st and 92nd bases and scored two runs.[41] Podres was credited with his seventh win of the season and his 136th and final win for the Dodgers. The Dodgers' tenth straight win kept them in a first-place tie with the Giants with six games left. The rapidly fading Reds fell four games off the pace.

	W	L	Pct.	GB
San Francisco	92	64	.590	—
Los Angeles	92	64	.590	—
Cincinnati	88	68	.564	4

Tuesday, September 28—Left-handers Claude Osteen and Jim O'Toole matched up in front of 38,424 fans at Dodger Stadium. Both dominated until Maury Wills broke a scoreless tie with a two-out, RBI single off O'Toole in the seventh inning. He promptly stole his 93rd base but was left on base when Jim Gilliam lined out. The Reds tied the game, 1–1, in the eighth when Osteen walked Tommy Harper, Pete Rose bunted him to second, and Vada Pinson doubled him in. The game remained tied, 1–1, as it moved to the bottom of the 12th inning. Johnson hit Jay's second pitch—a hanging curveball—into the left field stands for a walk-off home run four minutes before midnight. He was mobbed at the plate by his teammates, who were well aware of the significance of the moment.[42] The Giants had already been soundly beaten by the Cardinals, 9–1, at Candlestick Park. Only Willie Mays's 51st home run prevented a shutout.[43] The Dodgers' dramatic 2–1 win, their 11th in a row, gave them sole possession of first place.

In the wild post-game scene that was the Dodgers clubhouse, the master of understatement, Walter Alston, told reporters, "It's better than being tied, but we still have five to go."[44]

	W	L	Pct.	GB
Los Angeles	93	64	.592	—
San Francisco	92	65	.586	1
Cincinnati	88	69	.561	5

Wednesday, September 29—52,312 fans packed Dodger Stadium to watch Sandy Koufax (24–8) take on the Reds' ace, Jim Maloney (20–8). Both pitchers had already thrown no-hitters that season: Maloney a ten-inning no-hitter on August 19, and Koufax the September 9 perfect game. Both had shutouts through five innings. In the bottom of the sixth, a throwing error by Frank Robinson enabled the Dodgers to score an unearned run to take a 1–0 lead. In the bottom of the seventh, Maloney walked Parker, gave up a single to Roseboro, and walked Koufax to load the bases. Right fielder Robinson was over-shifted toward center when the spray-hitting Maury Wills pulled a ball into the right field corner for a bases-clearing triple that knocked Maloney out of the game. When Jim Gilliam followed with an RBI single off Reds reliever Ted Davidson, the game was out of reach at 5–0.[45] Koufax went on to pitch a two-hit, 5–0 shutout for his 25th win. He allowed just two singles, struck out 13 batters, and walked one.

Huddled around the radio in the clubhouse after the game, the Dodgers sweated out the Giants' game against the Cardinals at Candlestick Park. Shut out, 8–0, by Bob Gibson through the first eight innings, the Giants rallied for six runs in the bottom of the ninth as they knocked Gibson and Curt Simmons out of the game before obscure reliever Hal Woodeshick struck out Willie McCovey to end it with the tying runs on base.

With the Giants now two games behind, the Dodgers' magic number was reduced to three with four games to play. Dick Sisler's Cincinnati Reds were mathematically eliminated.

	W	L	Pct.	GB
Los Angeles	94	64	.595	—
San Francisco	92	66	.582	2

The season would conclude with a four-game weekend series with the Braves at Dodger Stadium.

Thursday, September 30—It was Drysdale's (22–12) turn to start on that Thursday night. His opponent was Hank Fischer (8–8), a tenacious little right-hander out of Seton Hall whom his teammates called Bulldog. The crowd of 36,006 saw the Dodgers extend their winning streak to 13 on an overpowering clutch performance by Drysdale: a three-hit, 5–0 shutout, with no walks and eight strikeouts. He retired the first 14 batters before Felipe Alou singled with two out in the top of the fifth. Bulldog Fischer was chased in the fifth when the disruptive Maury Wills singled, stole his 94th base, and caused an unearned run to score when Braves All-Star catcher Joe Torre made a hurried throw into center field.

It took Drysdale only 89 pitches to dispose of the Braves, the top home-run-hitting team in the National League. As a batter, he had two hits—including an RBI single in the second inning—to raise his average to .302. It was his seventh shutout of the year and his fifth consecutive victory. Drysdale told reporters after the game, "I was in the groove."[46]

At Candlestick Park, the game between the Giants and the Reds went to the bottom of the ninth tied, 3–3, before Orlando Cepeda ended it with a two-run, walk-off home run off Joe Nuxhall. But the Dodgers' magic number was still reduced to two.

Friday, October 1—50,813 fans turned out on a Friday night to watch a battle of left-handers: Claude Osteen (15–14) against Milwaukee's Denny Lemaster (6–13), from nearby Oxnard High School. It was Lemaster who prevailed, holding the Dodgers to five singles in a 2–0 shutout that snapped their 13-game winning streak. Osteen pitched well enough to win, but the breaks did not go his way. He was hurt by two throwing errors that cost him an unearned run in the sixth inning. With two out and a runner on third in the seventh, Felipe Alou beat out a slow ground ball by an eyelash, allowing the second Braves run to score. Down 2–0, Osteen was removed for a pinch-hitter in the bottom of the seventh. Largely unsupported all year, he would finish the season with an even 15–15 record despite an outstanding earned run average of 2.79. Dodgers hitters provided Osteen with a grand total of 29 runs in his 15 losses.[47] At Candlestick Park, the Giants were wiped out, 17–2, by the Reds, thereby reducing the Dodgers' magic number to one. Giants starter Bobby Bolin lasted but a third of an inning, giving up two home runs, including the last one hit by Frank Robinson for the Cincinnati Reds. Willie Mays, suffering from "delayed exhaustion," was now skipping batting practice.[48] He managed an innocuous single against Reds right-hander Sammy Ellis, who recorded his 22nd win.

With the pennant not yet in the bag, the Dodgers were still haunted by the possibility of another playoff with the Giants. In the clubhouse after the game, Alston asked Koufax, who was scheduled to pitch the final game on Sunday, October 3, if he would consider moving his turn up a day to start Saturday afternoon on two days' rest. That would make it possible to use Drysdale—if needed—on Sunday, also on two days' rest. The Dodgers would thus have two chances to clinch by using their best. Koufax, who had already made 40 starts and pitched over 326⅔ innings, told Alston that he would have to sleep on it.[49]

Saturday, October 2—When Koufax arrived at Dodger Stadium on Saturday morning, Alston asked him how he felt about taking the mound at 2:15 p.m. that day. His response was not exactly reassuring: "I'll give it a try and hope for the best."[50] He would be going up against Tony Cloninger, who had already won 24 games for the Braves.

In the bottom of the first inning, Jim Gilliam walked, stole second, went to third on a wild throw and scored an unearned run on a wild pitch by Cloninger to give the Dodgers a 1–0 lead. Koufax hyper-nemesis Gene Oliver tied the game in the top of the fourth with a leadoff home run into the left field stands. Dodgers fans flashed back to the final day of the 1962 season when Oliver—then playing for the Cardinals—hit a devastating, eighth-inning solo home run off Johnny Podres to beat the Dodgers, 1–0, and force the ill-fated playoff with the Giants.

The game moved to the bottom of the fifth as a 1–1 tie. By that time, everyone in the park was aware that the Giants had defeated the Reds at Candlestick Park. Cloninger had retired 11 batters in a row when he opened the door by walking leadoff man Lou Johnson. Jim Lefevbre promptly singled Johnson to third. Wes Parker hit a routine ground ball to first baseman Joe Torre, who threw home to get Johnson, heading for the plate. But Johnson reversed course and got himself in a rundown before diving back into third base safely under the tag of Mike de la Hoz. De la Hoz engaged in a heated, but unsuccessful, argument with third base umpire Tony Venzon. The bases were loaded with nobody out. The turn of events so unnerved Cloninger that he forced in two runs by walking Roseboro and Koufax before Braves manager Bobby Bragan could bring in Ken Johnson from the bullpen to stop the bleeding. But the damage was done. Though he had given up only one hit, the Braves' best pitcher was out of the game. And Sandy Koufax had a 3–1 lead.

In each of the last three innings, the Braves had the tying run at the plate. In the seventh, Frank Bolling, who hit a grand slam homer off Koufax at County Stadium on September 22, fouled out to end the inning with a runner on first. In the eighth, the inescapable Oliver singled with two out. But Koufax blew away Joe Torre on strikes. With two out in the ninth, Koufax walked shortstop Woody Woodward, cousin of actress Joanne Woodward, on five pitches.[51] When Koufax fell behind, 1–0, to Denis Menke, Alston went out to the mound. Though he had Ron Perranoski ready in the bullpen, Alston stayed with Koufax. With the count even at 2–2, Menke lifted a fly ball to left field. Lou Johnson alternately punched his glove and waved away Willie Davis before squeezing the ball and leaping high into the air. On the mound, Koufax was engulfed in a wave of white uniforms that swept him into the clubhouse as a torrent of seat cushions rained down on the field.

At 4:57 p.m. it was over. The Dodgers had clinched the pennant by beating the

Braves, 3–1, with only two singles—both by Jim Lefebvre. It was the 26th win of the season for Sandy Koufax. There would be no need for Drysdale to go on two days' rest the next day.

Sunday, October 3—The last day of the season was a mere formality as six Dodgers pitchers shut out the Braves, 3–0—the pitching staff's 23rd shutout of the year. Tommy Davis got a standing ovation when he came up to pinch-hit in the bottom of the eighth inning. Making his first appearance since he broke his ankle on May 1, Davis painfully hobbled about halfway to first base before he was thrown out on an infield tap.[52]

Up north at Candlestick Park, the Giants went through the motions in a meaningless 6–3 win over the Reds. Mays exited the game after he hit his 52nd home run of the season in the fourth inning. San Francisco, in first place by 4½ games on September 16—the day their winning streak reached 14—finished two games behind the Dodgers.

	W	L	Pct.	GB
Los Angeles	97	65	.599	—
San Francisco	95	67	.586	2

Twenty-four hours after Sandy Koufax's pennant-clinching performance, it began to sink in: the Dodgers were on their way to Minnesota to meet the Twins in the World Series. It was the most unlikely result after being declared dead and buried in mid–September, when they were 4½ games behind a red-hot Giants team. Remarkably, they turned it around by winning 15 of their last 16 games.

That same day, President Johnson signed the Immigration and Nationality Act of 1965 (also known as the Hart-Celler Act) into law in New York on Liberty Island, at the foot of the Statue of Liberty.[53] The Act discarded national origin as the criterion for admission to remedy the discriminatory national-origins quota system in place since 1921. It would cause significant changes to the demographics of the country.[54]

9

The World Series with the Twins

No use saving anything for tomorrow. This is it. There ain't no tomorrow.[1]—Ron Fairly, before Game 7, October 14, 1965

We were beaten by a great pitcher, and he had to be great to beat us. He's the best I've ever seen.[2]—Sam Mele, after Game 7, October 14, 1965

The 1965 World Series began on Wednesday, October 6. Since that day was also Yom Kippur, the Day of Atonement, the holiest day of the Jewish year, Sandy Koufax told Alston that he would not be available to pitch. Instead, the Dodgers would have to go with Don Drysdale against the Twins' number one right-hander, Jim "Mudcat" Grant. It was concerning that Drysdale, who hadn't pitched since September 30, was 1–2 with three no-decisions the last five times he pitched on five days' rest.

The Mudcat

James Timothy Grant was born August 13, 1935, in the lumber mill town of Lacoochee, Florida. One of seven children, Grant was a three-sport star (football, basketball, and baseball) at Moore Academy in Dade City. He was awarded an athletic scholarship to Florida A&M—a historically black university—to play football and baseball, but left during his sophomore year to help his struggling family with their financial problems.

While working as a carpenter's helper for $26 a week in New Smyrna Beach, Fred Merkle, the Cleveland scout who had tracked him in high school, offered Grant a tryout with the Indians and signed him as a free agent before the 1954 season.[3] It was at the Daytona Beach tryout camp that he was given the nickname, "Mississippi Mudcat," by LeeRoy Bartow Irby, a white player

Jim "Mudcat" Grant beat Drysdale and the Dodgers, 8–2, in Game 1 of the 1965 World Series on October 6, 1965, at Metropolitan Stadium.

who mistakenly assumed that the Negro Grant was from Mississippi. After spending four years in the Indians' farm system, he came up to stay with the big club in 1958. He was a member of Cleveland's starting rotation for six years, compiling a so-so record of 64–59 through 1963. After getting off to a rocky 3–4 start with a 5.95 ERA the next year, he was traded to the Twins on the trade deadline of June 15. Grant, who had always been a thorn in the side of Calvin Griffith's teams, with a 26–9 career record against the Senators and Twins, thus switched sides.[4] He blossomed in 1965 as an All-Star under Sam Mele in Minnesota, leading the American League with 21 wins and six shutouts. But he also led the league in home runs allowed with 34.

Game 1—Wednesday, October 6
at Metropolitan Stadium

Twins shortstop Zoilo Versalles had eight hits in the 1965 World Series including a crushing three-run homer off Drysdale in Game 1.

Vice President Hubert H. Humphrey, former Mayor of Minneapolis, threw out the ceremonial first pitch in front of a Metropolitan Stadium record crowd of 47,797. In the second inning, the Dodgers' Ron Fairly and the Twins' Don Mincher traded solo home runs to produce a 1–1 tie. Things fell apart for Drysdale in the third. Rookie second baseman Frank Quilici, a .208 hitter, led off by skipping a roller over the third base bag for a double.[5] Mudcat Grant then laid down a bunt in front of the plate. Drysdale fielded the ball but fell down when his left knee buckled on the soft turf. He threw from a sitting position, on a hop to first base, but everyone was safe when Lefebvre bobbled the ball. The error opened the floodgates. The Twins' star shortstop, Zoilo Versalles, followed with a crushing three-run homer into the left field stands to put Minnesota ahead, 4–1. Before the inning was over, the Twins got to Drysdale for three more runs on three singles, a double, and a walk before Alston removed him. At the end of three innings, the game was out of reach at 7–1, Minnesota. Grant went on to pitch an 8–2, complete-game win.[6] It was the first World Series defeat for Drysdale. Sandy Koufax attended Yom Kippur services at a St. Paul synagogue and then watched the game on television in his hotel room.[7]

Game 2—Thursday, October 7
at Metropolitan Stadium

True, Drysdale wasn't sharp, and the Dodgers were down a game. But not to worry; they had Sandy Koufax going in Game 2 against a 26-year-old left-hander named Jim "Kitty" Kaat. The lanky, 6'4" Kaat debuted with the Washington Senators in 1959 at the age of 20. By 1961 he was part of the Twins' starting rotation. He was 18–11 with a 2.83 ERA for the 1965 regular season. But Koufax would be pitching on four days' rest for the first time since September 14, when he lasted six innings in a loss to the Cubs at Wrigley Field.

It was a miserable day for baseball. Before the game, a helicopter had to hover over the outfield to fan the grass dry after an all-night and all-morning rain. The grounds crew turned flame-throwers on the mud along the sidelines. The lights were already on when the first pitch was thrown as another record Metropolitan Stadium crowd of 48,700 huddled under dark clouds in a 17-mile-per-hour wind and a 56-degree chill.[8]

The game was a scoreless tie as it moved to the top of the fifth. Ron Fairly led off with a single to right field—the first hit off Kaat. Lefebvre hit a fastball on a line toward the left field foul pole. The ball kept sinking and curving away from the sprinting Twins left fielder, Bob Allison, who had been positioned toward center field. The 6'3", 205-pound former Kansas Jayhawks fullback closed a remarkable amount of ground as he backhanded the ball with a desperate headlong dive and slid some 30 feet on the wet turf. Left field umpire Ed Vargo, right on top of the play, thrust his right arm and hooked thumb into the air to call Lefebvre out. It was not only one of the greatest plays in World Series history, it was a turning point in the game. Sam Mele later said, "Had it gone through for a double or a triple, I might have made a quick pitching change. We couldn't afford to give Koufax any cushion."[9] Wes Parker followed with an infield single, but Kaat got Roseboro and Koufax to foul out. The Dodgers did not score, and Kaat was still in the game.

Koufax was cruising with a one-hit shutout with eight strikeouts through five innings. In the bottom of the sixth, Zoilo

Above: **Jim Kaat beat Koufax and the Dodgers, 5–1, in Game 2 of the 1965 World Series on October 7, 1965, at Metropolitan Stadium.** *Below:* **A spectacular diving catch by Minnesota Twins left fielder Bob Allison was a turning point in Game 2 of the 1965 World Series.**

Versalles led off with a sharp grounder down the third base line that ricocheted off Jim Gilliam's arm and shoulder before it landed in left field. Versalles glided into second base, and a merciless official scorer charged Gilliam with a two-base error. Twins center fielder Joe Nossek bunted Versalles to third. American League batting champion Tony Oliva hit Koufax's 2–2 pitch for a slicing double to left field to score Versalles.[10] The error had clearly broken Koufax's rhythm. Harmon Killebrew lined Koufax's next pitch through the hole between third base and shortstop to score Oliva. After catcher Earl Battey also hit the first pitch for a single, Walter Alston came out to the mound to steady Koufax. Alston returned to the dugout, and Koufax calmed down to retire Allison and Mincher to end the inning. But the Twins were up, 2–0.

In the top of the seventh, Roseboro singled in Fairly to cut the Twins' lead to 2–1. With runners on second and third and one out, Alston brought in Drysdale to pinch-hit for Koufax. But Kaat struck him out and got Wills to pop out to shallow center field. The Dodgers had squandered their best opportunity to score. Worse, Sandy Koufax was out of the game.

Kaat went on to pitch a complete-game seven-hitter. And he even knocked in the Twins' last two runs with a single in the bottom of the eighth to make the final score 5–1. While Koufax struck out nine batters in six innings, he suffered his first World Series loss since 1959.

The Dodgers had thrown Drysdale and Koufax at the Twins, and they were down, two games to none. In the visitors' clubhouse after the game, the unflappable Walter Alston reminded reporters that the Dodgers had lost the first two games of the 1955 World Series to the Yankees before coming back to win it in seven: "It seems that we're always behind, but we did it in '55."[11] The odds makers in Las Vegas were not convinced. The odds shifted in Minnesota's favor to win the Series as the Dodgers flew home to Los Angeles. It would now be up to Claude Osteen, a 15–15 pitcher with no World Series experience, to save the Dodgers from sinking into a three-games-to-none hole—a position from which no team in Series history had ever recovered. The good news was that Osteen had a 5–0 career record against the Twins going back to the expansion year of 1961.[12]

Game 3—Saturday, October 9 at Dodger Stadium

Osteen's opponent was the 31-year-old, 5'11", Cuban right-hander, Camilo Pascual. Back on June 8, the perennial All-Star was 8–0 with a 2.49 ERA, but he didn't feel right. In the next six weeks, he was 0–3 with five no-decisions. Finally, on July 28 the team doctor found a lump below his right shoulder. Five days later, he underwent surgery to repair what was determined to be not a tumor, but a mass of torn muscles. He came off the Disabled List on September 1 and got permission from Commissioner Ford Frick to be eligible to play in the World Series. Six weeks after the operation, he was throwing his fastball harder than he had in the last two years. But the American League's "Mr. Curve Ball" was having trouble controlling his famous out pitch: the big overhand curveball which Ted Williams once called the most feared pitch in the league. From Labor Day, when he made his first post-op start, to the end of the regular season, he won one game and had five no-decisions.[13] Still, Sam Mele was hopeful that Pascual could give him some quality innings on that day in Chavez Ravine.

The record Dodger Stadium crowd of 55,934 fell silent when Twins leadoff man Zoilo Versalles lashed Osteen's first pitch down the left field line. The ball took one bounce before coming to rest to the right of the foul pole in the lower box seats for a ground rule double. Joe Nossek advanced Versalles to third with a groundout to the right side. With the Dodgers' infield drawn in, Tony Oliva was thrown out on a ground ball to Lefebvre. With two out, Osteen walked the dangerous Harmon Killebrew. With Earl Battey at the plate with a 2–0 count, Mele put on the hit-and-run play. But Battey did not swing at the next pitch, and the slow-moving Killebrew was hung up between first and second. Wills ran him back to first, then threw to the plate as Versalles broke for home. Versalles was caught in a rundown and eventually tagged out by third baseman Junior Gilliam to end the inning. The top of the first inning was a turning point. The Twins had Osteen on the ropes, but couldn't put him away. It would be their last serious threat.[14]

The Dodgers beat Camilio Pascual, "Mr. Curveball," in Game 3 of the 1965 World Series at Dodger Stadium to avoid sinking into a three-games-to-none hole.

Pascual and Osteen both had shutouts until the Dodgers got to Pascual in the bottom of the fourth inning. Fairly led off with a double down the third base line. After Lou Johnson bunted him to third, Lefebvre hit a sharp ground ball headed through the drawn-in infield. Versalles made an acrobatic backhand stop to prevent a run, but Lefebvre was safely aboard with an infield single. Pascual walked Wes Parker on four pitches to load the bases. Roseboro followed with a line drive inches out of second baseman Frank Quilici's reach for a single to drive in Fairly and Lefebvre and give the Dodgers a 2–0 lead.[15] The Dodgers increased their lead to 3–0 in the fifth inning when Lou Johnson hit a two-out double to drive in Willie Davis. It was the fourth of five doubles in the game for the Dodgers, and the end of the line for Camilio Pascual. He was removed for a pinch-hitter in the sixth and would not appear again in the Series. The Dodgers added an insurance run in the sixth against the Twins' 21-year-old, 6'5" left-hander from nearby West Covina, Jim Merritt.

Osteen went on to complete a five-hit, 4–0 shutout in a must-win situation. The win guaranteed that three games would be played in Los Angeles. The previous October, Claude Osteen was working for a building supply firm in Washington, D.C., and had paid little attention to the World Series.[16]

Game 4—Sunday, October 10 at Dodger Stadium

Game 4 was a rematch between Don Drysdale and Mudcat Grant before a capacity crowd of 55,920 at Dodger Stadium. Drysdale was a different pitcher on his normal three days' rest. He came through with a complete-game, 7–2 win, allowing only five hits and striking out 11. Two of the Minnesota hits were solo home runs: Harmon Killebrew in the fourth inning and Tony Oliva in the sixth. Grant lasted only five innings. The Dodgers played classic small-ball with six infield hits—including three bunts—stole two bases, and rattled the Twins into making two costly errors.[17]

The tone of the game was set in the first inning. Wills led off by boldly bunting Grant's second pitch wide of first base. Don Mincher fielded the ball in no man's land and lobbed it toward the bag as Grant, Wills, and Twins second baseman Quilici all arrived at the same time. Wills, an outstanding high school football player, met Quilici in a collision that sent both players sprawling. Wills was ruled safe and promptly stole second. He soon scored the first run of the game on Ron Fairly's ground out.

In the bottom of the second, Wes Parker led off with a bunt single, stole second, and scored when Quilici booted Roseboro's grounder to make it 2–0, Dodgers.

The game moved to the bottom of the sixth inning with the Dodgers clinging to a narrow 3–2 lead. Grant appeared to be tiring as he walked leadoff man Jim Gilliam. After Willie Davis followed with a line single to right field, Grant was done. Sam Mele removed him and brought in former Giant Al Worthington. With runners on second and third, Ron Fairly drove a ball through the drawn-in infield to score Gilliam and Davis. When Lou Johnson beat out a bunt, Fairly scored all the way from second on a throwing error by Worthington to put the game out of reach at 6–2.

In the bottom of the eighth, Lou Johnson pulled a pitch thrown by Minnesota's third pitcher, Bill Pleis, down the left-field line just fair and into the lower box seats for the Dodgers' seventh run. Before the inning was over, even catcher John Roseboro beat out a bunt.[18]

Game 5—Monday, October 11 at Dodger Stadium

Fifty-five thousand, eight hundred one fans turned out to watch Sandy Koufax and Jim Kaat meet for the second time in the Series. This time Koufax avenged his Game 2 defeat by taking complete charge of the Twins[19] with a four-hit, 7–0 shutout to give the Dodgers a three-games-to-two lead in the Series.

The game was all but over after the Dodgers scratched out two runs in the bottom of the first inning. By the end of the fourth, Koufax was out in front, 5–0, and he had a perfect game until slugger Harmon Killebrew led off the fifth inning with a harmless pop single into short center field. Willie Davis, who was playing deep, lost the modest fly ball in the background of white shirts and made a frantic lunge for the ball, but it popped out of his mitt as he rolled over. Davis would later say that he legitimately caught the ball before it became dislodged, but the official scorers called it a hit after a brief huddle. It mattered not a whit. On the next pitch, Earl Battey grounded into a double play to erase Killebrew, and Koufax blew away Bob Allison on strikes to end the inning.

The Dodgers knocked Kaat out of the game before he could complete the third inning and collected 14 hits. Maury Wills started three double plays, stole a base, and had four hits, including two doubles. Willie Davis stole three bases to tie a Series record set 56 years before to the day by the great Honus Wagner.

Sandy Koufax struck out ten batters and even drove in a run with a single with the bases loaded in the seventh inning. Of the four hits he allowed, only one was a clean blow. It wasn't until the ninth inning that the Twins had a man reach second base. After the game, Walter Alston told reporters, "It was a wonderful feeling, looking up at the scoreboard and seeing seven runs up there for us with Sandy Koufax pitching."[20]

In the three games played in Los Angeles, the Dodgers outscored the Twins 18 runs to two. They were now hitting .302 as a team for the Series, a whopping 57 points above their season average. There would be a travel day before the Series resumed in Minneapolis.

Game 6—Wednesday, October 13
at Metropolitan Stadium

With his team's backs to the wall, Mudcat Grant pitched a six-hitter on two days' rest and hit a three-run homer to beat the Dodgers, 5–1, to even the Series and force a seventh game. His opponent, Claude Osteen, pitched well enough to win, but was removed for a pinch-hitter in the sixth inning with the Dodgers behind, 2–0.

The night before the game, under cover of darkness, the Metropolitan Stadium groundskeepers brought in loads of sand and carpeted the base line from home plate to first base in a blatant effort to slow down the Dodgers' running attack. After an inspection tour by the umpires, crew chief Ed Vargo ordered the embarrassed head groundskeeper to remedy the situation. Before the game could begin, attendants brought out scrapers to scoop up the loose sand and shovel it into wheelbarrows for removal.[21]

Both pitchers were throwing shutouts when the game moved to the bottom of the fourth inning. Leadoff batter Earl Battey reached base safely when Dodgers second baseman Dick Tracewski bobbled his routine ground ball. Osteen got ahead, 0–2, on the next batter, Bob Allison, hitting .100 for the Series with seven strikeouts. While delivering the third pitch, Osteen's spikes caught in the dirt, causing him to make an awkward, truncated stride that left his fastball up in the strike zone. Osteen said, "The moment I let the ball go I said to myself, 'Oh no!'" It was a mistake—a letter-high fastball—that Allison hit into the left-field pavilion to put the Twins ahead, 2–0.[22]

In the bottom of the sixth, Howie Reed, pitching in relief of Osteen, walked Allison with one out. As Don Mincher took a third strike, Allison stole second. With first base open, Alston ordered Reed to walk Frank Quilici intentionally to get to the pitcher. The strategy blew up when Mudcat Grant hit Reed's first pitch deep into the left-center field bleachers for a crushing three-run home run to put the ballgame away at 5–0. Grant gleefully clapped his hands repeatedly as he rounded the bases. But the lead vocalist in the nightclub act of "Mudcat and the Kittens" restrained himself from singing.[23]

Despite being weakened by a lingering cough and a bad cold, Grant went all the way, striking out five and walking none.[24] He didn't give up a hit until Ron Fairly led off the fifth inning with a single. He lost his shutout when Fairly led off the seventh with a home run—his second off Grant in the Series. Claude Osteen lost to the Twins for the first time in his career.

That night Walter Alston wrestled with the question of who would pitch Game 7: Drysdale on his normal three days' rest, or Koufax on two days' rest. In the clubhouse after the game, Alston had told reporters, "It will be either be Sandy Koufax or Don Drysdale tomorrow. I won't decide until morning—maybe not until game time because I want to think about it." When told Alston might use him in Game 7 on two days' rest, Koufax said it was all right with him: "There's nothing to save my arm for after tomorrow."[25] Rain was forecast for the next day in Minneapolis–St. Paul. If the game was rained out and postponed for a day, Alston's choice would be much easier. It would be a tall order no matter which pitcher was chosen. The road team had lost each of the first six games of the Series.

Game 7—Thursday, October 14
at Metropolitan Stadium

"It's going to be the left-hander."[26] That was the laconic instruction Walter Alston gave Sandy Koufax and Don Drysdale in front of his locker the morning of the seventh game of the 1965 World Series. He would employ a Left-Right-Left strategy. Koufax would start on two days' rest. If he faltered, Drysdale would come in to neutralize the Twins' right-handed hitters. If they brought in their left-handed batters against Drysdale, Alston would bring in Ron Perranoski.[27] Jim Kaat would oppose Koufax for the third time in the Series.

As Koufax warmed up with John Roseboro, something unsettling was immediately evident to both of them: Koufax did not have a curveball. The standing-room-only crowd of 50,596 was unusually quiet, perhaps resigned to the enormity of the challenge of having to beat Koufax a second time to prevail.

Koufax got off to a shaky start in the first inning. With two out he walked Oliva on a 3–2 pitch. When he walked Harmon Killebrew on four straight balls, Drysdale started to heat up hurriedly in the bull pen. But Drysdale sat down when Koufax struck out Earl Battey to get out of the inning.[28]

Drysdale began throwing again after Zoilo Versalles singled with one out in the third inning. Versalles stole second, but home plate umpire Ed Hurley ruled that the batter, Joe Nossek, was out for interfering with the catcher, Roseboro, and Versalles was ordered back to first. Koufax escaped by blowing away Oliva on three pitches.

In the top of the fourth, leadoff batter Lou Johnson connected with a Jim Kaat fastball, sending a towering drive down the left field line. It was curving foul when it struck the screen high up on the fair side of the foul pole and ricocheted back onto the field. The crowd was frozen in silence as a jubilant Johnson circled the bases, clapping his hands. Ron Fairly followed with a line drive just fair into the right field corner for a double. With the Twins' infield set for a bunt, Alston instructed Wes Parker to swing away. Parker promptly bounced a single over the head of the onrushing first baseman, Don Mincher, to score Fairly and increase the Dodgers' lead to 2–0.[29] Jim Kaat, the hero of Game 2, had to be replaced by Al Worthington before he could get anyone out in the inning.

In the fifth, Drysdale got up again in the bullpen after Koufax gave up a one-out double off the left field wall to Quilici and walked pinch-hitter Rich Rollins on a 3–2 pitch that sailed way up out of the strike zone. The crowd finally came alive, sensing that Koufax was on the ropes with Versalles coming to the plate, already with eight hits in the Series. The eventual MVP of the American League ripped a 1–2 pitch down the third base line that looked like a sure game-tying double.[30] But Jim Gilliam made a great diving stop and beat the runner to the third base bag for the force out to get Koufax out of the jam. After surviving the fifth, Koufax found a rhythm and set down the Twins in order in the sixth through eighth innings. The Metropolitan Stadium crowd grew progressively quieter as their team ran out of outs.

Still clinging to a 2–0 lead, Koufax had to go through the heart of the Twins' order in the bottom of the ninth. After he got Tony Oliva to ground out to third, he made a mistake to Harmon Killebrew, who had already hurt him twice in the Series on low-inside fastballs.[31] Koufax fell behind 2–1 before missing his location on the third pitch, another low-inside fastball. Killebrew rocked him with a ringing single to left field. Fortunately for Koufax, the ball had stayed in the park. But with the tying run coming to the plate, Drysdale began throwing again in earnest in the bullpen. Even though Koufax had already thrown 124 pitches, his only pitch—the fastball—was still blazing. Earl Battey swung feebly at the first two pitches, then froze as he looked at strike three on the outside corner. Bob Allison was next, with the Twins down to their last out. Allison fouled the first pitch back to the screen, then took two balls, both high. Allison swung and missed on the next pitch for strike two. With the count 2–2, Koufax reached back and blew a fastball by him to end it. The Dodgers mobbed Koufax as the crowd watched in silence. It would be a 22 years before Minneapolis hosted another World Series.

Seven hours after the last pitch, the Dodgers' team plane arrived at Los Angeles International Airport, with Maury Wills waving from the cockpit window to a frenzied crowd of 10,000. Lou Johnson, the first player to emerge from the plane, was quickly swallowed up by autograph seekers. Sandy Koufax, who was named the Most Valuable Player of the Series, had to be escorted by ten airline stewardesses through the surging mob to his escape car.[32]

October 21 was "Lou Johnson Day" in Lexington, Kentucky. "Lexington Lou" was presented with a key to the city and paraded through downtown Lexington in a convertible with his wife and mother. Not even Adolph Rupp or Paul "Bear" Bryant, the legendary basketball and football coaches at the University of Kentucky, had ever received such an honor.[33]

10

How in the World Did They Do It?

Lou Johnson gave the team the lift at the time it had to have it. That's the kind of season we had—everyone did what had to be done to win it.[1]—Sandy Koufax

We won a pennant with a team batting average of .245. I think that shows the kind of team we had.[2]—Jeff Torbog

The 1965 Los Angeles Dodgers had to deal with two devastating early setbacks: Sandy Koufax's elbow flare-up that threw his career status into question before the season began, and the loss of their best hitter, Tommy Davis, on the first day of May.

Sandy Koufax

When the season started, the physical condition of Sandy Koufax was again the biggest question looming over the Dodgers: Would the game's best pitcher be relegated to the status of a "Sunday Pitcher" with an arthritic elbow? As we have seen, the trainers came up with an ingenious hot-cold regimen, employing a pre-game Capsolin ointment and a post-game "ice bath" that restored Koufax to an every-fourth-day starter. In fact, the erstwhile Sunday Pitcher did not miss a single turn all year—starting 41 games and completing an amazing 27. A year that began in uncertainty turned into a tour de force season of historic proportions with 26 wins, a perfect game, and a major league record 382 strikeouts. He led National League in ten categories (**bold**).

	G	GS	CG	W	L	W-L%	IP	SHO	SO	ER	HR	BB	ERA
Koufax	43	41	**27**	**26**	8	.765	**335⅔**	8	**382**	76	26	71	**2.04**

His WHIP (Walks + Hits per Innings Pitched) of 0.855 was the lowest in the major leagues since 1913. His career-best strikeouts-to-walks ratio of 5.38 was also the best in baseball since 1913.

	WHIP	H9	BB/9	SO/9	SO/BB
1965	**0.855**	5.8	1.9	**10.2**	**5.38**

Lou Johnson

Lou Johnson was a major reason for the Dodgers' success in 1965. He took over Tommy Davis's left field position in mid–May to end a chaotic six-player, revolving-door situation. He was one of the team's best clutch batters, hitting .320 in "Late & Close" plate appearances (in the seventh inning or later with the batting team tied, ahead by one, or the tying run at least on deck). In the last four games of the team's 13-game winning streak at end of September, he hit .556 (10-for-18). He came up big against the team's biggest competition, hitting .325 against the Giants and .339 against the Reds. He hit two home runs in the World Series against the Twins—the second one decided Game 7.

Hitting or Lack Thereof

The 1965 Dodgers finished eighth in the league in runs scored and last in home runs. They hit just .245 as a team and had only one .300 hitter: pitcher Don Drysdale. And he was responsible for seven of their 78 home runs.

Dominant Team Pitching

How could a team win a pennant and a World Series with such an anemic offence? The answer: Dominant pitching.

Category	Result	Rank in the NL
Earned Run Average	2.81	1st
Fewest Runs Allowed	521	1st
Strikeouts	1,079	2nd
Shutouts	23	1st
Fewest Hits Allowed	1,223	1st
Complete Games	58	1st
WHIP	1.117	1st
Fewest Hits Per 9 Innings	7.5	1st

The Dodgers' pitching staff led the National League in Earned Run Average, Fewest Runs Allowed, Shutouts, Fewest Hits Allowed, Complete Games, WHIP, and Hits Per 9 Innings. For the first time since 1949, the team did not lead the league in strikeouts—despite the record total by Koufax. Instead, Jim Maloney and the Cincinnati Reds edged them out by 34.

The Koufax & Drysdale Express

With a combined 49–20 record, the 1965 left-right combination of Koufax & Drysdale remains the best of their era. To illustrate their impact, the balance of the Dodgers pitching went 48–45.

	G	GS	CG	W	L	W-L%	IP	SHO	SO	ER	HR	BB	ERA
Koufax	43	41	27	26	8	.765	335⅔	8	382	76	26	71	2.04
Drysdale	44	42	20	23	12	.657	308⅓	7	210	95	30	66	2.77
K&D	87	83	47	49	20	.710	644	15	592	171	56	137	2.39
All Others	75	79	11	48	45	.516	832	2	487	290	71	288	3.14

As we have seen, the Dodgers won 15 of their last 16 games of the season from September 16 through October 3. Sandy Koufax and Don Drysdale both won all four of their starts in that period. Koufax threw three shutouts, saved one game in relief, and broke Bob Feller's major league record for most strikeouts in a season on September 25. He struck out 47 batters over his last 38 innings with an ERA of 1.38. Drysdale threw two shutouts, gave up only one earned run, and batted .429.

Captain Maury Wills

Had his battered right leg on which he slid not deteriorated to the point of hemorrhaging in late August, Maury Wills would have easily broken his own single-season stolen base record of 104. Wills would later say that he could have stolen 150 "because I was a better base stealer in 1965 than I was in 1962."[3] As it was, he stole 94, 31 more than the league runner-up, Lou Brock. After Alston named him captain in spring training, the veteran shortstop provided much-needed stability to an infield comprised of a rookie second baseman (Lefebvre), a second-year first baseman (Parker), and five different third basemen. Wills finished third in the voting for league MVP behind Mays and Koufax.

The Ageless Junior Gilliam

On May 25, the Dodgers reactivated their first base coach, Jim Gilliam, in what they thought would be a limited utility role. Gilliam ended up playing in 111 of the last 120 games, at third base and in left field. He hit a respectable .280, the second-highest batting average on the team.

Claude Osteen

Claude "Gomer" Osteen, the left-hander who came over from the American League in the Frank Howard trade the previous December, was 15–15 with a 2.79 ERA. In the September-October stretch run, he was 4–2 with a 1.80 ERA. His saving shutout in Game 3 of the World Series turned the Series around.

At the end of May 1965, the Dodgers reactivated first base coach Jim Gilliam. Gilliam hit a clutch .280, playing in 111 of the last 120 games at third base and in left field.

Jim Lefebvre

Twenty-three-year-old Jim Lefebvre took over the second base position on Opening Day and played 157 games. He hit .400 in the three games he started in the World Series (before he was sidelined by injury in Game 3), and was voted National League Rookie of the Year.

Walter Alston

Thanks to the masterful managing of Walter Alston, the Dodgers were able to overcome a multiplicity of challenges and win their third World Championship on the West Coast. He was named National League Manager of the Year by the *Associated Press*.

INTERLUDE

The period from the 1965 World Series to the end of that year was a time of rapidly escalating changes in baseball and in the country.

A Lock on the Cy Young Award

On November 2, 1965, Sandy Koufax became the first two-time winner of the Cy Young Award, when for the second straight year a special committee of the Baseball Writers' Association of America made him their unanimous choice. They cast all 20 of their ballots for him even before he turned in his stunning World Series performance. A humbled Koufax told reporters from his home in Studio City, "To have this kind of a year and to win this kind of award after wondering at times last spring whether I'd be able to pitch once a week or at all, it adds up to the most gratifying season I've ever had."[1] Koufax and Drysdale had now won three of the last four awards. A week later, the same BBWAA named Willie Mays the National League's Most Valuable Player by a vote of 224 to 177 over Koufax.[2]

A New Commissioner Called Spike

On November 17, the major league owners unanimously elected William E. "Spike" Eckert, a retired Air Force three-star general, as the new commissioner to succeed Ford Frick.[3] Frick retired after serving two seven-year terms, beginning in 1951 after commissioner Albert "Happy" Chandler was dismissed by the owners. Frick, who was best known for putting a mythical "asterisk" next to Roger Maris's 1961 home run record, led the game through a period of major change that included television, continued integration, and West Coast expansion. The 56-year-old Eckert became the game's fourth commissioner. He had been called "Spike" ever since he was given the nickname as a plebe at the U.S. Military Academy in 1926.

The First Large-Scale Vietnam War Demonstration

On November 27, an estimated 25,000 demonstrators circled the White House, carrying signs protesting against the war in Vietnam. After the leaders of the demonstration met with three White House aides, the crowd moved on to the Washington Monument, where counter demonstrators tore Vietcong flags from the hands of anti-war protestors. From his ranch in Texas, President Johnson said that while he respected the right of U.S. citizens to protest, he was confident that the great majority of Americans supported his policies in Vietnam.[4]

The Reds Give Up on Robby

On December 9, the Cincinnati Reds traded 30-year-old Frank Robinson to the Baltimore Orioles for pitchers Milt Pappas and Jack Baldschun and outfielder Dick Simpson. Robinson, who broke the major league record for most home runs by a rookie as a 20-year-old with 38 in 1956, averaged 32 home runs, 101 runs batted in, and a .303 batting average in ten seasons with Cincinnati. Robinson turned in a workman-like 1965 season, batting .296 with 33 homers. But teammate Deron Johnson had supplanted him as the team's top run producer with 130 runs batted in to Robby's 113. Reds President Bill DeWitt defended the trade, calling Robinson "an old 30."[5]

Goodbye to Trixie

On December 15, 1965, the Dodgers traded their superb defensive infielder, Dick Tracewski, to the Detroit Tigers for a fading right-handed pitcher named Phil Regan.

On December 15, the Dodgers traded superb defensive infielder Dick Tracewski to the Detroit Tigers for pitcher Phil Regan. When Jim Lefebvre went down midway through Game 3 of the World Series with the Twins, Tracewski stepped up to take over the position for the remainder of the Series. Regan had gone 42–44 in five full years as a starter for the Tigers. Bavasi and Alston had another role in mind for him.

Changes at the Players Association

The Major League Baseball Players Association (MLBPA) had been slowly evolving since 1946, when it was first registered as the American Baseball Guild by Robert E. Murphy, a Massachusetts attorney and labor organizer. At that time, a players pension plan was created, to be funded by World Series and All-Star Game television and radio revenues.[6] In 1953, each team selected a player representative to represent their interests. The player reps in turn elected Ralph Kiner (Pittsburgh Pirates) to represent the National League and Allie Reynolds (New York Yankees) to represent the American League.

By 1960, the Association had established an office in New York City with Frank Scott, former traveling secretary for the Yankees, as part-time director. Judge Robert Cannon, of the Circuit Court of Wisconsin, was the players' popular part-time, unpaid legal advisor.

In late 1965, the Executive Board of the MLBPA, recognizing the need for more comprehensive representation, authorized the hiring of a full-time Executive Director. The Association created a Search Committee comprised of Robin Roberts, a pitcher with the Astros; Jim Bunning, a pitcher with the Phillies; and Harvey Kuenn, an outfielder with the Cubs.[7] Shortly before Christmas, the Search Committee conducted interviews with the three leading candidates for the new position: Judge Cannon, Hall of Fame pitcher Bob Feller; and Marvin Miller, a 48-year-old economist with the United Steelworkers' Union. Miller had been recommended to Roberts by Dr. George W. Taylor, Dean at the Wharton School at the University of Pennsylvania and labor advisor to LBJ.[8]

Koufax at 30

On December 30, Sandy Koufax turned 30. After deciding to give it "one more year" after a 7–13 1960 season, he had turned in five straight world-class seasons. Only those closest to him knew that he was considering making 1966 his last season.

LBJ Consumed by Vietnam

The next day, December 31, 1965, President Johnson, speaking at his year-end news conference at the LBJ ranch, told the American people that they *could* and *must* continue to afford both the war in Vietnam and the war on poverty at home.[9] At the same time, world leaders were speaking out against the U.S. intervention: UN Secretary General U Thant called for an unconditional halt to the bombing of North Vietnam,[10] and French President Charles de Gaulle urged the U.S. to end its "detestable" intervention.[11] As a fragile, 48-hour bombing halt began for the New Year, there were now an estimated 184,300 U.S. troops in Vietnam—a 161,000 (691 percent) increase over the past year.[12]

11

Holding Out in a Gathering Storm

For my part, I was no longer giving us better than a 50 percent chance of playing ball.[1]—Sandy Koufax

If one of us had gone to spring training and signed, the Dodgers would have let the other one dangle and twist in the wind.[2]—Don Drysdale

As the whole spring training season went by, Walter O'Malley and I were nowhere near as cool about the missing pitchers as we were letting on.[3]— Buzzie Bavasi

The 1965 Dodgers had three of the top five players in the 1965 Most Valuable Player Award voting. But none of the three stars were among the 36 Dodgers on the team's Electra Jet II when it arrived in Vero Beach on February 26, 1966. Dodgers captain Maury Wills (third in the voting) was in Japan for a nightclub engagement.[4] Sandy Koufax (runner-up to the MVP, Willie Mays) and Don Drysdale (fifth in the voting) were back in Los Angeles, where they formed a two-man contract negotiating team.

Two days before, Koufax and Drysdale bought breakfast for Dodgers General Manager Emil Joseph "Buzzie" Bavasi at a restaurant in the Hollywood Roosevelt Hotel, where they rejected out of hand his offer that would have made them the highest paid pitching duo in baseball history: Koufax was offered an estimated $105,000 (a 31 percent raise) and Drysdale an estimated $95,000 (27 percent). At the same time, Koufax and Drysdale presented Bavasi with an unprecedented demand: $1,000,000 to be split evenly over three years at $166,667 per year. The proposal was shocking on many levels. The Dodgers had always had a strict one-year contract policy. Even Walter Alston, with his three World Championships, was signed for one year at a time. Contract negotiations had always been between the Dodgers' general manager and the individual player; but Koufax and Drysdale were negotiating together—as a team. What's more, they told Bavasi that they would be represented by an "agent," Los Angeles attorney J. William Hayes. At the time, only Hollywood stars had agents; baseball players were on their own. In his autobiography, Koufax said that he and Drysdale decided to join together as "an entry" because they were tired of the Dodgers playing them off against each other in alternate years.[5]

On Sunday, February 27, Bavasi, concerned about the effect of the star holdouts on the morale of the team, made a clubhouse address to the players before their first workout. Bavasi told them that there was no way Koufax and Drysdale were going to get what they were asking for, describing their contract demands as "fantastic." He said that "under no circumstances will anyone get more than a one-year contract,"[6] and assured them that they could field a team without their two principal starters who were responsible for 49 wins the year before—51 percent of the team's total. The players were not convinced, the prevailing view being that there was no way to win without them.

Since the infamous reserve clause was in effect, Koufax and Drysdale were taking a huge risk. Their only options were: sign the contract the Dodgers offered to them or retire. The onerous clause allowed owners to practice what amounted to a form of "legalized blackball." If you didn't agree with your owner's contract terms, you could not play for anyone else. Even after your contract expired, you were "reserved" for the owner and his team in perpetuity.[7]

The Dodgers were in a bind. Bavasi was appalled that he was being asked to pay Koufax and Drysdale what he described as "four times more than John Roseboro and five times more than Ron Fairly."[8] Bavasi could not suspend or fine Koufax and Drysdale for missing spring training, because, in his mind, you weren't a "holdout" until you missed the first game of the regular season. What's more, the situation with the Dodgers was threatening to shake up baseball's salary structure. Top-flight NL starters such as Jim Maloney of the Reds and Juan Marichal of the Giants were waiting to see what the Dodgers did with Koufax and Drysdale.

Back in Los Angeles on Day 5 of the "holdout," Koufax and Drysdale authorized their representative, J. William Hayes, to give an update to the press. Hayes told the *Los Angeles Times* that the Dodgers had made no attempt to resume negotiations after the initial breakfast meeting on February 24 between Bavasi and Team K&D. Hayes told the *Times*, "management has the ball" and that the next move was up to the club.[9] At this point, it was evident that communications had broken down between the two sides.

Drysdale caused a buzz when it was reported that he called Dodgers trainer Wayne "Doc" Anderson in Vero Beach on Saturday, March 5, from his Hidden Hills ranch in California. "Keep my stuff in the clubhouse dusted off, "[10] he told Anderson. It set off speculation that Drysdale was getting itchy to settle the contract impasse.

By Day 11, March 9, the *Los Angeles Times* reported that Claude Osteen was being groomed to be the starter for the opening game of the season on April 12.[11] Maury Wills, who arrived at LAX the night before after a ten-day, banjo-playing act in Japan, confidently told the press that he didn't expect any problems coming to terms with Bavasi and the Dodgers. Wills was seeking a $90,000 contract—a whopping $30,000 (50 percent) increase—and wanted to conclude the contract negotiations in L.A. to avoid having to deal with Bavasi under pressure in Vero Beach with his teammates already fully engaged in pre-season games.[12]

On March 11 in Los Angeles, Bavasi offered Wills $75,000, a 25 percent increase. Wills' response was prompt and abrupt: "I'm sorry, but that's not enough. It doesn't look like I'll be down for spring training."[13] The day before their first spring exhibition game, all three of the Dodgers' top stars were holdouts.

In the intervening 48 hours, things had begun to weigh heavily on Wills. Bavasi—as publicly backed up by O'Malley—had told the L.A. press that his offer to Wills was "final." Then young John Kennedy put in a sterling performance at shortstop in the first Grapefruit League game. On Sunday, March 13, the 33-year-old Wills relented and called Bavasi. He agreed to come to Vero Beach for a face-to-face meeting with the Dodgers' general manager in two days.[14]

On the night of March 15, Bavasi picked Wills up at the Melbourne airport, 33 miles from Vero Beach. At the airport, they made a verbal agreement for Wills to be paid the previously rejected salary offer of $75,000 for 1966, and worked out the details as they drove together to Dodgertown.[15] At the time, that made Wills the third highest-paid player after Willie Mays ($125,000) and Mickey Mantle ($100,000). Twenty-three of the 25 Dodger players who were expected to make the Opening Day roster were now signed.

On Wednesday, March 16, Day 19 of the holdout, *Los Angeles Times* columnist Jim Murray—after repeated attempts—reached Sandy Koufax by phone at his home in Sherman Oaks. Koufax told Murray that he and Drysdale had actually made two counteroffers to Bavasi after the initial three-year $1 million proposal, only to get dead silence from the Dodgers. Koufax said he was anxious to play, but that the last thing he heard from Bavasi was "we'll miss you boys."[16]

On March 17, Koufax and Drysdale signed a contract with Paramount Studios to do a movie called "Warning Shot," starring Dodgers fan David Janssen. Drysdale was to play a television commentator and Koufax a detective sergeant, with shooting scheduled to begin on April 4. Their agent, J. William Hayes, told the press that their movie contracts did not have "escape" clauses that would allow K&D to get out of the deal if they reached an agreement with the Dodgers before the project got under way.[17] The next day, Day 21 of the holdout, Koufax sold his biography to Viking Press for an $110,000 advance against royalties. *Look* magazine immediately purchased the serial rights for another $40,000.[18] The Dodgers' star pitching duo did not appear to be in a hurry to settle.

In Florida, with nine pitchers in camp with a combined 1965 record of 48–45 and nine complete games, panic had begun to set in. Dodgers pitching coach Harold "Lefty" Phillips, who had signed Drysdale out of Van Nuys High School in 1954, warned that a year's layoff could be career-threatening for Koufax and Drysdale. "At their age [Drysdale to turn 30 on July 23, and Koufax 31 on December 30], they'd probably be through," Phillips told the press. Phillips cited possible problems with shoulder adhesions and weight. It was a move clearly intended to nudge the holdouts.[19]

On Day 24, March 21, one half of the K&D team implied that he was ready to settle. Drysdale told the *Los Angeles Times* that he and Koufax could come to terms with the Dodgers in a couple of hours if the two sides could sit down and talk, but that he and Koufax hadn't heard from Bavasi since their February 24 breakfast meeting. When asked if he had been working out, Drysdale said, "I've been working around my ranch, and that keeps you in pretty good shape."[20]

On Day 25, March 22, Koufax and Drysdale went over Buzzie Bavasi's head and called owner Walter O'Malley directly. The maneuver failed to move the negotiations forward as O'Malley, in Vero Beach, merely repeated the Dodgers' earlier offer (Koufax $105,000 and Drysdale $95,000); K&D rejected it again. An angered Bavasi told the press, "If the boys prefer doing business with Mr. O'Malley, it's perfectly agreeable with me. It's his money."[21] That same day, Drysdale began more formal workouts at Pierce College in Woodland Hills with Pierce baseball coach Bill Ford, who was his coach at Van Nuys High.

In Los Angeles on March 26, Sandy Koufax told the *New York Times*, "Don and I are fighting for the principle that ballplayers aren't slaves; that we have a right to negotiate."[22]

By Day 30, March 27, with no further communications between the two sides and Opening Day fast approaching, Koufax and Drysdale—and the Dodgers—were losing public support. "I can see Drysdale and Koufax have not considered their lowly fans who helped make them what they are today; all they have is $ signs in their eyes,"[23] said a fan in a letter to the *Los Angeles Times*. "We would like to see them go down as the greatest pitchers in baseball history—not the greediest,"[24] said another. A more neutral, exasperated fan wrote, "Who are the baseball fans in Los Angeles going to want to get rid of more if NOBODY gives in, Koufax-Drysdale or O'Malley?"[25]

On March 28, Koufax and Drysdale began rehearsals at Paramount Studios for their movie, *Warning Shot*.[26]

On Monday, March 29, the 33-day communication freeze ended when Bavasi called K&D agent Hayes and made a new offer $210,000 offer: Koufax $112,500, and Drysdale $97,500, only to have it rejected. Things looked bleak. Bavasi told the press, "This is our final offer." In Vero Beach, Walter O'Malley confirmed that the team had given up their attempts to sign K&D for 1966, telling reporters, "The incident is being closed." That day in Orlando, Florida, the Dodgers' World Series opponents, the Minnesota Twins, shut them out, 2–0.[27] Alston and the Dodgers were now resigned to not having Koufax and Drysdale for 1966.

However, things had begun to move behind the scenes. Attorney Bill Hayes and his law firm were preparing to sue the Los Angeles Dodgers and Major League Baseball to challenge the reserve clause under a California statute that said personal service contracts were only legal for seven years, after which they had to be renegotiated. Mervyn LeRoy, a prominent film producer and friend of Walter O'Malley, got wind of the plan.[28] Chuck Connors, a former Brooklyn Dodger turned actor, intervened by calling Bavasi and urging him to meet with Koufax and Drysdale. Connors then called Drysdale, who called Bavasi. Bavasi had a close relationship with Drysdale, whom he always addressed as Donald. The two arranged to meet at Nikola's restaurant on Sunset Boulevard near Dodger Stadium. Koufax declined to participate, leaving it in Drysdale's hands.

The next day, March 30, as the Dodgers' new number one starter, Claude Osteen, shut out the Reds, 2–0, on two hits in Vero Beach, Buzzie Bavasi quietly met with Don Drysdale at Nikola's. Bavasi, relieved not to have to negotiate with K&D as a two-man package, presented yet another offer to Drysdale: Koufax $120,000 and Drysdale $105,000 for a total of $225,000.[29] Drysdale responded by telling Bavasi, "I'll sign for $110,000 (a 38 percent increase), and Sandy will sign for $125,000 (a 47 percent increase)."[30] With only two weeks left to prepare for the season, Bavasi relented and accepted the counter-offer from Drysdale. In a bizarre scenario, at the insistence of Bavasi, Drysdale had to call Koufax, inform him of the deal, and obtain his concurrence. After deliberating briefly over the phone, K&D agreed to accept the deal. The ordeal was over, the season saved. A collective sigh of relief was heard from Los Angeles to Vero Beach. Koufax and Drysdale agreed to begin working out together later that day at Dodger Stadium. Paramount Studios immediately—and graciously—let Koufax and Drysdale out of their movie contracts.

A jubilant Walter Alston, who suddenly inherited 49 victories from last season, told the press his two Cy Young Award winners would report to the team in its Arizona leg of spring training that weekend.[31] He would now have a formidable starting rotation including three future Hall of Famers: Koufax, Drysdale, and a 20-year rookie named Don Sutton. In one day, the Dodgers were transformed from likely also-rans to NL pennant favorites.

The Gathering Storm

While the Dodgers were going through their ordeal with Koufax and Drysdale, Marvin Miller, recently nominated for Executive Director of the Major League Baseball Players Association, was making a tour of the Florida spring training camps in a rented car. On leave from his present position as the assistant to the president of the United Steelworkers' Union, Miller urged the players to seek an increase in their "unreasonably low" minimum salary of $6,000 ($7,000 if they were on a major league roster at the end of June).[32] Miller was nominated on March 5 by a players' screening committee after Judge Robert Cannon turned down the job to preserve his judicial tenure and pension rights.[33] Miller's nomination was still subject to ratification by the players and the owners of the 20 major league clubs, who would have the final say. The players would be asked whether they wanted to establish an office of Executive Director; and if so, whether they would ratify the selection of Miller at a salary of $50,000 per year.[34] In the 20th year of its existence, the Major League Baseball Players Association had no full-time employees, did not engage in collective bargaining, had never challenged the reserve clause, and had only $5,400 in the bank.[35]

Koufax and Drysdale joined the team in Mesa on April 2. They saw their first action three days later, each pitching three innings against the Giants. Drysdale started and gave up four runs and four hits, including a three-run home run by Jim Ray Hart. Koufax gave up five hits, including a home run by Tom Haller, a double and two runs. The Dodgers lost the meaningless exhibition game, 7–2, but they were a complete team for the first time since the World Series.[36]

Koufax's second and final pre-season start came on April 9 against the Cleveland Indians at Dodger Stadium. He pitched a near-perfect six innings with nine strikeouts and one walk. His eight-day spring training was over. Though he had thrown just three times on the sidelines, two batting practice sessions, and logged a total of nine innings in two exhibition games, Koufax told reporters he would be ready to start in the second game of the regular season in four days.[37] The next day, it was Drysdale's turn to throw six shutout innings as the Dodgers closed out the exhibition season with a 6–0 win over the Indians at Dodger Stadium. Drysdale gave up six singles, stuck out four, and did not walk a batter. Rookie sensation Don Sutton—who had just turned 21—blanked Cleveland over the final three innings.

12

Struggling in the Aftermath

I couldn't throw the ball where I wanted to, and I couldn't get anything on it.[1]—Sandy Koufax April 13, 1966

My arm was moving fast, but the ball wasn't.[2]—Don Drysdale April 19, 1966

The weekend before the opening of the season, an Associated Press poll of 43 baseball writers picked the Reds to win the National League and the Twins to win the American League. They discounted the chances of the defending World Champion Dodgers due to the late start of Drysdale and Koufax after their 32-day holdout. Los Angeles was picked to finish fourth behind Cincinnati, San Francisco, and Atlanta.[3]

Opening Day 1966

Ever since William Howard Taft began the tradition in 1910, for 55 consecutive years the President of the United States had thrown out the first ball to open the baseball season. But with President Johnson on his ranch in Texas, consumed by the war in Vietnam,[4] Vice President Hubert Humphrey stepped in to throw out the first ball on Monday, April 11, in the opening game between the Senators and the Cleveland Indians before 44,468 fans at DC Stadium in Washington. Humphrey, sitting with Chief Justice Earl Warren, actually threw out two "first balls." The first was caught by an unfortunate Senators pitcher, Jim Hannan, who would be optioned out to the minors the next morning; the second was caught by Senators third baseman and former Dodger Ken McMullen. The Senators, managed by Gil Hodges, were well stocked with former Dodgers. Left-hander Pete Richert made the start. Big Frank Howard put Washington ahead, 2–1, with a home run off the Indians' fire-balling left-hander, Sam McDowell, that struck the left field foul pole screen in the sixth inning. Emmett Ashford, who broke a color barrier that day by becoming the first Negro ever to umpire a major league game, waved the ball fair from his position behind third base. Richert carried the 2–1 lead into the ninth. But alas, the hapless Senators went down to a 5–2 defeat after a four-run Cleveland onslaught buried them. Hubert Humphrey stayed to the bitter end to witness the meltdown.[5]

On the same day, the players of the Major League Baseball Players Association—by a vote of 489–136—ratified the nomination of Marvin Miller as their first full-time Executive Director at an annual salary of $50,000 per year, plus a $20,000 expense budget.[6]

The Dodgers opened their season the following night, April 12, against the Houston

86

Astros at Dodger Stadium. Since it was only ten days since Koufax and Drysdale restored the Dodgers' chances by rejoining the team, neither star was ready to make the start. Instead, Alston called on Claude Osteen. This was the first time since the Dodgers moved to the West Coast that the triumvirate of former Brooklyn pitchers—Drysdale, Podres, and Koufax—did not get the opening game assignment. Osteen's only previous Opening Day start came in 1964, his last season with the Senators. On that day, the Angels beat him, 4–0, at D.C. Stadium. Houston manager Grady Hatton chose veteran right-hander Robin Roberts for his NL record 13th start in an opener.

For the tenth consecutive season, the Dodgers opened with a new third baseman. This time Jim Lefebvre had the honors, after opening at second base as a rookie the year before.

	April 12, 1966		*April 12, 1965*	
1	Maury Wills	SS	Maury Wills	SS
2	Wes Parker	1B	Wes Parker	1B
3	Willie Davis	CF	Willie Davis	CF
4	Ron Fairly	RF	Tommy Davis	LF
5	Jim Lefebvre	3B	John Roseboro	C
6	Lou Johnson	LF	Jim Lefebvre	2B
7	John Roseboro	C	Ron Fairly	RF
8	Nate Oliver	2B	John Kennedy	3B
9	Claude Osteen	P	Don Drysdale	P

In the first inning, Maury Wills started where he left off in 1965 by helping the team manufacture a run. He led off with a single, advanced to second and third on groundouts, and scored on a single by Ron Fairly. Fairly, who had led the Dodgers with a modest 70 runs batted in the prior year, got the honor of batting in the cleanup spot in the lineup. The redhead from USC responded by driving in all three of the Dodgers' runs, scoring Wes Parker with a sacrifice fly in the sixth inning and Wills again with a single in the eighth to give the team a 3–1 lead. Osteen gave up a run in the ninth, but hung on to record a 6-hit 3–2 win.[7]

Earlier that day at Fenway Park in Boston, Frank Robinson made his American League debut by hitting a home run and a single for Baltimore. In the top of the first, Red Sox starter Earl Wilson welcomed Robinson to the league by drilling him in the ribs with a pitch. The Orioles won the game, 5–4, in the 13th inning on a balk with the bases loaded by a 23-year-old Jim Lonborg, pitching in relief.

A Shaky First Start by Sandy Koufax

On Wednesday night, April 13, Sandy Koufax made his first start of the 1966 season against the Astros. There appeared to be a lingering anti-holdout effect as only 24,049 fans showed up at Dodger Stadium. In his 20 starts the prior year at Dodger Stadium, Koufax had drawn an average of 37,571.

The absence of a normal six-week spring training showed, as he lasted only three innings. Koufax was cuffed around for five runs on five hits, including a three-run home run by sophomore sensation Joe Morgan after two were out in the third inning. John Roseboro tied the game 5–5 with a three-run home run off 19-year-old Houston right-hander Larry Dierker in the bottom of the third, and Koufax gamely answered the bell for the fourth. But after Astros catcher John Bateman led off the inning with a booming triple, Alston brought in Phil "The Vulture" Regan. Regan, who came over from Detroit in the Dick Tracewski trade in December, pitched five solid innings, allowing only two hits and one run. The young Astros continued to shine. Center fielder Jimmy Wynn, "The Toy Cannon," tied the game 6–6 with a home run off Regan in the eighth. Rusty Staub, a flaming redhead dubbed the "Le Grande Orange" when he played later in Montreal drove in the winning run with a single off Ron Perranoski in the ninth.[8] Koufax, who got off the hook with a no-decision, gave up one earned run on five hits with two walks and two strikeouts in his brief three innings of work. After the game, Koufax told reporters that he was still in his mid-spring training "tired arm stage."[9]

The Vulture

Philip Raymond Regan was born April 6, 1937, in Otsego, Michigan. After earning varsity letters in football, basketball, and baseball at Wayland High School in Wayland, Michigan, he spent one year at Western Michigan University. The Detroit Tigers signed him as an amateur free agent for a small, $4,000 bonus before the 1956 baseball season.

Regan spent four and a half years in the Detroit farm system before being called up in July of 1960. He started seven games, completed none, and finished with a disappointing 0–4 record. He improved to 10–7 in 1961, 11–9 in 1962, and 15–9 in 1963. In 1964, new Detroit manager Charlie Dressen relentlessly pounded at Regan to throw more curveballs. As a result, he lost his best pitch, the slider, and his record plummeted to 5–10.[10] The decline continued into 1965. After going 0–4 through June 27, he was demoted to Triple-A Syracuse in the International League, where he contemplated leaving the game. He was recalled in September and made his last two starts for the Detroit Tigers, winning one and losing one to finish the year with a dismal 1–5 record.

Upon rejoining the big club, Regan informed Detroit general manager Jim Campbell that a Dodgers scout had been sent to Syracuse that summer to evaluate him. At 11:30 p.m. on December 15—a half-hour before the interleague trading deadline—Campbell called Regan to tell him he had been traded to the Dodgers for Dick Tracewski.[11]

While at Syracuse, Regan developed a new "super slider" that broke an amazing 15–16 inches. His new National League opponents had a different name for it: a "spitter." His Dodgers teammates would soon name him "The Vulture," for his propensity to hover in the bullpen while a starter was dying out on the mound before swooping in to scavenge the victory.[12]

Phil "The Vulture" Regan made his Dodgers debut on April 13, 1966, at Dodger Stadium in relief of Sandy Koufax.

On April 14, 21-year-old Don Sutton made his major league debut in a starting role against the Houston Astros. Only 18,550 fans showed up on this Thursday night at Dodger Stadium to see Sutton match up against big right-hander Bob Bruce, representing an Astros team that had never finished higher than ninth place since coming into the league as an expansion team in 1962.

Don Sutton, Southern Boy in L.A.

Don Howard Sutton was born into a devout Southern Baptist family on April 2, 1945, in Clio, Alabama. The family moved to Florida, where young Sutton attended elementary school. He started throwing a curveball at the age of 11 when his sixth grade teacher, Henry Roper, a former pitcher in the Giants organization, taught him the pitch. "I threw curves right from the start—I just had that kind of an arm," recalled Sutton in his rookie year.[13] Sutton starred in baseball, basketball, and football at Tate High School

in Pensacola. An army of major league scouts converged on the Sutton house at the end of his senior year. The Dodgers were actually his 20th choice. He intended to sign with the Kansas City Athletics for a package including a $21,000 bonus, a new car, and a college scholarship. But the deal fell apart when scout Whitey Herzog called Athletics owner Charles Finley for approval and was told that the player procurement fund was empty. Sutton decided to give the Dodgers a chance. After all, his mother always liked Duke Snider. Sutton was impressed that "the Dodgers let you know they thought you had an inner self; while the other scouts made you feel like a piece of merchandise."[14] On September 11, 1964, Dodgers scouts Monty Basgall and Bert Wells signed Don Sutton to a contract as an amateur free agent. The terms included a smaller bonus of $15,000, but guaranteed him a paid college education.[15]

With his impressive work in spring training, right-hander Don Sutton earned a spot in the Dodgers' starting rotation. He made his debut on April 14, 1966, at Dodger Stadium 11 days after his 21st birthday.

The following spring, Sutton launched his career in the Class-A California League with the Santa Barbara Dodgers. After going 8–1 with a 1.50 ERA and 101 strikeouts in 84 innings, he was promoted to Class-AA Albuquerque in the Texas League. There he compiled a 15–6 record with a 2.78 ERA and won a post-season playoff game for the Dukes. After just one year in the minors—albeit at the Class A-AA level—Sutton looked like a "can't miss" prospect with a combined 23 wins and 239 strikeouts.

G	GS	CG	W	L	W-L%	IP	ERA	SHO	SO	BB	SO/BB
31	31	24	23	7	.767	249	2.35	3	239	45	5.31

Looking at next year, the question for the Dodgers was simple: Is Triple-A experience even necessary for this kid?

When Sutton arrived at Vero Beach in February, two things stood out: his confidence and his curveball. Duke Snider observed, "I think he has the best curve on the staff, other than Koufax."[16] On April 3, Sutton's 21st birthday, Alston selected him to start against the Giants in one of the final exhibition games at Mesa, Arizona. Sutton came through with a strong, five-inning, winning performance.[17] In the Dodgers' last exhibition game on Sunday afternoon, April 10, at Dodger Stadium against the Cleveland Indians, Sutton threw the last three shutout innings.[18] The Triple-A question was now moot. Not only had the kid right-hander made the roster, he would be part of the starting rotation with Sandy Koufax, Don Drysdale, and Claude Osteen.

Sutton read his Bible before the April 14 game and took a cold shower for invigoration before coming out to warm up.[19] He gave up an unearned run in the top of the first inning and then cruised through the next six innings, striking out seven batters with no walks.

Jim Lefebvre continued his torrid start by rocking Bruce for solo home runs in the second and fourth innings. Sutton took a 2–1 lead into the eighth. After he gave up his only walk to leadoff batter Sonny Jackson, Alston came out to the mound to settle him down with Perranoski up and throwing in the bullpen. Alston's decision to stay with his confident rookie backfired when Jimmy Wynn doubled home Jackson with the tying run. It would be Sutton's last pitch, as Alston immediately came back out and brought in Perranoski. After Joe Morgan was thrown out on a bunt attempt, the irrepressible Rusty Staub sent Perranoski's next pitch into the right-field pavilion for a game-winning two-run homer. Don Sutton thus lost his first major league game, 4–2. In seven innings he gave up seven hits, struck out seven, and walked one.[20]

It was an inauspicious start to the 1966 season for the World Champion Dodgers, losing the opening series two games to one to the lowly Astros, thanks to two game-winning blows delivered by Rusty Staub. They would reunite with old friend Leo Durocher and his new team, the Chicago Cubs, over the weekend.

The Return of Leo

Back on October 25, 1965, Leo Durocher signed a three-year contract to manage the Chicago Cubs, replacing "head coach" Lou Klein. After four years as the Dodgers' third base coach (1961–1964), the flamboyant Durocher spent the summer of the 1965 season as a television commentator on ABC's "Game of the Week" program. Frustrated by 19 consecutive years in the second division of the National League, Cubs owner Philip K. Wrigley scrapped his multiple coach system and turned the reins over to Durocher.[21]

Durocher brought his Chicago Cubs into Dodger Stadium for a weekend series beginning Friday night, April 15. Don Drysdale was scheduled to make his first start against Cubs left-hander Dick Ellsworth. As third base coach for the Dodgers, Durocher was famous for defiantly obliterating the chalk boundaries of the coaching box with his shoe. On this night, Durocher, still wearing his familiar number 2—albeit with Chicago on the front of the jersey—remained in the dugout and turned over the third base coaching duties over to crony Whitey Lockman (a former player on his New York Giants' championship teams of 1951 and 1954).

Drysdale got off to a rocky start. In the top of the second inning, Ron Santo led off

After spending the 1965 season as a commentator on ABC's Game of the Week, Leo Durocher returned to the dugout as manager of the Chicago Cubs in 1966.

with a single. Drysdale promptly balked Santo to second and hit Ernie Banks with a pitch. Cubs center fielder Ty Cline beat out a bunt to load the bases. Successive sacrifice flies by Randy Hundley and Don Kessinger put Drysdale behind, 2–0. Though the visibly fatigued Drysdale managed to make it through the next four innings without giving up another run, Alston took him out after the sixth inning and brought in Bob Miller.[22]

In the bottom of the seventh inning, after Ellsworth gave up a leadoff single to Ron Fairly, the Cubs' infield botched two double play ground balls that gave the Dodgers an unearned run and forced Durocher to remove Ellsworth and bring in the control-challenged Ted Abernathy.[23] In the bottom of the eighth, Abernathy walked his second and third batters, and gave up a single to Willie Davis, a double to Wes Parker, and a game-winning three-run homer to the red-hot Jim Lefebvre. It was Lefebvre's fourth home run in the first four games. Phil Regan got his first win as a Dodger in relief. Drysdale, who allowed eight hits and two earned runs in his six innings, escaped with a no-decision.

The next night, Claude Osteen matched up against fellow left-hander Bob Hendley. Hendley had pitched a brilliant one-hitter the last time he pitched at Dodger Stadium. But on that night (September 9, 1965) he had the misfortune of competing against a perfect game by Sandy Koufax.[24] On this April night, Osteen beat Hendley and the Cubs, 4–2, on a complete game with nine strikeouts. Tommy Davis got his first start in left field, but had to come out of the game when he pulled a thigh muscle in the fourth inning.[25] His thick leg muscles would make pulled muscles a chronic problem.

Sandy Koufax Finds His Bearings

On April 17, 32,772 fans came out to Dodger Stadium on an overcast Sunday afternoon to watch Sandy Koufax pitch the final game of the series with the Cubs against Larry Jackson. The Dodgers got to Jackson for four runs in the first inning, sparked by a crushing three-run homer by Lou Johnson into the left field bullpen. Alston allowed Koufax to pitch six scoreless innings and then brought in Bob Miller to pitch the last three for an easy 5–0 win over the hapless Cubs. Though Koufax had what for him was just "ordinary stuff," he recorded his first victory of 1966 with six strikeouts and one walk. In pre-game ceremonies, the Dodgers received their World Series rings and Koufax was presented with his second Cy Young Award.[26]

Don Sutton's First Win

The next day, the Dodgers began their first road trip. Houston was the first stop on Monday night, April 18. Don Sutton got the start against 39-year-old Robin Roberts for the Astros. Twenty-five thousand, one hundred eighty-two fans turned out to see the first official game played on the Astrodome's synthetic grass infield, made of tough nylon strips zippered together.[27]

The Dodgers knocked Roberts out of the game before he could get anyone out in the fifth inning, and Dodgers led, 5–1, after five. Sutton did not have his good curveball and had to rely on his fastball. But he made it through seven innings, holding on to 5–1 lead. He began to fade in the bottom of the eighth, giving up two singles and a two-run double to the Dodgers' arch-tormentor, Rusty Staub, that cut their lead to 5–3. Alston allowed Sutton to finish the eighth and brought in Phil Regan to save a 6–3 win for Sutton.[28]

Drysdale's Second Rocky Start

On April 19, Don Drysdale made his second start of the season. Big Houston right-hander Turk Farrell opposed him that night at the Astrodome. Though Drysdale was clearly still not in shape, he took a 5–2 lead into the bottom of the fifth inning before things unraveled.

It started when Wes Parker fumbled Joe Morgan's leadoff grounder. Sonny Jackson looped a single just beyond Parker's reach into right field. When Jim Wynn scratched out an infield single, the bases were loaded. Rusty Staub's sacrifice fly scored Morgan to cut the lead to 5–3. When right fielder Dave Nicholson hit a slow roller to Parker's right, Drysdale froze on the mound and did not cover first base. The result: Nicholson beat Parker to the bag for an infield single, scoring Jackson to make it 5–4. An irritated Walter Alston removed Drysdale and brought in Johnny Podres. Before Podres could retire the side, the Astros had surged to a 6–5 lead.[29] It would be his last appearance in a Dodgers uniform.

The Dodgers scored all five of their runs off Turk Farrell, knocking him out of the game in the fourth inning. But Mike Cuellar, a 165-pound, left-handed screwball pitcher from Cuba, came out of the Houston bullpen to shut them out over the last 5⅔ to get credit for the 8–5 win. The ultra-superstitious Cuellar, who would count off the same number of steps when he walked to the mound and again when he walked back to the dugout, would win 180 more games in his major league career. Drysdale was charged with his first loss after allowing four earned runs, six hits, and three walks, with no strike-outs in 4⅓ innings.

Osteen Continues to Fill the Void in the Clutch

Claude Osteen continued to step up and the fill void created by the K&D late start with his third consecutive complete-game win.[30] On Wednesday night, April 20, in Houston, Osteen beat Bob Bruce and the Astros, 3–2. Because Willie Davis, batting .346, was out of action after he re-pulled a leg muscle the night before, Alston moved Fairly to center field and started Al Ferrara in right. Ferrara responded with a solo home run off a high, hanging curveball by Bruce in the second inning and a run-scoring single off Bruce in the seventh.[31] Though Osteen walked five batters and gave up seven hits, he continually managed to pitch his way out of trouble. The Astros left nine runners on base—six were left in scoring position. The Dodgers were 6–3, and Osteen was 3–0 with a 1.33 ERA. Now it was on to Leo Durocher's new home, Wrigley Field.

The First Koufax Complete Game

The series in Chicago began on a chilly Friday, April 22, in front of a sparse crowd of 4,551 at Wrigley Field. Sandy Koufax faced fellow left-hander Dick Ellsworth. The Dodgers got on the scoreboard in the first inning against Ellsworth. With one out, Wes Parker and Lou Johnson singled. Al Ferrara drove in Parker with a sacrifice fly to give Koufax a 1–0 lead.

In the bottom of the fourth inning, Glenn Beckert, Billy Williams, and Ron Santo opened with consecutive singles. Santo's hit drove in Beckert to tie the score, 1–1. Koufax struck out Ernie Banks, but walked Byron Browne to load the bases. After Alston came out to the mound to tell Koufax not to press, he got catcher Randy Hundley to pop up for the second out. Leo Durocher called back his starting center field, Carl Warwick, and sent up Adolfo Phillips to pinch-hit. The Panamanian Phillips had not taken batting practice, having arrived late to the game from O'Hare Airport after being obtained from the Philadelphia Phillies the day before. Ever since Durocher had left the Giants after the 1955 season, he had been in search of "the next Willie Mays." Phillips was his latest candidate. Unfortunately for Phillips, his debut for Durocher's Cubs would be against Sandy Koufax. And Koufax welcomed him to Chicago by blowing him away on strikes to get out of the inning. After the game, Durocher commented to reporters about Phillips' first encounter with Koufax, "I admit I didn't put him up there in an easy spot."[32]

With one out in the sixth inning, Lou Johnson got aboard on a throwing error by Cubs shortstop Roberto Pena, filling in for the injured Don Kessinger. After Ferrara followed with a single, Jeff Torborg singled home Johnson to make it 2–1, Dodgers.[33]

Koufax appeared to be getting stronger as the game progressed. He struck out the first two batters in the bottom of the ninth. The speedy Phillips blooped a hit to shallow center field and put himself in scoring position by stretching it into a double. Durocher sent up utility man John Boccabella to pinch-hit for Ellsworth. Koufax struck out the overmatched Boccabella on three pitches to end the game. In his complete-game 2–1 win, Koufax allowed six hits, one earned run, walked three, and struck out 11.

The Dazzling Debut of Ferguson Jenkins

Don Sutton and Bob Hendley squared off the next day on a 45-degree Saturday afternoon. After Hendley survived based-loaded jams in the second and third innings, 22-year-old Canadian right-hander Ferguson Jenkins made his major league debut when he took over in a scoreless tie with the bases loaded in the third inning.

Ferguson Arthur Jenkins came over from the Phillies two days before in the trade that sent him and Phillips to the Cubs for front-line starters Bob Buhl and Larry Jackson.

The 6'5" Jenkins was one of Canada's prime prospects in ice hockey until Phillies general manager John Quinn made him give up the sport.[34] Jenkins and his wife drove all night from Philadelphia to reach Chicago. With just two hour's sleep, he was in uniform for the series opener the day before, but Durocher didn't use him.[35]

Jenkins shut out the Dodgers for 5⅓ innings on four singles. He also hit a solo home run off Sutton in the bottom of the fifth inning to break the scoreless tie. Batting against Sutton in the seventh, he singled home Randy Hundley to make it 2–0.[36] The submariner Ted Abernathy, took over in the ninth inning to save the 2–0 win for Jenkins. It was the first of 284 wins for the future Hall of Famer.

The Dodgers tied a National League record by leaving 14 runners on base. Overshadowed by Jenkins, Sutton suffered his second loss of the season in a solid seven-inning, seven-hit performance.

The Dodgers first encountered Ferguson Jenkins on a frigid April 23, 1966, day at Wrigley Field. He came in from the bullpen to pitch 5⅓ scoreless inning and hit a home run and a single to boot.

Drysdale Loses to a Kid Left-Hander

The Wrigley Field series concluded on Sunday, April 24. Don Drysdale made his third start for the Dodgers. His opponent was a 20-year-old, part-time player named Kenneth Holtzman, a sophomore at the University of Illinois making his first major league start. After holding the Cubs scoreless in the first inning, Drysdale was victimized by the Dodgers' defense in the second. John Herrnstein led off with a single to center. After Byron Browne lined out to Al Ferrara in right field, Randy Hundley hit a double to left to put runners on second and third. Don Kessinger hit a sinking line drive to right field that Ferrara nearly made a shoestring catch on. But the bumbling, stumbling Ferrara kicked the ball out of his own glove, and it squirted out of his vision toward the right field foul line. He blindly whirled around twice, trying to find the ball, before center fielder Lou Johnson could retrieve it. By that time, both runners had scored and Kessinger was on third base with a freak triple.[37] After the game, Ferrara told reporters, "I blew the play; I should have caught the ball."[38]

Drysdale never recovered from the fatal second inning. He pitched a solid six innings, allowing just the two runs on five hits, and striking out seven. But he went down to a 2–0 loss as the Dodgers could manage just three hits against the kid left-hander, Holtzman, who won his first major league game before returning to his studies the next day.

The Dodgers Run Head-On into the Enigma of Larry Jaster

On Monday, April 25, the Dodgers returned home to Los Angeles in third place and opened a two-game series with the Cardinals at Dodger Stadium. Claude Osteen (3–0) would seek his fourth straight complete-game win against a 22-year-old rookie left-hander named Larry Jaster.

Larry Edward Jaster was born January 13, 1944, in Midland, Michigan. A standout, all-around athlete at Midland High School, he was prepared to accept a combination baseball-football scholarship to Michigan State when St. Louis Cardinals scout Mo Mozzali lured him away with a $50,000 bonus. Jaster spent the next four years in the St. Louis farm system before being called up at the end of the 1965 season. On September 21, 1965, the 21-year-old Jaster made his major league debut against the Dodgers at old Busch Stadium. He came in from the bullpen in the sixth inning to retire Lefebvre, Parker, and Torborg in order as the Dodgers came from behind to win, 3–2—the second win in their decisive 13-game winning streak. Jaster went on to pitch three consecutive complete-game victories, including a devastating 9–1 win over the Giants at Candlestick Park on September 28 that knocked them out of a first-place tie with the Dodgers.[39]

Twenty-two-year-old rookie left-hander Larry Jaster shut out the Dodgers for the first of five consecutive times on April 25, 1966, at Dodger Stadium.

Jaster came into the game this April night at Dodger Stadium with a 1–1 record and a hefty 5.25 ERA. The game was a scoreless tie for the first five innings. In the top of the sixth, Osteen walked Lou Brock, and Julian Javier singled him to third base. Curt Flood doubled home Brock, and Javier scored on a sacrifice fly by Charlie Smith to make it 2–0. That was the end of the scoring. Osteen allowed only five hits over eight innings but suffered his first loss of the season. Larry Jaster pitched a surprising seven-hit shutout with seven strikeouts and no walks. "That's the best game I've ever pitched in the big leagues," Jaster told reporters after the game.[40] The Dodgers had now gone 35 straight innings without scoring an earned run.[41] More importantly, Larry Jaster had their number.

The Return of the Devil

It was becoming a familiar pattern. Last year, the Dodgers made 12-year veteran infielder Jim Gilliam their first base coach, but by the end of May they had reactivated him. Gilliam was first called "Junior" as a Rookie of the Year second baseman for Brooklyn in 1953. But ever since he walked into a pool place in Vero Beach, laid down his money on the table, and announced, "Who's going to pay the Devil his due?" his teammates had rebranded him "Devil." Devil hit .280 in 111 games for the 1965 Dodgers, playing second base, third base, and the outfield. That October he saved Game 7 of the World Series with a dazzling backhand stab of a sure, game-tying smash by Zoilo Versalles. After this putative "final game," the National Baseball Hall of Fame asked for his glove.[42]

But now, after being shut out for three straight games to slip into the second division, Walter Alston realized he couldn't win without the Devil on the field. On April 26, he ordered the 37-year-old Gilliam to vacate his coaching box and find a new glove.[43]

The Final Koufax-Gibson Confrontation

That night, Sandy Koufax and Bob Gibson squared off at Dodger Stadium. The modest crowd of 25,121 did not realize that they were witnessing the last confrontation between the two future Hall of Fame pitchers.

The Dodgers got to Gibson early, scoring four runs on six hits in the first inning to stake Koufax to a 4–0 lead. An inconsistent Koufax pitched in and out of trouble the entire game as the Cardinals amassed 13 hits. It was ultimately the heavy marine layer that frequently descended on Los Angeles in the evenings that would save Koufax, as he took a 4–2 lead into the ninth inning. After leadoff batter Julian Javier was thrown out by Roseboro on a swinging bunt in front of the plate, Curt Flood singled to left field to bring the tying run to the plate in the person of Cardinals cleanup batter Alex Johnson. In succession, Johnson and Charlie Smith hit drives off Koufax that would have been home runs in most parks, but died on the warning track for outs.[44]

The Dodgers were fortunate to snap their scoreless streak in the first inning because Gibson shut them out on one hit the rest of the way. He retired the last 18 batters in order. After the game Koufax told reporters, "I had a lot of pain in my left elbow. My control wasn't good, and I was having trouble with my curve."[45] Remarkably, Koufax managed to pitch a complete game with eight strikeouts and only one walk. With a record of 3–0 and an ERA of 1.33, he was ten days ahead of his 1965 pace.

Sutton's First Complete Game Victory

On Wednesday, April 27, Don Sutton pitched against a Braves team playing their first game at Dodger Stadium with "Atlanta" on their jerseys. His opponent, right-hander Hank Fischer, lasted only 2⅓ innings. Sutton took a four-hit, 4–0 shutout into the ninth, having retired the last 13 Braves in a row by employing a wicked sinking fastball. Hank Aaron spoiled the shutout with a leadoff home run deep into the left-center field pavilion. After the game Sutton told reporters, "The ball I threw Aaron was a fastball that didn't sink until it landed somewhere around the twentieth row of the bleachers."[46] Sutton went on to win his first complete game, 4–1, to even his record at 2–2. He struck out ten batters and walked only one.

Wes Parker tripled home two runs and squeezed home another. Maury Wills returned to the lineup after a pulled leg muscle caused him to miss four games (of which the Dodgers lost three).[47] Wills had four hits, including an RBI single.

Drysdale Finally Gets Off the Schneid

Drysdale made his fourth start on Thursday night, April 28, at Dodger Stadium against the Braves. He came into the game with a 0–2 record and a 4.41 ERA, having not advanced beyond the sixth inning in his three previous outings. For the first time, Drysdale felt he had good stuff from the start. But in the first inning he left a ball up in the strike zone to old nemesis Hank Aaron. "Bad Henry" jumped on it for a ringing RBI double that put him behind, 1–0. He settled down and shut out the Braves over the next four innings until Aaron reared his head again with a solo home run in the sixth. By that time, the Dodgers had scored eight runs off Atlanta starter Wade Blasingame and reliever Arnold Umbach. Drysdale completed the game, an 8–2 six-hitter with ten strikeouts and no walks. His first win enabled the Dodgers to stay in a second-place tie with the Giants, only one game behind the Pirates.[48]

Osteen Continues His April Leadership

On Friday night, April 29, the Dodgers opened a three-game weekend series with the Reds at Dodger Stadium with Claude Osteen going up against fellow left-hander Jim O'Toole. In the bottom of the first inning, Lou Johnson staked Osteen to a 2–0 lead with a two-run homer off O'Toole. Osteen shut out the Reds on two hits through the first eight innings. With one out in the ninth, he walked Pete Rose. When Vada Pinson followed with a bloop single to left field, the tying runs were on. Osteen got Don Pavletich to ground out to Lefebvre at third to come within one out of a shutout. But the Reds' sophomore first baseman, Tony Perez, flared a single into center field to score both runners and tie the game, 2–2. Right fielder Ron Fairly saved Osteen with a lunging, one-handed catch of Deron Johnson's line drive for the third out.[49]

In the bottom of the ninth, Nate Oliver led off with a double to left field against Reds reliever Jack Baldschun. The Devil, Jim Gilliam, made his first appearance of the year as a pinch-hitter, and drew a walk. Wills bunted, but the Reds threw out Oliver on a force play at third. Baldschun walked Parker to load the bases for the Dodgers' top RBI man, Lou Johnson. Johnson popped up for the second out, leaving it up to Ron Fairly. Fairly came through with a walk-off single over Pete Rose's head at third base.[50]

Osteen got his fourth win, a complete-game four-hitter with seven strikeouts. The Dodgers went into a virtual tie with the Pittsburgh Pirates for first place.

The Reds Hand Koufax His First Loss

The series with the Reds continued with a matchup between Sandy Koufax and Joey Jay on Saturday night, April 30, before a Ladies Night crowd of 44,594 (the largest to date for 1966) at Dodger Stadium. Koufax was seeking to extend his winning streak to four straight for the season and eight straight since September 14, 1965.

The Dodgers gave Koufax a 1–0 lead to work with in the third inning. Wills walked and stole second after multiple unsuccessful pickoff attempts by Jay. With two out, Willie Davis drove him in with a single through the hole between shortstop and third base.

Koufax shut out the Reds on two singles through the first seven innings, striking out seven and not walking anyone. But after retiring 18 batters in a row, he began to tire and lose his control as he took the 1–0 lead into the eighth.[51] He walked Tony Perez and Tommy Harper. With one out, Reds manager Don Heffner brought in Lee May to hit for Jay. May hit a double play ground ball to third, but the Dodgers couldn't turn it as the runners moved up to second and third.[52] That brought up rookie second baseman Tommy Helms, who had not hit the ball out of the infield in three previous at-bats. With Helms behind 0–2, Roseboro called for a fastball. Koufax shook him off because, as he told reporters after the game, "I just wanted to shake off a pitch, though I still intended to throw the fastball."[53] At that point, he lost his concentration and threw the curve instead— a very un–Koufax one with no snap. Helms lined it into left field to score both runners. Pete Rose and Vada Pinson followed with singles to force Koufax to face the dangerous Deron Johnson with the bases loaded. Alston stayed with Koufax on the ropes, and he got out of the inning by getting Johnson to ground into a force play.

In the ninth, the Reds' little shortstop, Leo Cardenas, hit a two-out home run into the left field pavilion off a laboring Koufax to make the final score 3–1. Though Koufax suffered his first loss, he managed to go the distance and strike out nine batters.

Sutton and Perranoski Shut Out the Reds

On Sunday, May 1, the Dodgers closed out their weekend series with the Reds. Don Sutton (2–2) went up against Milt Pappas (0–1). The Dodgers scratched together three runs on three hits off Pappas in the third inning. The runs scored on a bunt single by Sutton, a groundout by Wes Parker, and a walk with the bases loaded by Lou Johnson. After Wills contributed his own bunt single to the rally, the Dodgers went hitless for the remainder of the game.[54]

Sutton breezed through the Cincinnati lineup with a 3–0 lead for the first eight innings, shutting them out on four singles. But when he gave up a leadoff double to Vada Pinson in the ninth, Alston brought in Ron Perranoski.[55] Perranoski had not pitched in the five consecutive complete games by the Dodgers' staff—and it showed. Don Pavletich hit a line shot right at third baseman John Kennedy for the first out. Perranoski wild-pitched Pinson to third before retiring Deron Johnson on a ground ball to Wills. Leo Cardenas, who hit .391 against the Dodgers in 1965 and had tagged Koufax for a home run the night before, threatened to ruin the shutout. Perranoski battled Cardenas to a full count before sneaking a called strike past him to save the game for Sutton, who improved his record to 3–2 and lowered his ERA to 1.85.

As the Dodgers prepared to leave town for a showdown in San Francisco, they were in a tie with the Giants for second place, a half-game behind the Pittsburgh Pirates. The Pirates had not held the top position on this date since their championship year of 1960.

	W	L	Pct.	GB
Pittsburgh	11	5	.688	—
Los Angeles	12	7	.632	½
San Francisco	12	7	.632	½

Domination by Marichal

The first series of 1966 with the Giants took place in San Francisco, beginning with a night game at Candlestick Park on May 3 pitting an unbeaten Juan Marichal against a struggling Don Drysdale. Drysdale almost did not survive the first inning. It started with a walk to the Giants' .077-hitting leadoff man, Dick Schofield.[56] Big D tormentor Willie McCovey followed with a single to center. When Mays got aboard on a fielder's choice, the Giants had the bases loaded with nobody out. Drysdale dug himself deeper into the hole by hitting Jim Ray Hart with a pitch to force in a run. But he got out of the inning by striking out Tom Haller and inducing Jesus Alou to ground into a double play. With Felipe now in Atlanta and Matty in Pittsburgh, Jay was the last of the Alou brothers in a Giants uniform.

In the fifth inning, Marichal faced John Roseboro for the second time since the Dominican Dandy split his head open with a bat on August 22, 1965. The crowd of 35,193 rose in anticipation when Roseboro hit a slow ground ball past the mound, and he and Marichal began a race to first base. Roseboro was safe when Marichal dropped second baseman Hal Lanier's throw for an error. There was no collision, no words, and no trouble between the two for the rest of the game. There was, however, a lawsuit still pending against Marichal and the Giants' organization for $110,000 in damages.

In the bottom of the inning, Drysdale again walked Schofield with two out and a runner on second. McCovey then put the game out of reach with a 400-foot, three-run homer to make it 4–0, Giants. It was the first home run Drysdale had given up to McCovey since September 7, 1963.[57]

Meanwhile, Marichal was working his magic on the Dodgers. Through the first eight innings, he gave up just three singles and no runs. He took an 8–0 shutout to the ninth before Lefebvre ruined it with a solo home run over the right field fence.[58] With the 8–1 win, Marichal had now beaten the Dodgers 11 consecutive times without a loss at Candlestick Park. For the year, he was 5–0 with five complete games and a microscopic 0.60 ERA. Drysdale saw his record fall to 1–3. There now was no doubt that Juan Marichal was the National League's premier right-hander.

Osteen Serves Up Home Run #512 to Willie Mays on a Platter

Left-handers Claude Osteen and Joe Gibbon squared off the next night. In the second inning, Osteen's throwing error opened the door for the Giants to score four runs with four hits to jump out to a 4–0 lead.[59] Osteen made it into the fifth inning and retired the first two batters before having to face Willie Mays for the third time. He had struck out Mays his first two times up. But this time Mays hit his first pitch—a high changeup—over the right field fence for the 512th home run of his career to break Mel Ott's National League record. It was the first changeup Mays had seen in ages, and the first home run Osteen had given up in 12 starts.[60] Tito Fuentes followed with a triple to knock Osteen out of the game. The Giants went on to win the game, 6–1. It took only one hour and 55 minutes for Gibbon to pitch a complete-game four-hitter with seven strikeouts and no walks.[61]

Koufax and Wills Can't Prevent a Giants Sweep

A crowd of 26,326 turned out on a Thursday afternoon to see the series finale at Candlestick Park. It fell on Sandy Koufax to prevent a sweep. Four times he had come through with a win to prevent a sweep in 1965, and six times in 1964. But today, Koufax didn't have it. The Giants routed him, scoring their first two runs in the first inning on a double by Orlando Cepeda. Alston considered pulling Koufax at that point but left him in, hoping he could loosen up and find a rhythm. In the second inning, after he walked the Giants' pitcher, Bob Bolin, with one out to put runners on first and second, Alston had seen enough and brought in Bob Miller. The Giants continued the onslaught against Miller, scoring five more runs to take a 7–0 lead. Four of the runs were charged to Koufax, who saw his ERA jump 90 points, from 1.75 to 2.65. His aborted, 1⅓-inning stint was his shortest since April 22, 1964, when an elbow flare-up forced him to come out of a game after one inning in St. Louis.[62]

Maury Wills, who missed the first two games of the series due to a pulled muscle, was back in the lineup at shortstop—albeit not at 100 percent. Wills was clearly the engine that made the Dodgers go. So far in 1966, the Dodgers had lost five of the six games without him in the lineup.[63] But on this day, four different San Francisco pitchers prevented Wills from reaching first base in his five plate appearances.

Even without Wills, by the end of the fifth inning the scrappy Dodgers had clawed back to tie the game, 7–7, to get Koufax off the hook with a no-decision. Both teams scored a run in the eighth, and the game went into extra innings as an 8–8 tie. In a disastrous bottom of the tenth, Ron Perranoski, the Dodgers' fifth pitcher, got leadoff man Jim Davenport to hit a routine ground ball to third that John Kennedy booted for a rare error. Ollie Brown hit a double play ball back to Perranoski, but the Dodgers couldn't turn it, leaving Brown safe at first. A passed ball by Roseboro allowed Brown to move into scoring position. Perranoski was lucky to get Willie Mays on a line drive right at Willie Davis in center field for the second out. The final indignity came when Jim Ray Hart, batting .344, hit a long—but clearly playable—fly ball into right center field. Davis got to the ball, but it was knuckling in the wind and bounced off the heel of his glove for a game-ending error.

With their 9–8 win, the Giants swept the series and sent the Dodgers into a fourth-place tie with Atlanta, three games back. The sweep in San Francisco caused the resentment over the holdout that had been simmering since late February to boil over in the Los Angeles press. Charles Maher ripped into Koufax: "Koufax still isn't ready to pitch. The reason that he still isn't ready to pitch is that he missed spring training."[64] He also turned his wrath on the Dodgers' management: "The reason he missed spring training is that the Dodger management took over a month to come up with a second salary offer. Having been content to wait for Koufax and Drysdale to come around to signing, the club must be content to wait for them to come around to pitching."[65] A disaster in San Francisco, a hostile press, and it was only the beginning of the road trip. There would be no day off to regroup. They had a date with the Reds the next night in Cincinnati.

	W	L	Pct.	GB
San Francisco	15	7	.682	—
Pittsburgh	13	6	.684	½
Houston	13	9	.591	2
Los Angeles	12	10	.545	3
Atlanta	12	10	.545	3

Welcome to Sixth Place

Five days after Don Sutton shut out the Reds (with Perranoski's help) at spacious Dodger Stadium, it was a different story when he faced them in their cracker box, Crosley Field, on May 6. The Reds jumped on Sutton for three runs in the first inning, including a two-run homer by Tony Perez. He escaped further damage until the sixth inning, when Art Shamsky hurt him with a three-run homer that barely cleared the 387-foot barrier in center field to make it 6–1, Reds.[66]

Milt Pappas, pitching his first game in Crosley Field, pitched a complete-game eight-hitter to beat the Dodgers, 7–1.[67] The Dodgers' starting rotation of Drysdale-Koufax-Osteen-Sutton came up empty for the fourth straight game, sending them careening into sixth place. Sutton was now 3–3 for the year. Charged with six earned runs in six innings, his ERA ballooned from 1.85 to 2.80.

The Bats Come Alive Behind Drysdale

On Saturday afternoon, May 7, Don Drysdale and Sammy Ellis matched up in the second game of the Cincinnati series. The previous year, the two right-handers totaled 45 wins between them: Drysdale, 23, and Ellis, 22. Today they began the game with identical 1–3 records.

On this day, behind a solid seven innings by Drysdale, the Dodgers pounded the Reds, 14–2, to climb out of sixth place. With the wind blowing out to left field, Drysdale and three other Dodgers hit home runs. Lefebvre hit two, one from each side of the plate.[68] Drysdale and the Dodgers avenged the 18–0 thrashing by the Reds the last time they played in Crosley Field in August 1965.[69]

Osteen and O'Toole—A Pitcher's Duel Decided by the Wind

In contrast to the Saturday blowout, the Sunday finale was a pitchers' duel between left-handers Claude Osteen (4–2) and Jim O'Toole (0–1). A change in the wind at Crosley Field cost the Dodgers the game and the series. Instead of blowing out to left, the wind on May 8 blew toward right field. The Dodgers had O'Toole on the ropes in the first inning, but they couldn't put him away. After walking two batters, he hit Lefebvre with a pitch with two out to load the bases. Ron Fairly hit a drive to center field that, under normal conditions, would have been a grand slam home run. But the cross-wind slowed it down, allowing Tommy Harper to catch the ball at the barrier.[70] O'Toole recovered and blanked the Dodgers over the next five innings. Five of the six innings Osteen pitched were scoreless. But he faltered in the fourth, giving up two runs on three singles. After 14 runs on 16 hits the day before, the Dodgers could produce only one unearned run off O'Toole and went down, 2–1. Osteen lost his third game and the Dodgers—now only one game over .500—fell into a fifth-place tie with Atlanta. They were now five games behind the Giants, who completed a three-game sweep of the Cardinals in St. Louis.

	W	L	Pct.	GB
San Francisco	18	7	.720	—
Pittsburgh	14	8	.636	2½
Houston	15	10	.600	3
Philadelphia	11	9	.550	4½
Los Angeles	13	12	.520	5
Atlanta	13	12	.520	5

The Giants Give Up on Orlando Cepeda

Also on May 8 in St. Louis, the Giants and Cardinals consummated a major trade: 28-year-old Giants slugger Orlando Cepeda for 25-year-old Cardinals left-hander Ray

On May 8, 1966, the Giants traded Orlando Cepeda to the Cardinals for left-hander Ray Sadecki. They would regret their decision.

Sadecki. The Giants were in need of a left-handed starter to complement right-handers Juan Marichal, Gaylord Perry, and Bobby Bolin. But they were really rolling the dice with this deal.

Sadecki had won 20 games for the Cardinals in their pennant year of 1964 but slumped to 6–15 for the seventh-place Cardinals in 1965. He was 2–1 so far for 1966 and had a 67–64 record with a 4.17 ERA since breaking in with St. Louis in 1960.

Cepeda had been one of the National League's premier hitters since his Rookie of the Year season of 1958. In 1961, he led the league with a dazzling 46 home runs and 142 runs batted in, finishing second to Frank Robinson in the MVP voting. For the next three years, he averaged 33 home runs and 103 runs batted in with a .309 batting average. Following the 1964 season, he underwent surgery to remove cartilage in his knee. He could play in only 33 games in 1965, batting .176 with one home run. To this point in the season, he was batting .286 with three home runs and 15 runs batted in. A Giants spokesman told the press, "Orlando is a great hitter, but we have a duplication of ability at first base with Willie McCovey."[71] The knee problem had apparently foreclosed the option of playing Cepeda in the outfield. By the following October, the Giants would regret their decision.

Johnny Podres Is Sold to the Tigers

In the Dodgers' first six years on the West Coast, Johnny Podres was a stalwart of their rotation, averaging 15 wins and 33 starts. But after elbow surgery sidelined him after only two starts in 1964, he came back to win only seven games in a limited role in 1965.[72]

Don Sutton's emergence as the fourth starter at the beginning of 1966 made the 33-year-old Podres expendable. As we have seen, he pitched an inning and two-thirds out of the bullpen on April 19 in Houston. That was his only appearance for the Dodgers in 1966. They put his name on the waiver list, but sadly, no National League team claimed him. That allowed Buzzie Bavasi to offer him to American League teams. The Red Sox wanted him, but Bavasi respected Podres' wishes to play for his old manager, Charlie Dressen, in Detroit. In his rookie year of 1953, Podres had played for Dressen in Brooklyn, his last year as Dodgers manager. On May 9, the Dodgers announced that the Tigers had agreed to pay the $20,000 waiver price for Podres and deliver "a player to be named later."[73] It was a fate all too familiar to Dodgers fans. Three years before, the Dodgers sold their beloved Duke Snider to the Mets for $40,000 cash. Now they sold Johnny Podres, who delivered their first World Championship by shutting out the Yankees in Game 7 of the 1955 World Series, for half that amount.

Koufax Bounces Back in Philadelphia

On May 10 in Philadelphia, Sandy Koufax made his first start after being knocked out in the second inning by the Giants at Candlestick Park. His opponent, Chris Short, was a chronic problem for the Dodgers. He was 15–5 against them since coming into the league in 1960 and had beaten them five of the six times he faced them in 1965. What's more, Short had won four of the six previous meetings with Koufax. But this time, Short lasted only two innings as the Dodgers ran wild in Connie Mack Stadium, stealing six bases. Wills stole three and scored three runs. Even with subpar control (he walked three batters), Koufax pitched a complete-game six-hitter with ten strikeouts for a 6–1 victory to advance his record to 4–1.[74] It would mark the start of a personal eight-game winning streak. But for a run the Phillies scored in the fourth on a double play ground ball hit by catcher Bob Uecker, Koufax would have had a shutout.[75]

The next night, May 11, rookie Don Sutton put on a dazzling show. He shut out the Phillies, 5–0, on six singles with eight strikeouts and one walk. As a batter, he had three hits to raise his average to .455. Sutton gave himself a 1–0 lead in the third inning with an RBI single.[76] His opponent, veteran right-hander Larry Jackson, said in admiration after the game, "The kid pitched a great game; he can get the breaking stuff over."[77] Sutton's first major league shutout improved his record to 4–3.

Don Drysdale and Jim Bunning met in the Thursday night series finale of May 12. The Dodgers were looking for their first series sweep in Philadelphia since July of 1961. It was not to be. Bunning, with relief help from Darold Knowles, beat the Dodgers, 5–1. For good measure, Bunning went 3-for-3 as a batter against Drysdale.[78]

Jim Lefebvre gave Drysdale a 1–0 lead with a home run off the right field foul pole in the second inning. Bunning was on base with two out in the third when the power-challenged Dick Groat hit an 0–2 pitch over the left field fence to put the Phillies ahead, 2–1. It was first home run Groat had hit off Drysdale since they began facing each other in 1956.[79] Alston took Drysdale out of the game after he loaded the bases in the fifth. Consecutive singles by Johnny Callison and Doug Clemens off Perranoski drove in three more runs (charged to Drysdale) to make it 5–1.

Drysdale had now lost ten of his last 11 decisions against the Phillies. His record for the year slipped to 2–4, and his ERA was 4.43. As the Dodgers moved on to Pittsburgh, they were stuck in fourth place, six games out.

Hitting Bottom on Friday the Thirteenth
   in Pittsburgh

The Dodgers met a resurgent Pittsburgh Pirates on May 13—Friday the Thirteenth—at Forbes Field. After spending 20 of the first 23 days of the season in first place, the Pirates were in a rough patch, losing six out of seven—including their last three games at home to the Giants. But this Pittsburgh team was still a legitimate pennant contender, albeit now 5½ games off the pace in third place. Giants castoff Matty Alou was batting .326 on his way to a surprise batting title. Roberto Clemente was batting .312 and driving in, what was for him, an unusually high number of runs. This was a power-laden team. Not only was Willie Stargell blossoming into one of the league's top power hitters, Clemente and first baseman Donn Clendenon would have career years in home runs. To complement their perennial All-Star second baseman, Bill Mazeroski, they had a Gold Glove shortstop in Gene Alley. They had one of the league's premier left-handers in the intimidating, 6'6" flame-thrower, Bob Veale. Thirty-six-year-old Vern "Deacon" Law was still a reliable right-hander who would contribute 12 wins and four shutouts.

Claude Osteen was on the mound for the Dodgers, looking to snap a two-game losing streak. The odds looked good for Osteen. The Pirates went with rookie left-hander Woody Fryman, a tobacco farmer from Ewing, Kentucky, who was making his first major league start.

The Pirates scored two runs off Osteen in the second inning on RBI singles by Mazeroski and Fryman (his first major league hit). Osteen left the game midway through the fifth inning with no chance to win, down 3–0. Fryman, who wasn't even on the Pirates' roster when spring training opened, shut out the Dodgers for the first five innings.[80] Two throwing errors by the Pirates' infield allowed the Dodgers to tie the game, 3–3, in the sixth, but Fryman survived. Phil Regan came in to pitch the seventh inning. Clemente greeted him with a booming triple and scored the deciding run on a sacrifice fly by catcher Jim Pagliaroni.[81] Fryman went all the way to win the game, 4–3. Regan was charged with his only loss of the season.

May 13 would be the low point of the year for the Dodgers. They were now 3–7 on the road trip and once again only one game above .500. That night, the Giants won, 4–3, at Shea Stadium on a home run in the 17th inning by Jim Davenport to extend their winning streak to 13 games. That put the Dodgers seven games off the pace in fourth place. It would be their largest deficit of the year. To make matters worse, Jim Lefebvre—among the league leaders in home runs and runs batted in—sustained a self-inflicted hairline fracture of his big toe when he fouled a Woody Fryman pitch off his left foot.[82] He would be out of action at least for the remainder of the series.

	W	L	Pct.	GB
San Francisco	22	7	.759	—
Houston	17	11	.607	4½
Pittsburgh	15	11	.577	5½
Los Angeles	15	14	.517	7

The next afternoon, May 14, it would be up to Koufax to keep the Dodgers from falling further off the cliff. The Pirates went with 24-year-old right-hander Steve Blass, from Housatonic, Connecticut. After a 5–8 rookie year in 1964, Blass was demoted to Triple-A Columbus, where he won 13 games with four shutouts in 1965.

Despite not having his best stuff, Koufax came through with a gritty performance that day. The Dodgers scratched together a run in the third inning on an RBI groundout by Wills to give Koufax a 1–0 lead. They chased Blass in the sixth, scoring three more runs to go up, 4–0. It was fortunate for Koufax that he did not walk anyone, for the Pirates hit him hard. The pesky leadoff man and future Dodgers pinch-hitter extraordinaire, Manny Mota, belted two doubles. Clendenon added a double, and Mazeroski tagged him for a booming, 455-foot triple.[83] Each time, Koufax bore down and left them stranded. He got to the ninth inning with a 4–0 shutout before the great Clemente put the Pirates on the scoreboard. Koufax threw him an outside fastball that Clemente reached out and drove into the upper deck in right field. Dodgers right fielder Ron Fairly didn't even bother to move. Koufax hung on to complete the game for a 4–1 win. He struck out nine batters and improved his record to 5–1.[84]

Right-handers Don Sutton and Don Cardwell met in the deciding game of the series on Sunday afternoon, May 15. After a turbulent night in which he had nightmares of choking in this key assignment, the 21-year-old Sutton rose to the occasion. He turned in a solid seven innings, allowing only one run, on five singles, with no walks.[85] The sultry Pittsburgh weather sapped his strength, and Phil Regan came in to pitch the last two innings. The Dodgers scored single runs off Cardwell in the fourth and fifth innings. Behind 2–1, the Pirates were forced to remove him for a pinch-hitter in the person of the great Jerry Lynch in the bottom of the seventh, with two out and the tying run on base. Lynch, who held the major league record with 17 pinch-hit home runs, lined out to Ron Fairly. The Dodgers added an insurance run in the ninth against Pirates reliever Bob Purkey. Lou Johnson led off with a bunt single and Wills drove him in with a two-out triple over the drawn-in Clemente's head in right field.[86] Gene Alley hit a triple off Regan in the bottom of the ninth, but he was left on third as Regan hung on to save a 3–1 win for Sutton. Sutton was now 5–3 with a 2.21 REA.

It was a disastrous road trip for the Dodgers. They began in second place, a half-game behind the Giants, and returned in third place, five games back. But it could have been worse. Only the clutch performances by Koufax and Sutton at the end of the trip prevented a further slide toward a double-digit deficit that could have proved fatal to the Dodgers' chances going into a rematch with the league-leading Giants. Fortunately for the Dodgers, the Giants lost their last two games that weekend to the Mets at Shea Stadium.

	W	L	Pct.	GB
San Francisco	22	9	.710	—
Houston	18	12	.600	3½
Los Angeles	17	14	.548	5
Pittsburgh	15	13	.536	5½

The next day, May 16, a travel day for the Dodgers, Bob Dylan released a strange new album titled *Blonde on Blonde* that he recorded in Nashville. On the cover was a blurry photograph of Dylan in a suede coat and checkered scarf standing outside on a cold winter day in New York City. In a burst of creativity, he had composed and recorded so much material that Columbia Records had to present it on two discs—the first great double album.

Climbing to First on the Back of #32

No club can stop the Dodgers in 1966 because of the closeness of the Dodger players.[1]—Maury Wills June 12, 1966

Coming off their disappointing 5–7 road trip of May 3–15, the Dodgers would begin a home stand with a three-game series with the Giants, to be followed—without a break—by four games with the Pirates.

Marichal's Return to L.A.

On May 17, a huge crowd of 53,561 turned out on a Tuesday night at Dodger Stadium to see the opening game of the second series of the year between the Dodgers and the Giants. It was Don Drysdale's turn to take on a red-hot Juan Marichal. Marichal was making his first start in Los Angeles since NL President Warren Giles barred him from pitching there the previous September for attacking John Roseboro with a bat. At this point in the season, Marichal was a perfect 7–0 with a 0.76 ERA. Drysdale was still struggling with inconsistency at 2–4 with a 4.43 ERA. Despite the apparent statistical mismatch, this one was a classic one-on-one pitchers' duel. Only a seventh-inning error by Lefebvre prevented Drysdale from throwing a shutout. Instead, it was Marichal who took a 1–0 shutout to the bottom of the ninth. Maury Wills, a perpetual irritant to Marichal, beat out a bunt with one out. After the Devil-Coach, Jim Gilliam, now back in the lineup at third base, singled Wills to third, Willie Davis scored Wills on a sacrifice fly to tie the game, 1–1, and send it into extra innings.

Marichal, who heard thunderous boos whenever he warmed up on the mound or walked to the batter's box, continued on through the tenth inning. He left the game with no visible sign of animosity between him and John Roseboro.[2] Perranoski took over for Drysdale in the tenth. The Giants had him on the ropes with two out and the bases loaded in the 11th, but he struck out Willie McCovey to preserve the tie. Phil Regan blanked the Giants in the 12th and 13th innings. Wes Parker led off the bottom of the 13th with a single against Giants reliever Frank Linzy. The great Willie Mays had already thrown out three Dodgers base runners in the game. When Wills singled to right field, Parker decided to challenge rookie Ollie Brown's arm by making a dash for third. Brown cut loose with a tremendous throw, but it skipped past third baseman Jim Ray Hart and into the Dodgers dugout, allowing Parker to waltz home with the winning run.[3]

The Dodgers dodged a bullet as Marichal pitched another gem: ten innings of seven-hit ball with no walks. Drysdale went nine innings, walking none and scattering 11 singles. Both pitchers had no-decisions to show for their efforts. It was Phil Regan who got credit for his second win.

A Comedy of Dodgers Errors

Claude Osteen and Ray Sadecki pitched game two of the series in front of a Dodger Stadium crowd of 41,726 on Wednesday night, May 18. Sadecki was making his second start as a Giant after throwing five scoreless innings against the Mets the weekend before at Shea Stadium. In contrast to the tight pitchers' duel of the night before, this one was a sloppy, error-laced affair.

Errors by Gilliam and Osteen gifted the Giants two unearned runs in the first inning. The Dodgers came back with three runs in the fourth on a two-run homer by Fairly and a run-scoring double by Osteen to knock Sadecki out of the game. Once past the first inning, Osteen settled into a rhythm as he took a 3–2 lead to the eighth inning. After he induced Giants catcher Bob Barton to ground back to the box for the first out, he had retired 20 of the last 22 batters he faced.[4] He then walked pinch-hitter Don Landrum. Three hits, two more errors, and an intentional walk later, Osteen was out of the game as the Giants scored four runs to surge ahead, 6–3. In the bottom of the inning, the Dodgers scored a run off San Francisco reliever Bill Henry before Frank Linzy came in from the bullpen to retire Roseboro with two out and the bases loaded.

The Dodgers went down, 6–4, and the series was tied at one game apiece. Osteen lost his third straight game. With 30 errors in their first 33 games, the Dodgers' defense was now a glaring problem.[5] Once again five games behind the Giants, it would again be up to Sandy Koufax to prevent the Dodgers from falling further behind in the race.

Saved by Koufax and His Rediscovered Curve

On Thursday night, May 19, Koufax was matched against Giants left-hander Joe Gibbon in the deciding game of the series before 49,409 at Dodger Stadium. The 6'4" Gibbon, who came over from Pittsburgh in the off-season trade for Matty Alou, was a perfect 2–0 with a 1.27 ERA. This was arguably the most important game of the season to this point. If the Dodgers lost, they would drop back into fourth place, six games behind.

It sometimes took a few batters for Koufax to loosen up fully on cool night games at Dodger Stadium early in the season. This night was no exception. Koufax struggled in the top of the first. After he got the Giants' leadoff man, Tito Fuentes, to fly out, he gave up a single to Jesus Alou and walked Willie Mays. With runners on first and second, cleanup batter Jim Ray Hart hit a smash heading for left field. But Wills made a great play on the ball and turned it into an inning-ending double play. The Giants had missed their best scoring chance of the night.

Wills led off the bottom of the first with an infield single, stole second, and scored on a single by Willie Davis to stake Koufax to a 1–0 lead. The third inning was a near replay of the first. Wills led off with another infield single, stole second, and scored the Dodgers' second run on a single by Gilliam.

In the fourth inning, two Giants errors followed by a run-scoring single by Jeff Torborg, and Gibbon was gone before he could finish the inning. Wes Parker added a fourth run leading off the eighth with a home run off Giants reliever Bob Shaw. In three weeks, Shaw would be sold to the Mets.

Once past the first inning, Koufax put on a show. He shut out the Giants, 4–0, on three singles with ten strikeouts and two walks—both to Mays.[6] He finally found his curveball, the pitch he had been struggling with for seven weeks. On this night, it was so devastating that five batters swung at pitches that broke into the dirt in front of the plate.[7] In the post-game locker room, he told reporters, "My curve ball was the best it has been all year, and my fast ball was 'OK' too. It was the first time this season that I had two consistently good pitches working for me."[8] Bad news for the league, indeed. Koufax was now 6–1 with a 1.82 earned run average. His clutch performance won the series, two games to one, and moved the Dodgers to within four games of the Giants. San Francisco had now lost four of its last five.

	W	L	Pct.	GB
San Francisco	23	11	.676	—
Houston	20	13	.606	2½
Los Angeles	19	15	.559	4
Pittsburgh	16	14	.533	5

On Friday night, May 20, the Dodgers began a four-game series with the Pittsburgh Pirates at Dodger Stadium. Don Sutton could retire only one batter in the first inning, as the Pirates jumped on him for five runs.[9] Even though Jeff Torborg knocked Woody Fryman out of the game with a two-run homer in the fifth, the first inning proved to be fatal. The Dodgers went down to a 7–3 defeat,[10] and Sutton sustained his fourth loss. For the first time, he failed to complete the first inning.[11] Charged with five earned runs in only one-third of an inning, Sutton's ERA jumped 72 points to 2.93.

Six foot six inch fireballing left-hander Bob Veale was the ace of the 1966 Pittsburgh Pirates' pitching staff.

The second game of the series pitted Don Drysdale against Steve Blass on Saturday night, May 21. Hard-luck Drysdale struck out 13 Pirates—including the great Roberto Clemente four straight times—and still couldn't win. He took a 4–2 lead into the ninth inning. But after he gave up singles to the first three batters, Walter Alston came out to get him with the lead cut to 4–3. Ron Perranoski allowed the tying run to score (charged to Drysdale) on a sacrifice fly by Manny Mota, sending the game into extra innings.

Perranoski settled in to hold the Pirates scoreless over the next three innings. The Dodgers pulled it out, 5–4, in the bottom of the 12th on a clutch RBI single by Maury Wills. Perranoski picked up his first victory of the year.[12] It was another disappointing no-decision for Drysdale, whose record remained frozen at 2–4 for the second straight game.

Claude Osteen, who had not won in his last four starts, tried to get back on track in the Sunday afternoon game of May 22. Unfortunately for Osteen, he had to go up against Bob Veale who was overpowering that day, pitching a five-hit, 4–0 shutout with 11 strikeouts. The only Dodger who wasn't overwhelmed was old pro Jim Gilliam, who somehow solved Veale for two singles and a double. Though Osteen gave up only one earned run, his record fell to 4–5 as he sustained his fourth straight defeat in May.[13]

The loss sent the Dodgers into a virtual tie for third place with the Pirates. It would now be up to Sandy Koufax to prevent the Pirates from taking the series three games to one, thereby allowing Pittsburgh to take over sole possession of third place. The Dodgers would drop into fourth.

The Dodgers Salvage a Split Thanks to Koufax— and the Fates

The fourth and concluding game of the series was played on Monday night, May 23. Koufax went up against Pittsburgh right-hander Don Cardwell. The last confrontation between Koufax and Cardwell, on August 14, 1965, was a classic pitchers' duel. On that day at Dodger Stadium, Koufax came out on top, 1–0, in ten innings.

On this Monday night, Ron Fairly's home run off Cardwell in the sixth inning gave the Dodgers a 2–0 lead. Koufax shut out the Pirates on three scattered singles through the first seven innings. He saw his lead wiped out by Gene Alley's two-out, two-run double in the eighth. The game went to the ninth tied, 2–2.

In the bottom of the ninth, Pirates reliever Pete Mikkelsen retired the first two batters before John Roseboro doubled off the right-field fence. Then fate intervened. While Derrell Griffith was pinch-hitting for John Kennedy, Pirates catcher Jim Pagliaroni was ejected for arguing a ball-two call. After "Pag" was replaced mid-batter by backup catcher Jerry May, things got bizarre. With the count at 2–2, Griffith topped a slow roller down the first base line. The ball was a good three feet foul when it reached the halfway point between home plate and first base. It suddenly took a crazy hop and rolled back across the foul line into fair territory with Mikkelsen, May, and first baseman Donn Clendenon in hot pursuit. By the time Mikkelsen retrieved the ball, he had no alternative but to toss it to second baseman Bill Mazeroski, who was standing several feet behind first base with no chance to get Griffith.[14] When Roseboro rounded third, he saw that no one was covering home plate and made a dash for home. All Mazeroski could do was hold the ball and watch Roseboro cross the plate with the winning run. After the game, Walter Alston told reporters, "I've been in baseball over thirty years, but I never saw anything like that."[15]

Thanks to another clutch performance by Koufax—and one fateful bounce—the Dodgers held on to preserve a split in the series and moved back into sole possession of third place. With his fourth straight win, Koufax improved his record to 7–1.

	W	L	Pct.	GB
San Francisco	25	13	.658	—
Houston	21	16	.568	3½
Los Angeles	21	17	.553	4
Pittsburgh	18	15	.545	4½

That day, the Dodgers announced that plans were completed for their second postseason tour of Japan. The team had been designated by Commissioner William Eckert to make the trip. They toured Japan for the first time in 1956 as the Brooklyn Dodgers.[16]

From Washington, D.C., Vice President Hubert Humphrey dashed off a letter to Walter O'Malley, telling the Dodgers' owner how pleased he was that the team would be making the trip. Oddly, it included an admonishment: "I know you realize, Walter, that it is especially important that all the Dodger players make this trip. As you know, these visits to Japan are an important part of our American foreign relations. I would hope that the Japanese fans could avoid the disappointment of missing any of the Dodger players."[17]

The Dodgers opened a two-game series with the Phillies on Tuesday night, May 24, at Dodger Stadium, with 21-year-old rookie Don Sutton (5–4) taking on 37-year-old veteran Bob Buhl (0–1).

The Phillies nicked Sutton for a run in the second inning. He gave up singles to Doug Clemens and Clay Dalrymple and struck out Tony Gonzalez and Cookie Rojas. Sutton labored to a full count on Buhl, a lifetime .089 hitter, before allowing him to serve a run-scoring single into left field. On the mound, Buhl had given up only three singles when he took the 1–0 lead into the bottom of the seventh. After Alston removed Sutton for a pinch-hitter, the Dodgers knocked Buhl out of the game with a two-out, two-run rally to take a 2–1 lead. A red-hot Ron Fairly hit a solo home run in the eighth inning to make it 3–1. It was Fairly's fourth home run in his last five games.[18]

Perranoski pitched the last two innings. He gave up a run in the ninth but hung on to save a 3–2 victory for Sutton. In seven innings of work, Sutton gave up one earned run with nine strikeouts and no walks to improve his record to 6–4.[19]

Don Drysdale (2–4) took on the Phillies' ace left-hander, Chris Short (4–3), on May 25 to conclude the series. Drysdale fell behind, 1–0, in the second inning on an RBI single by Short, who still clung to the 1–0 lead as he entered the bottom of the ninth inning. After Gilliam lined out to center field, the door was opened when Phillies first baseman Bill White booted Willie Davis's ground ball to put the tying run aboard. Lou Johnson followed with a single to left. Fairly got behind 0–2 before turning it into a base on balls. Short, who appeared to be throwing harder than any time in the game, blew Lefebvre away on strikes for the second out. Wes Parker was 0-for-3 when he stepped in to face Short for the fourth time as a right-handed batter. With the count 0–1, Parker went with a low and outside fastball, lining it into right field to score both Davis and Johnson for a walk-off 2–1 win.

Saved by Parker's ninth-inning heroics, Drysdale got his first victory in four starts. It went into the record book as a complete-game eight-hitter with six strikeouts and one walk. The third-place Dodgers moved to within three games of the Giants.

Before the game, the Dodgers announced the addition of the 34-year-old veteran outfielder Wes Covington. The left-handed power hitter had been given his release by the Chicago Cubs two weeks before after producing one single in 11 at-bats. Covington was hailed as "the left-handed Hank Aaron" on the Milwaukee Braves' pennant winning teams of 1957–1958. In 1958, he hit .330 with 24 home runs in only 90 games. On August 20, 1959, the Braves' chances for a third straight pennant were greatly diminished when Covington tore a ligament in his ankle. Covington was done for the season, and the Braves went on to lose a pennant playoff series to the Dodgers. Covington was never the same. For the next five years, he bounced between four different teams before landing with Leo Durocher's Cubs in January.

Thursday, May 26, was an off-day for the Dodgers. Up north at Candlestick Park, Juan Marichal pitched a magnificent, 14-inning, 1–0 shutout against these same Phillies.

Marichal was now 9–0 with an incredible 0.59 ERA. The idle Dodgers dropped another half-game to 3½ behind the Giants.

The New York Mets came into Los Angeles for a weekend series beginning Friday night, May 27. Wes Westrum, a former catcher on Leo Durocher's New York Giants championship teams, was in his first full season as Mets manager (Westrum had replaced Casey Stengel back on July 25, 1965, after Stengel broke his hip). For the first time in their five-year existence, the Amazin's were not in last place at this point in the season. That distinction now belonged to Durocher's Cubs. Still, they were only marginally less inept. Claude Osteen, who had not won in his first five starts in May, seized the opportunity to get back on track with a trouble-free, three-hit shutout. As 76-year-old Stengel—a resident of nearby Glendale—watched from the stands, the Dodgers capitalized on three Mets errors in the sixth inning to cobble together four runs for Osteen.[20]

This easy 4–0 win came at a cost. Dodgers right fielder Ron Fairly came into the game as the team's leading hitter with a .291 batting average. In the fourth inning, he went hard into second base in an unsuccessful attempt to break up a double play. In the process, he took a knee to the ribs from Mets second baseman Ron Hunt. Two innings later, Fairly had to come out of the game. The bruising to his ribs was so severe that he would be unable to play—even in a pinch-hitting role—for the next 28 games.

Koufax Toys with the Mets

Sandy Koufax pitched the second game of the series before a large Ladies Night crowd on May 28. Dennis Ribant, a little right-hander with a 3–8 career record, drew the unenviable assignment of opposing him. Poor Ribant didn't fool anyone. After he walked the first three batters, Tommy Davis hit a sharp ground ball headed for left field that third baseman Ken Boyer stopped and threw to home plate to start a double play. That was the only batter Ribant could retire. Lefebvre followed with a two-run single, Lou Johnson singled him to third, and Ribant was gone. Things only got worse for the Mets. They used five more pitchers that the Dodgers pounded for five more runs.

Koufax appeared to be toying with the hapless Mets as he pitched a dazzling three-hitter for his fifth straight win. Only an unearned run the Mets were lucky to score in the sixth inning—on a double play ground ball—prevented a shutout.[21] Koufax struck out ten batters and lowered his ERA to 1.64. It was also the fifth straight win for the second-place Dodgers, who moved to within a game and a half of the Giants.[22]

The rookie, Don Sutton, got the call to close out the series with the Mets and the homestand on Sunday, May 29. The Mets sent out their 21-year-old sophomore left-hander, Rob Gardner. Two weeks before, Gardner (2–2) had pitched an impressive, complete-game four-hitter against the Giants at Shea Stadium. From the start, it was evident that Sutton did not have it. He turned in a ragged seven innings in which he twice lost the lead.

In a seesaw game, the Dodgers went ahead 6–4 in the bottom of eighth inning on a two-run, inside-the-park home run by Jim Lefebvre. It was Lefebvre's second home run of the day off Gardner. Dodgers bullpen aces Phil Regan and Ron Perranoski collapsed in the ninth.[23] Regan, who had pitched the seventh and eighth innings, gave up a leadoff single to Cleon Jones and was promptly removed. Alston brought in Perranoski, who walked Dick Stuart on four pitches. After Perranoski struck out Ken Boyer, Hawk Taylor tied the game with a two-run double down the left field line.[24] Perranoski walked Ed Krane-pool intentionally and stuck out Jerry Grote. Now all he had do to preserve the tie was to put away the Mets' 36-year-old, .144-hitting shortstop, Roy McMillan. But McMillan threaded a grounder through the hole between shortstop and third base to score Taylor with the go-ahead run. The Dodgers had lost the lead for the third time and went on to lose the game, 7–6. Perranoski was charged with his second loss. Worse, the Dodgers fell back to two and a half games behind the Giants as they prepared to go back out on the road.

On the Road to First

The Dodgers opened their third road trip of the season in Atlanta with a night game on Memorial Day, May 30, before a holiday crowd of 40,702. Don Drysdale and Tony Cloninger opened the two-game series. Both teams' premier right-handers were still struggling. Cloninger believed that he was never the same after pitching a Herculean 13 innings in a tough 1–0 loss to the Pirates on Opening Day.[25] On this night in Atlanta, Drysdale was cuffed around for six earned runs on nine hits—including three home runs—and still came out with a win. That's because the Dodgers pounded five Braves pitchers for ten runs on 16 hits. The tone was set when Maury Wills hit Cloninger's second pitch of the game over the right field fence for a home run. The Braves' beleaguered manager, Bobby Bragan, removed Cloninger in the middle of the third inning after he gave up four more runs on three doubles, a single, and a wild pitch. Drysdale contributed a double and a single to the Dodgers' attack[26] and evened his record at 4–4.

Claude Osteen (5–5) and Wade Blasingame (3–3) pitched the second game the following night. Blasingame didn't make it out of the first inning. He gave up three runs on a double, triple, two walks, and a wild pitch before Bragan walked out to the mound amidst a chorus of boos to replace him with Billy O'Dell. Osteen pitched a solid six innings and took a 5–2 lead into the seventh. After he walked the leadoff batter, Mack Jones, a finger blister on his pitching hand forced him to come out of the game. Phil Regan took over and shut out the Braves over the last three innings. Osteen, who hit the third home run of his career over the center field fence in the fourth inning, got credit for his sixth win.[27]

The Dodgers closed out the month of May in second place, two and a half games behind the Giants. Bobby Bragan's days were numbered as the Braves sank into an eighth-place tie with the Mets. In August, he would be replaced by Billy Hitchcock and never given another chance to manage at the major league level.

	W	L	Pct.	GB
San Francisco	30	16	.652	—
Los Angeles	27	18	.600	2½
Pittsburgh	24	20	.545	5
Houston	25	21	.543	5

In St. Louis on June 1, Sandy Koufax shut out the Cardinals, 1–0, in the Dodgers' first game in the new Busch Memorial Stadium in St. Louis. Though it was another dominating performance by Koufax, the game could have gone either way. For the first six innings, he was locked in a scoreless pitchers' duel with the Cardinals' little left-hander, Al Jackson. In the seventh, Willie Davis became the first Dodger to get past first base when he lined a ball into the right field corner that caromed off the wall past rookie Bobby Tolan, who slipped while trying to field it. Davis, the fastest man in the league, had an easy stand-up triple. When Tolan's errant relay throw evaded second baseman Julian Javier, Davis kept on going to score the only run of the game.[28] Koufax relied on his fastball to mow down the Cardinals over the final two innings.[29] His walk of pitcher Jackson in the fifth inning was his only walk of the game. Koufax scattered seven singles and struck out nine for his sixth straight complete-game victory. He was now 9–1 with a 1.48 ERA. Orlando Cepeda's harmless first-inning single off Koufax was his first hit against the Dodgers in a Cardinals uniform.

The next night, Don Sutton and Ron Perranoski combined for another shutout of the Cardinals. Sutton was working on a six-hitter when he ran out of steam in the seventh inning. With two out, he walked Tito Francona to put runners on first and second. It was only his 12th walk in 12 starts, but it brought Alston out of the dugout with the hook. Perranoski came in to get Phil Gagliano on a groundout to Wills to end the inning. Perranoski retired six of the last seven batters to save the 2–0 win for Sutton, his seventh of the year.[30]

Wes Covington made his Dodgers debut in left field, wearing Frank Howard's old number 25. Acquired to add some "pop" to the lineup, Covington was a quiet 0-for-3.

When the Dodgers left St. Louis, they had won nine of their last ten games.[31] They remained two and a half games behind the Giants, who won their fifth game in a row that night in Atlanta.

A Missed Opportunity in New York

On June 3, the Dodgers arrived in New York for a four-game series with the ninth-place Mets, having won nine of their last ten games. Alston expected Drysdale to continue the momentum. After all, Drysdale was 18–2 in his career against the Mets, and his opponent, Jack Fisher, was 0–7 against the Dodgers. But this Friday night at Shea Stadium, 49,414 would see a different Jack Fisher.

A disputed double unsettled Drysdale in the first inning. With one out, Ron Hunt went with an outside pitch and hit a ball down the right field line that appeared to land several inches foul. First base umpire Frank Secory started to call it foul and then changed his signal. All hell broke loose as Dodgers Wes Parker, Lou Johnson, Walt Alston, and Drysdale converged on Secory to engage in a heated protest—to no avail. Before the inning was over, the Mets had gotten to Drysdale for three more hits and two runs.[32] Drysdale never recovered. They pounded him for three more runs in the fifth inning. A two-out, two-run homer by the Mets' 35-year-old third baseman, Ken Boyer, brought Alston out of the dugout with the hook. It was the first time since August of 1962 that the Mets had driven Drysdale from a game.

Fisher completely outpitched Drysdale. After giving up an unearned run in the second inning, he retired 20 Dodgers in a row until John Kennedy singled with two out in the eighth inning. The Dodgers' third and final hit off Fisher was Wes Parker's meaningless solo home run in the ninth that made the final score 6–2. The combination of Drysdale's continued failure to deliver and Jack Fisher's surprise performance was a double jolt to the Dodgers. Fisher beat them for the first time ever on a complete-game three-hitter. Drysdale now had a losing record: four wins and five losses.

On Saturday afternoon, June 4, Claude Osteen—with help from Phil Regan—beat the Mets, 6–3, to even the series. It was another costly win, as the Dodgers lost two more outfielders to injury. In the first inning, Lou Johnson was struck on the left hand for the second time that season by Mets starter Jack Hamilton. Johnson had to be taken to Roosevelt Hospital for X-rays. While the results showed no broken bones, his playing status was uncertain.

In the fifth inning, Willie Davis's RBI single gave Osteen a 2–0 lead. While Davis was diving back into first base, the Mets' 6'4", 220-pound first baseman, Dick Stuart, landed on his left arm after leaping to catch Hamilton's pickoff throw. Already with a bruised arm, Davis then pulled a hamstring muscle while stealing second. He limped off the field at the conclusion of the inning and was replaced by Tommy Davis, who put the game out of reach with a three-run homer in the sixth inning—his first home run since September 25, 1964.[33]

Osteen struggled to make it through the first six innings, allowing nine hits and walking two batters. After Osteen gave up a leadoff single to Cleon Jones in the seventh, Alston brought in Phil Regan. Regan survived the inning despite walking a batter and giving up two RBI singles that cut the Dodgers' lead to 6–3. Supported by an injury-depleted makeshift defense, Regan shut down the Mets over the last two innings to save Osteen's seventh victory. The game was a testament to the ingenuity of Walter Alston and to the team's versatility. Three players played left field (Lou Johnson, Derrell Griffith, and Tommy Davis); three players played center field (Willie Davis, Griffith, and Wes Parker). And in a bizarre twist, with Parker needed in center field in the ninth inning, Jim Gilliam had to play first base for the first time in his 14-year career.[34]

The next day at 7:00 a.m., Mets fans were already in line to snap up 10,000 unreserved seats for that day's Sunday doubleheader, with Sandy Koufax announced to pitch the first game. The crowd would eventually reach a standing room 57,332, only 843 short of the Shea Stadium record.[35] Koufax, who had eked out a 1–0 win in his last start in St. Louis, was given a laugher. The Dodgers disposed of Mets starter Gerry Arrigo in the sixth inning on their way to a season-high 16 runs on 19 hits, with four home runs. Wes Parker hit two—one from each side of the plate. Tommy Davis was a perfect 5-for-5 with a triple and four singles to raise his batting average to .328. Koufax cruised into the seventh inning with an 11–0 lead. An error by Wills cost him two unearned runs and a shutout. With two out in the eighth, Ron Hunt lined a ball into center field that took a kangaroo bounce over Wes Parker's head and rolled to the flagpole 410 feet from home plate. By the time Parker could retrieve it, Hunt had a freak inside-the-park home run for New York's third and final run. The Dodgers won it, 16–3. Koufax won his seventh straight complete game, a five-hitter with nine strikeouts. He improved his season record to 10–1, even with Juan Marichal.[36]

Alston had to go with Joe Moeller in the second game of the doubleheader against Mets right-hander Dennis Ribant. Moeller, who was making his first start of the year, shut out the Mets for the first four innings. The Mets tied the game in bottom of the fifth on RBI singles by Roy McMillan and Ribant. The game was still tied, 2–2, as it moved to the bottom of the ninth with the usually reliable Perranoski on the mound. But Perranoski, who took over in the eighth, could not close the deal. With the bases loaded and two out, Wes Westrum brought in his old New York Giants teammate, Ed Bressoud, to pinch-hit. With the count 1–1, Perranoski bounced a curveball in front of the plate that evaded John Roseboro and went to the backstop. Ken Boyer scored the winning run on the wild pitch.

New York in June was a missed opportunity for the Dodgers. They could only manage a series split with a ninth-place team. The 3–2 loss in the second game of a doubleheader—in which they scored 18 runs—caused them to slip a half-game, to two games behind the Giants, who dropped three out of four to the Phillies in Philadelphia that weekend.

Drysdale Can't Come Through in Chicago

On June 6, the Dodgers flew to Chicago for a three-game series with Leo Durocher's tenth-place Cubs. Don Sutton and Bob Hendley started in the opener the next afternoon. The travel day caused Sutton to skip his regularly scheduled day in the rotation. In his previous 12 starts, he had averaged one walk per game. On this day at Wrigley Field, he walked four, which he attributed to the extra day off: "Being a control pitcher, I don't like to skip a day."[37]

It was a rough afternoon for both starters. Ferguson Jenkins relieved Hendley before he could finish the finish the fifth inning, down 5–2. Sutton gave up six earned runs on seven hits, including a triple and two home runs in 5⅓ innings. The second home run—a two-run shot by Adolpho Phillips in the sixth inning—put the Cubs in front, 6–5, and knocked him out of the game.

The game went to the tenth inning tied, 6–6, with workhorse Jenkins still on the mound for the Cubs. Jim Lefebvre hit his first pitch into the right field bleachers to break the tie. On Jenkins' second pitch, Al Ferrara lifted an innocent pop fly into shallow center field. Cubs center fielder Byron Browne misjudged the ball, starting back before reversing course and sprinting in toward the infield, where he collided with shortstop Don Kessinger behind second base. As Browne and Kessinger lay unconscious on the grass, Ferrara circled the bases for an inside-the-park homerun to make the final score 8–6.[38] Phil Regan, who pitched the last 4⅔ innings, picked up his third win.

Don Drysdale took on Dick Ellsworth the next day, June 8, at Wrigley Field with a chance to move the Dodgers into a first-place tie with the Giants. But he again failed to deliver. In the fourth inning, he hit two batters, gave up two singles, an RBI double to Ron Santo, and a grand slam home run to rookie catcher Randy Hundley.[39] He was already in a 5–0 hole after four innings. Alston stayed with Drysdale until Ellsworth (batting .107) finished him off with a two-run single in the eighth that put the Cubs up, 8–1. Ellsworth, who had won only one game in 11 previous starts, pitched a complete-game eight-hitter.[40] Lou Johnson returned to the lineup after missing two games due to a bruised hand after Jack Hamilton drilled him with fastball in New York. Johnson prevented an Ellsworth shutout with an RBI single in the fifth. The June 9 series finale with the Cubs was rained out.

That night in Houston, the Giants beat the Astros, 3–1, on a two-run double by Jim Davenport in the 11th inning. It put the Giants one game ahead of the Dodgers as the two teams prepared to meet the next night in San Francisco.

Koufax Lifts the Dodgers to the Top at Candlestick

The Dodgers' second trip to San Francisco began on Friday night, June 10, with Sandy Koufax (10–1) making his 14th start of the season. Herman Franks chose spot starter Joe Gibbon (2–2) to go up against Koufax.

The game was a hitless, scoreless tie after four innings. Lou Johnson led off the fifth with the first Dodgers hit, a single to left field. Lefebvre bunted him to second. An angry crowd of 40,048, recalling last year's notorious bat episode, showered John Roseboro with boos as he walked to home plate.[41] Roseboro answered by sending a 1–2 pitch from Gibbon over the center field fence to put the Dodgers ahead, 2–0.

The Dodgers broke the game open in the sixth inning. Wills ignited things with a leadoff infield single. Gibbon was chased before he could get anyone out. By the time the inning was over, four more Dodgers runs had scored on an error, three hits, and two walks—one with the bases loaded. John Kennedy delivered the key blow, a two-out, two-run double off Giants reliever Bob Priddy to make it 6–0.

It looked like Koufax was breezing as he went to the bottom of the ninth with a two-hit, 6–0 shutout. But after he blew away the leadoff batter, Tito Fuentes, on strikes, he walked Jim Davenport and gave up a single to Willie Mays to put runners on first and third. Cleanup batter Jim Ray Hart ruined the shutout by scoring Davenport with a single to left. That was it for the Giants, as Koufax got Cap Peterson to ground into a game-ending double play.

The Giants, who had been in first place for 35 straight days, now trailed the Dodgers by .004 percentage points. Koufax's four-hit, 6–1 win was his eighth straight complete-game victory. He struck out 11 batters and walked two. He now led the majors with a record of 11–1 and an ERA of 1.40.[42]

Claude Osteen (7–5) pitched the second game of the series on Saturday afternoon, June 11. He hadn't pitched in a week, having missed his last turn due to the rainout in Chicago. He gave up a solo home run to Jim Ray Hart in the second inning and a run-scoring single to Tito Fuentes in the third. For the first six innings, Giants starter Bobby Bolin (4–4) shut out the Dodgers on five hits.

In the top of the seventh, Bolin walked leadoff batter Roseboro and then struck out Covington. Gilliam followed with a single, sending Roseboro to third. Herman Franks brought in 38-year-old left-hander Bill Henry to pitch to Maury Wills. Batting right-handed, Wills hit a 410-foot double over the head of the drawn-in Willie Mays to score both runs and tie the game, 2–2.[43]

The score was still 2–2 going to the top of the ninth inning. Gilliam drew a lead-off walk against Giants reliever Frank Linzy. Wills bunted Gilliam to second. With two out, Willie Davis singled home Gilliam to break the tie. An infield single by Tommy Davis put runners on first and third. Lou Johnson executed a perfect squeeze bunt down the third base line to score Willie Davis with an insurance run. In the bottom of the ninth, Phil Regan walked the first batter, Don Landrum, bringing Alston out to the mound. Alston brought in left-hander Jim Brewer to pitch to Willie McCovey, representing the tying run.[44] McCovey hit a towering fly ball into a swirling wind in center field that Willie Davis dropped for an error. The tying runs were on with none out. Ollie Brown and Bob Barton hit fly balls to center that Davis was able to stay with for outs. Brewer, who was making only his third appearance of the year, struck out pinch-hitter Ozzie Virgil to end it.

The Dodgers, who just a month before were seven games out in fourth place, were in first by a game over a San Francisco team that had now lost six of their last seven games. Completing the sweep on Sunday, they could pull ahead of the Giants by two games. There were only two problems: first, they would have to beat Juan Marichal, who was a perfect 11–0 against them at Candlestick Park; second, the struggling Don Drysdale would have to come through.

The Sunday afternoon finale on June 12 was played in front 42,402 people, the largest crowd to date at Candlestick. The Dodgers' best chance to beat Marichal came in the second inning. After he struck out the leadoff batter, Tommy Davis, Marichal hit Lou Johnson with a pitch. Lefebvre followed with a single to center, sending Johnson to third. Roseboro struck out, but Parker walked to load the bases. Marichal escaped by getting Drysdale to ground into a force play to end the inning without giving up a run.

Giants catcher Tom Haller broke the scoreless tie with a solo home run off Drysdale in the fifth inning. In the sixth, Drysdale gave up singles to the first two batters, Tito Fuentes and Len Gabrielson. Alston allowed Drysdale to pitch to Willie Mays, whom he induced to pop out to first baseman Parker. Alston brought in left-hander Nick Willhite to pitch to Willie McCovey. Willhite's first pitch to McCovey skipped past Roseboro to the backstop. Instead of covering home, Willhite stood frozen on the mound as Fuentes scored from third on the wild pitch to put Marichal and the Giants up, 2–0.[45]

Marichal gave up a solo home run to Lefebvre in the seventh inning that cut the Giants' lead to 2–1. Perranoski, the Dodgers' fourth pitcher, came in to pitch the bottom of the eighth. With one out and Fuentes on first, he got pinch-hitter Cap Peterson to hit a harmless nubber down the third base line. Perranoski fielded the ball and threw it beyond Parker's reach and down into the right field corner. The speedy Fuentes came all the way around from first to score the game's deciding run on a three-base error.

Marichal went to the ninth with a 3–1 lead. Tommy Davis led off with a sharp ground ball between shortstop and third, headed for left field. But Giants shortstop Hal Lanier threw out the gimpy Davis from deep in the hole. It was the key play of the game as Lou Johnson followed with what would have been a game-tying home run. Instead, Marichal struck out the last two batters, Lefebvre and Roseboro, to put the Dodgers away.

Marichal's 11th win of the season tied him with Koufax for best in the majors. Drysdale's third straight loss made his record 4–7. Drysdale's problematic start was starting to raise eyebrows, since he was 11–3 at this point in the 1965 season. At the end of play on June 12, the Dodgers and Giants were again locked in a virtual tie for first, separated by just .004 percentage points.

	W	L	Pct.	GB
Los Angeles	34	22	.607	—
San Francisco	35	23	.603	—
Pittsburgh	32	23	.582	1½

The next day, the U.S. Supreme Court issued its landmark *Miranda vs. Arizona* decision extending the Fifth Amendment's right against self-incrimination to criminal suspects in "custodial interrogation."[46] From now on, before suspects in police custody could be questioned, they had to be read their Miranda rights: they must be informed that they have the right to remain silent, that anything they say may be used against them, that they have the right to have a lawyer present, and the right to have a lawyer appointed to defend them if they cannot afford one.[47]

14

Staggering into the Break

Last year the elbow didn't bother me when I was pitching, but it would hurt between starts. This year it only hurts when I pitch.[1]—Sandy Koufax, Los Angeles, June 15, 1966

The ascent to first place in San Francisco was short-lived. Not only was Drysdale's inability to beat the Giants in the June 12 series finale at Candlestick Park a missed opportunity to take a two-game lead over San Francisco, it precipitated a slide. The Dodgers returned home to drop two straight games to the Houston Astros, including a stunning two-hit shutout by 19-year-old Larry Dierker on June 14 that handed Sandy Koufax his second loss of the year. That was followed by the split of a two-game series with the last-place Cubs at Dodger Stadium.

Koufax Turns Around the Second Series with the Giants at Dodger Stadium

The Giants came into Los Angeles on June 17 for the three-game weekend series with a five-game winning streak and a three-game lead. Fortunately for the Dodgers, Juan Marichal won his 12th game the day before in San Francisco and would not available to start in the series.

Don Sutton (7–4) and Gaylord Perry (7–1) opened the series on Friday night, June 17, in front of a crowd of 50, 316 at Dodger Stadium. Willie Mays put the Giants in front, 1–0, in the third with a two-out RBI double off the center field fence. Jim Lefebvre led off the bottom of the fifth with a double to left-center. Roseboro followed with a slicing drive into left field. After a long run, Len Gabrielson got to the ball, but it glanced off his glove for another double to tie the game at 1–1.

With one out in the top of the eighth, Lefebvre, playing third base, fumbled Tito Fuentes' ground ball for a costly error.[2] Sutton got Gabrielson to pop up to Wills for the second out. Fuentes stole second and went to third on Sutton's wild pitch. Sutton then walked Willie Mays to bring up Willie McCovey with runners on first and third. McCovey parked Sutton's first pitch into the last rows of the right field pavilion for a decisive three-run homer.

Given a gift 4–1 lead, Gaylord Perry held the Dodgers scoreless over the final two innings to pick up his eighth win and increase the Giants' winning streak to six. Perry was fast coming into his own as one of the league's top right-handers. Sutton dropped to

7–5 despite giving up only one earned run. With the fifth loss in their last six games, the Dodgers fell into third place, four games off the pace. Again, it would be up to Sandy Koufax to stop the slide.

Koufax (11–2) took on Ray Sadecki (3–4) the next night in front of a standing-room-only crowd of 54,567 at Dodger Stadium. The stakes were high. With another loss, the Dodgers would fall five games behind. In the bottom of the first inning, Tommy Davis drove in Wes Parker with a two-out single to stake Koufax to a 1–0 lead. Koufax retired the first ten batters in order before Jim Davenport homered into the left field pavilion to tie the game, 1–1, in the fourth. Tommy Davis broke the 1–1 tie with another two-out single to score Parker in the sixth. Lefebvre led off the seventh with a home run off Sadecki to increase the Dodgers' lead to 3–1.

Koufax, who was having trouble keeping his pitches down all night, walked Mays to open the ninth inning.[3] Jim Ray Hart singled to right field, sending Mays to third. Cap Peterson followed with a solid line drive to right field—right at Lou Johnson for the first out. Alston let Koufax pitch to McCovey with the potential tying runs on and Perranoski and Regan warming up in the bullpen. McCovey just got under a rising fastball up in the zone and hit a moon shot to center field. It stayed in the park, allowing Willie Davis to make the play, but Mays scored on the sacrifice fly to cut the lead to 3–2. Koufax reached back and blew away Ollie Brown on strikes for the second time in the game to close it out.

Again, Koufax had come through in a critical game. His 12th win—and third straight over the Giants—snapped a six-game San Francisco winning streak and prevented the Dodgers from falling five games behind.[4]

The next day, Sunday, June 19, the Dodgers, buoyed by Koufax's performance, beat the Giants, 2–1. Facing Claude Osteen in the first inning, Willie Mays doubled home Jim Davenport to put the Giants in front, 1–0. Giants starter Bobby Bolin shut out the Dodgers through six innings on five singles. Herman Franks removed Bolin with one out in the seventh after Johnson and Lefebvre got on with back-to-back singles. Joe Gibbon was brought in and faced pinch-hitter Al Ferrara. Gibbon got Ferrara to hit a ground ball to third, but he beat the relay to first, allowing Johnson to score from third to tie the game at 1–1.[5]

The score was still 1–1 going to the bottom of the eighth inning. Drysdale came off the bench to hit a pinch single up the middle. Wills moved pinch-runner Bart Shirley to second with a sacrifice bunt. After Parker flied out to right field for the second out, Willie Davis bounced a 1–2 curveball from Gibbon through the left side of the infield to score Shirley with the winning run.[6]

Osteen allowed only one earned run in 7⅓ innings but came out with a no-decision. Phil Regan, who pitched two-thirds of an inning in relief of Osteen in the eighth, got credit for his fifth victory. By winning the series two games to one, the Dodgers pulled to within two games of San Francisco, albeit still in third place.

	W	*L*	*Pct.*	*GB*
San Francisco	40	25	.615	—
Pittsburgh	37	25	.597	1½
Los Angeles	37	26	.587	2

The Dodgers would lose six of their next ten games on the road to close out June in third place, five games behind the Giants. While Sandy Koufax helped to keep the team in contention with his six complete-game wins in the month, Drysdale lost an alarming six straight starts. Only with the gift of an early eight-run lead was Drysdale finally able to snap his losing streak with a so-so, six-inning performance in Cincinnati on June 29.

The Dodgers began the month of July with a ten-game homestand beginning with a weekend series with the St. Louis Cardinals. Sandy Koufax took on little left-hander Al "Toy Tiger" Jackson on Friday night, July 1, in the first game of the series. Koufax was 14–2, having thrown three straight complete-game victories. Jackson was 6–6 for the season and 1–10 in his career against the Dodgers. But he was Koufax's match on this night at Dodger Stadium.

The game was a scoreless tie going to the top of the seventh inning. After Curt Flood grounded out on a come-backer to the box, Orlando Cepeda singled for the second time in the game. Koufax went 3–1 to Mike Shannon, who was hitless in his last 17 at-bats against him. Since a walk would have put a runner in scoring position, Koufax tried to blow a fastball past Shannon. But Shannon hit what Koufax described as "a good pitch"[7] into the left field pavilion to put St. Louis up, 2–0. That was all Jackson needed, as it took him just one hour and 53 minutes to shut out the Dodgers on six singles. Koufax gave up five hits and struck out ten batters in eight innings, leaving for a pinch-hitter in the bottom of the eighth. Though the two hits he gave up in the seventh were the only solid Cardinals hits, they cost Koufax his third loss of the year. The Dodgers fell 6½ games back in third place.

On July 1 in New York, Marvin Miller officially assumed his position as Executive Director of the Major League Baseball Players Association. The Association had a bank balance of $5,700, no office, and a single file cabinet.

The next night, Claude Osteen—with help from Phil Regan—beat Bob Gibson, 7–2, to even the series. The Cardinals got to Osteen for two earned runs on nine hits, including a home run by Cepeda, before Regan relieved him with runners on first and third with two out in the seventh. Regan retired the last seven batters to save Osteen's tenth win. The Dodgers beat Gibson for the second straight time by pounding him for six runs on eight hits.[8]

Drysdale Is the Victim of Another Larry Jaster Shutout

Don Drysdale pitched the finale of the Cardinals series on Sunday, July 3. He was opposed by Larry Jaster, who had been recalled from Triple-A Tulsa ten days before.[9] Drysdale turned in a fine complete-game six-hitter. Unfortunately, the Dodgers' hitters could manage just three singles against Jaster as he shut them out, 2–0. It was a truly dominating performance by the 22-year-old, rookie left-hander. No Dodger made it past first base.[10] The loss dropped the Dodgers into fourth place behind the Phillies.

That day in San Francisco, the Braves crushed the Giants, 17–3, at Candlestick Park. Not only did Braves right-hander Tony Cloninger pitch a complete-game seven-hitter, he drove in nine of the runs himself with two grand slams and a single.[11]

	W	L	Pct.	GB
San Francisco	49	30	.620	—
Pittsburgh	45	31	.592	2½

	W	L	Pct.	GB
Philadelphia	43	34	.558	5
Los Angeles	42	34	.553	5½

After being shut out in two out of three games by the seventh-place Cardinals, the Dodgers caught a break when a struggling Cincinnati Reds team limped into town for a three-game series beginning on the Fourth of July. Don Sutton (7–7), who had not won a game since June 2, got the start against the Reds' Jim O'Toole (1–2).[12] Consecutive singles by Wes Parker, Willie Davis, and Lou Johnson after two were out in the third inning put the Dodgers in front, 1–0. After Tommy Helms singled to left with one out in the fifth, Deron Johnson hit a vicious line drive back to the box. Sutton tried to get out of the away, but it struck him just below the back of his right elbow. It was already the fifth time Sutton had been hit by a batted ball in the first 77 games of the season.[13] After a conference on the mound with Alston and the trainers, Sutton was allowed to stay in the game. He struck out two of the last three batters in the inning, but Johnny Edwards singled in Helms to tie the game, 1–1. The game was decided in the bottom of the sixth. Fairly led off the inning with a double. After O'Toole struck out Lefebvre, Roseboro went the opposite way with a single to left to score Fairly with the tie-breaking run. Sutton shut down the Reds on one hit over the last three innings for a complete-game, 2–1 win. He gave up five singles and struck out ten batters to move his record back over .500 to 8–7.

Can a Shutout Be Ugly?

Sandy Koufax (14–3) took on the Reds' ace right-hander, Jim Maloney (9–3), the night of July 5. Koufax struggled with his curveball for the first six innings, often throwing it well above the strike zone.[14] Fortunately, the Dodgers were able to cobble together a run in the second inning. Lefebvre led off with a walk and Roseboro followed with a single. After Jim Barbieri, in his first major league at-bat, lined out to Deron Johnson in left field, John Kennedy scored Lefebvre with a single to left. It was the only run of the game. Koufax went on to pitch an "ugly" ten-hit, 1–0 shutout for his 15th victory. He had to pitch with men on base in every inning but the fifth. The potential tying and winning runs were on in the ninth when he struck out Dick Simpson, the .125-hitting "throw-in" from Baltimore in the Frank Robinson trade, to end the game.[15] It was a tough loss for Maloney, who gave up only four hits in six innings before leaving for a pinch-hitter.

Claude Osteen pitched the final game of the series with the Reds on Wednesday night, July 6, against Milt Pappas. This game would be the Osteen-Kennedy show at Dodger Stadium, featuring two players who came over from the Washington Senators for Frank Howard.

Through the first six innings, neither Osteen nor Pappas was scored upon. Osteen got into trouble in the seventh. After Pete Rose led off with a single, Vada Pinson hit a ground ball to second that Lefebvre booted for an error. Tony Perez advanced the runners with a groundout. Alston ordered Osteen to walk Don Pavletich intentionally to load the bases for Deron Johnson, the major league leader in runs batted in for 1965.[16] Johnson hit a troublesome, high bouncer down the third baseline that had "two-run double" written on it. Kennedy leapt high to snag it, stepped on the bag to force Pinson for the second out, and fired the ball to Roseboro, who tagged Rose out in a collision at home plate to end the inning with the scoreless tie preserved.

Kennedy led off the bottom of the eighth inning with a double. Osteen twice tried to bunt the ball to Reds third baseman Chico Ruiz, but fouled off both pitches from Pappas. The Reds expected Osteen to attempt another bunt and had Perez playing in at first base. But Osteen swung away on the next pitch, grounding a ball between Perez and Rose to score Kennedy from second with the winning run.[17]

Osteen got three groundouts in the ninth to complete a four-hit, 1–0 shutout, and a three-game sweep of the rapidly disintegrating Reds, who had now lost eight games in a row. Alston placed the little rookie, Jim Barbieri, in the leadoff spot in the lineup for this game and moved Maury Wills down to the number two hole. It was only the second time Wills had batted second since he took over the leadoff spot from Junior Gilliam in 1960. After three Dodgers starters pitched complete-game wins—allowing a combined one run—the Dodgers remained four games out in third place.

The Dodgers split a four-game weekend series with the Atlanta Braves before the All-Star break. They eked out two one-run wins before the Braves beat both Koufax and Osteen to even the series.

In the July 7 opener on a Thursday night at Dodger Stadium, Don Drysdale pitched a strong eight innings for a 3–2 win. His third hit of the game, a two-out infield single in the bottom of the eighth, broke a 2–2 tie. Phil Regan came in to strike out the side in the ninth and preserve Drysdale's sixth victory.[18]

The next night, the Dodgers won their fifth straight one-run game, albeit a ragged 7–6 affair. Don Sutton was cuffed around for four runs in the second inning as he gave up three doubles, a single, and a walk. He lasted only one more inning but was let off the hook with a no-decision when the Dodgers scored six runs off Tony Cloninger in the third inning. With the score tied 6–6 in the bottom of the eighth, Lefebvre doubled home Parker with the winning run. After Perranoski held the Braves scoreless in the seventh and eighth innings and retired the first batter in the ninth, Alston took him out and brought in Regan. Why? The next batter was Hank Aaron. Bad Henry was a ridiculous 10-for-13 (.769) to that point in his career against Perranoski. Regan got Aaron to ground out to Wills for the second out, but he put the potential tying run on base by walking Rico Carty. Regan hung on as Joe Torre lined out to John Kennedy at third base to end the game.

The Braves Hammer Koufax for Three Homers

On Saturday evening, July 9, a turn-away Ladies Night crowd of 55,170 (47,962 paid) packed Dodger Stadium to watch Sandy Koufax go for his 16th victory. Koufax, who had not lost a decision to the Braves since 1962, shut them out through five innings on one hit—Felipe Alou's double to lead off the game. At the same time, the Dodgers were unable to score against Braves right-hander Ken Johnson.

A lucky break turned a scoreless game in Atlanta's favor in the sixth inning. Alou led off with a routine pop foul behind the plate. Johnny Roseboro, usually automatic on such plays, muffed it. Given a new life, Alou hit Koufax's next pitch into the left field seats. After Koufax got nemesis Gene Oliver to ground out, Hank Aaron lowered the boom on him with a line shot over the right-center field fence to make it 2–0. The next inning, Alou homered again with a man aboard, giving him ten total bases in the game against Koufax. Down 4–0 as the result of the three bombs, the Dodgers pinch-hit for Koufax in the bottom of the seventh. They knocked Johnson out of the game in the eighth when Willie Davis homered with Wills aboard. Tony Cloninger came in to end the rally and retired the Dodgers in order in the ninth to save a 5–2 win for Johnson.

Koufax sustained his fourth loss in a largely lackluster performance. In seven innings, he gave up two singles, a double, and the three home runs—the first time he had given up that many since June of 1963. He struck out only three batters.

Denny Lemaster shut out the Dodgers, 2–0, in the series finale on Sunday, July 10. The left-hander from Oxnard held them to five singles. No Dodger made it past first base. The Braves beat Dodgers starter Claude Osteen with two runs in the fifth inning on four consecutive singles.[19] Osteen's record fell to 11–7.

That day at Candlestick Park, the Reds snapped an 11-game losing streak by beating the Giants, 2–1, on a complete-game eight-hitter by Milt Pappas. Consequently, despite two straight losses to the eighth-place Braves, the Dodgers were able to remain in third place, five games behind the Giants at the All-Star break.

	W	L	Pct.	GB
San Francisco	54	33	.621	—
Pittsburgh	52	33	.612	1
Los Angeles	47	36	.566	5

At the break, Sandy Koufax was 15–4, with 165 strikeouts and a 1.61 ERA, the major league leader in all three categories. The Dodgers sent three players, in addition to Koufax, to the All-Star Game: Jim Lefebvre with 15 home runs; Maury Wills with a .292 batting average and 30 stolen bases; and Phil Regan, with a 5–1 record, ten saves, and a 1.47 ERA.

The second-place Pirates had the top four batters in the National League: Manny Mota, .352; Matty Alou, .338; Willie Stargell, .337; and Roberto Clemente, .328. Clemente, Stargell, and starter Bob Veale, with a 10–5 record and a 2.73 ERA, made the All-Star team.

The Giants sent six players to the All-Star Game: Willie Mays with 20 home runs; Willie McCovey with 17 home runs; Jim Ray Hart with 20 home runs; Tom Haller with 19 home runs; Juan Marichal with a 14–4 record and a 2.04 ERA; and the blossoming Gaylord Perry, who after winning his last seven decisions had a 12–1 record and a 2.51 ERA.

The Frank Robinson Trade Alters the Balance of Power in the American League

Back on June 7, the Baltimore Orioles took over sole possession of first place in the American League on a bases-loaded, walk-off single by Frank Robinson in the 12th inning at Memorial Stadium. Robinson's fourth hit of the game raised his batting average to .351. By the All-Star break, Baltimore had a commanding eight-game lead over the second-place Detroit Tigers. The Minnesota Twins, who lost Game 7 of the 1965 World Series to Sandy Koufax and the Dodgers, were mired in fifth place, 17 games off the pace. Twins manager Sam Mele, in St. Louis as manager of the AL team, told reporters that if Frank

On June 7, 1966, the Baltimore Orioles took over first place on a 12th-inning walk-off single by Frank Robinson. The Orioles would never be displaced, and Robby would go on to win a Triple Crown.

Brooks Robinson was voted the Most Valuable Player of the 1966 All-Star Game in St. Louis.

Robinson had not been traded to Baltimore, "it would still be a race in the American League."[20]

The American League batting leaders were packed with Orioles. Russ Snyder led the league with a .347 batting average. Brooks Robinson led in runs batted in with 70, and John "Boog" Powell was second with 67. Frank Robinson was tied with Al Kaline for most home runs with 21. Left-hander Steve Barber was 10–3 with a league-leading 1.97 ERA.

The All-Star Game in St. Louis

On July 11 in St. Louis, the day before the All-Star Game, Marvin Miller held his first formal meetings, first with the player reps, followed by a joint meeting with the owner reps. At issue was where the $150,000 needed to fund Miller's salary, his annual expenses, and the cost of the new MLBPA headquarters in New York should come from: 1. the owners, or 2. the players' pension fund.[21]

The 37th All-Star Game was played the next day in front of 49,936 fans at the new Busch Memorial Stadium in oppressive heat. The temperature was 100° when the game began and climbed to 105°. Vice President Hubert H. Humphrey made a quick exit after throwing out the first ball. An estimated 400 people required medical aid.[22]

Sandy Koufax made his first All-Star start against 22-year-old Detroit right-hander Denny McLain. Koufax needed only five pitches to retire the side in the first inning, but it took him 26 to get through the second. With one out, Brooks Robinson hit a sinking line drive in front of Hank Aaron in left field. Instead of letting the ball fall in for a single, Aaron raced in to try to make a shoestring catch. The ball got past Aaron and rolled to the wall, turning a single into a stand-up triple for Robinson. After Koufax got George Scott to foul out, he overthrew a pitch high over the head of catcher Joe Torre. Robinson trotted home on the wild pitch to put the AL up, 1–0.[23]

The Nationals tied the game, 1–1, in the fourth inning. The first two batters, Willie Mays and Roberto Clemente, singled off Twins left-hander Jim Kaat. After Aaron fouled out, Willie McCovey advanced Mays to third on a groundout. Ron Santo came to the plate wearing an improvised protective flap attached to his helmet after being hit in the face by a pitch just three weeks before. Santo hit a slow bouncer toward third base. Brooks Robinson raced in to pick up the ball with his bare hand but had to hold onto it as Mays scored on the infield single.

The game went into extra innings, tied 1–1. With Gaylord Perry pitching his second inning in the top of the tenth, Brooks Robinson led off with his third hit of the game, a single to left-center field. After Perry wild-pitched him to second and walked Earl Battey, Walter Alston left the shade of the dugout for the first time to talk to Perry. Alston offered to spell him with Phil Regan, but Perry declined to come out. He worked his way out of the jam by getting Bobby Richardson to foul out and striking out Jim Fregosi.

In the bottom of the tenth, Tim McCarver lined Washington left-hander Pete Richert's first pitch into right field for a single. On the next pitch, Ron Hunt made a perfect sacrifice bunt to advance McCarver to second. Maury Wills, batting right-handed, followed with an opposite-field single to right field. Tony Oliva fielded the ball but made a poor throw to the plate—high and several feet up the first base line. Catcher Earl Battey had no chance to attempt a tag on McCarver, who slid in with the winning run. It was ironic that Wills, who didn't even want to come to the game after Cincinnati's Leo Cardenas was voted over him as the starting shortstop, had the game-winning hit.[24]

Brooks Robinson, who had three of the AL's six hits and made two spectacular defensive plays at third base, was voted the game's Most Valuable Player. He set a new All-Star Game fielding record by handling eight chances, including four putouts. After the game, a dazzled Ron Santo told reporters, "Brooks Robinson is the greatest I've ever seen."[25] Sandy Koufax gave up only one hit—the tainted triple by Brooks Robinson—in his three innings of work. Gaylord Perry got credit for the win.

After the All-Star break, the Dodgers headed to New York to begin the second half with a three-game series with the Mets. With one day's rest after pitching three innings in the heat in St. Louis, Koufax pitched a complete game to win the opener, 4–2, on Thursday night, July 14, at Shea Stadium. In an erratic performance without a curveball, he threw 158 pitches, walked three batters, struck out 11, and gave up eight hits—including a home run to Eddie Bressoud in the seventh inning that cut the Dodgers' lead to 3–2. Lou Johnson's three run homer off Mets' starter Bob Shaw with two out in the first inning proved to be insurmountable.[26]

The Dodgers prevailed, 4–3, the next night in front of 50,423 at Shea. Dick Stuart, released by the Mets the prior month, had the game-winning single in the eleventh inning. Drysdale gave up eleven hits in six innings, but escaped with no decision. Phil Regan won his sixth game by coming in from the bullpen in the eighth to pitch 2⅔ scoreless innings.[27] Maury Wills sprained his right knee running out a bunt in the fifth, and had to be removed from the game. The next day he would be flown back to Los Angeles for X-rays.[28]

Don Sutton completed the three-game sweep of the Mets with a 7–1 complete game 5-hitter with eleven strikeouts on Saturday, July 16. With Wills back in L.A., John Kennedy filled in at shortstop. The game was decided in the first inning when Roseboro hit a two-run homer batting in the cleanup spot for the first time.

On July 17, the Dodgers split a Sunday doubleheader with the Phillies in Philadelphia. It took Chris Short one hour and 37 minutes to shut them out on two hits in the opener, 3–0. Joe Moeller matched Short for the first five innings with his own one-hit shutout. Cookie Rojas and Dick Groat opened the bottom of the sixth with singles. After Nate Oliver threw out Rojas at home plate on Short's ground ball, Tony Taylor hit a likely inning-ending, double play grounder to Dick Stuart at first base. Stuart threw to Kennedy to force Short at second base for the first out, but Taylor beat the throw back to first. While Moeller went berserk, arguing with first base umpire Mel Steiner, Groat broke for home. Stuart and second baseman Pee Wee Oliver screamed at Moeller, "Groat! Home!"[29] But by the time he regained his senses and threw the ball to the plate, it was too late. The Phillies had scored the only run Chris Short would need.[30] In the second game, Osteen won his 12th game by beating Philadelphia, 3–1. Osteen pitched the first seven innings, allowing the Phils their only run on six singles. Phil Regan shut them out without a hit for the last two innings.

The Dodgers were dealt a blow the next night when Larry Jackson bested Sandy Koufax with a five-hit, 4–0 shutout to close out the series and the brief 4–2 road trip. Pitching in front of the standing-room-only crowd of 34,755 at Connie Mack Stadium, Koufax lasted five innings and struck out only two batters. The Phillies finished him off in the fifth with three runs on four line shots—a double and three singles plus a bunt single.[31] Jackson, who came over from the Cubs in the April trade for Ferguson Jenkins, had now pitched 24 consecutive scoreless innings for Gene Mauch.[32] Despite losing two out of three games in Philadelphia, the Dodgers remained three games back in third place. July 19 was an off-day as the team travelled back to Los Angeles for a nine-game home stand.

The home stand began with a two-game series with Pirates, who were still locked in a virtual tie with the Giants for first place. Drysdale pitched against Vern Law in the opener of July 20 in front of 39,545 fans on a Wednesday night at Dodger Stadium. Drysdale took a 5–2 lead to the seventh inning. He got the first two batters to pop out. But things began to fall apart when he hit the league's leading hitter, Matty Alou, with a pitch. After Gene Michael singled and Clemente followed with a single to score Alou, Drysdale was done. Alston brought in Jim Brewer, who in turn exited after walking Manny Mota. Alston turned to the trusty Phil Regan, who had saved ten games. Regan was promptly rocked by Jose Pagan's two-run single and Donn Clendenon's crushing three-run homer— both on 0–2 pitches. By the time Regan finally got the third out, the Pirates had scored six runs to take an 8–5 lead. The Pirates' little right-hander, Al McBean, blanked the Dodgers over the last three innings. Drysdale escaped with a no-decision. In a cruel twist of the scoring rules, Brewer was hung with the loss despite having pitched to only one batter. After spending the previous four days back in Los Angeles having the fluid in his injured right knee drained by Dr. Robert Kerlan, Maury Wills returned to the lineup and had three hits.[33] With the loss, the Dodgers fell to four games off the pace.[34]

July 21 was a key date for the 1966 Dodgers. Another loss to the Pirates at Dodger Stadium, and they would fall five games behind. The burden fell on their rookie right-hander, Don Sutton, who could get only one out in his last start against Pittsburgh.

Sutton had a 1–0 lead with nine strikeouts after seven innings but was knocked out when the Pirates went out in front, 2–1, in the eighth. The Dodgers were down to their last out in the bottom of the ninth when Willie Davis tied the game with an RBI single off Elroy Face.

Pinch-hitter Bob Bailey led off the tenth inning with a home run against Phil Regan to put the Pirates back in front, 3–2. Wills opened the bottom of the tenth with a single off Face, but was forced out at second base on Lou Johnson's unsuccessful sacrifice bunt. When Face fell behind 2–0 to Wes Parker, Harry Walker pulled him and brought in Pete Mikkelsen. After Mikkelsen completed the walk to Parker, pinch-hitter Jim Barbieri bounced a single through the infield to tie the game.[35] Walker ordered Mikkelsen to walk the red-hot Johnny Roseboro, loading the bases for John Kennedy. Mikkelsen's first pitch to Kennedy hit him squarely in the back, allowing Parker to walk home from third base with the winning run.[36] By salvaging a split with the Pirates, the Dodgers were able to stay within three games of the lead.

After surviving the Pirates, the Dodgers had to take on a surging New York Mets, on a six-game winning streak. In the first game of a four-game weekend series on July 22, the Amazin's made it seven straight on Bob Friend's eight-hit, 3–0 shutout. Only a month before, the 35-year-old Friend had been sold to the Mets by the Yankees.[37] Claude Osteen hung with him until he was tagged for a two-run homer by Ron Swoboda in the eighth inning.

With four losses in their last six games, the Dodgers needed a stop the next day from Sandy Koufax. And Koufax came through with a complete-game, 6–2 win to break the Mets' seven-game win streak. But it was a struggle. He did not have his good fastball; he could not control his curve; he walked five batters and had to throw 168 pitches. "It seemed like I was 3-and-2 on the hitters all day," he told reporters.[38] Maury Wills' two-run single in the bottom of the second inning put the Dodgers up, 4–1, and drove Mets starter Bob Shaw from the game. This gutty win from a sub-par Koufax, in which he pitched with runners on base in every inning but the first, changed the team's momentum.

Buoyed by the Koufax stop, the next day the Dodgers swept a Sunday doubleheader from the Mets, shutting them out in both games. In his first shutout of the year, Drysdale blanked them, 5–0, on six hits with ten strikeouts in the first game. As a batter, he hit a single and a home run, the 29th and last of his career. Game number 94 for the Dodgers was clearly Drysdale's best effort of the year so far, giving them hope that he could still regain his top form, considered essential for them to repeat as NL champs.[39] In the second game, the tandem of Joe Moeller and Phil Regan shut out the Mets, 6–0. Moeller's fine four-hit performance over the first seven innings gave him his first win since August of 1964.[40] Regan shut down the Mets on one hit in the last two innings. This was the first time in Walter Alston's 13-year tenure with the Dodgers that his pitchers had given him back-to-back shutouts in a doubleheader.[41]

The Dodgers continued the momentum with a three-game sweep of the Phillies to close out the home stand. The bullpen won all three games. On July 25, Don Sutton left the game in the eighth inning after he gave up a solo home run to Johnny Briggs that tied the game, 3–3. Perranoski took over and picked up the win when the Dodgers rallied for three runs in the bottom of the inning.[42] The next night, Briggs knocked Claude Osteen out of the game with a double in the seventh inning. The Dodgers came from 2–1 behind with two runs in the bottom of the ninth to beat Larry Jackson, 3–2. Perranoski, who held the Phillies scoreless over the last two innings, was credited with his fourth win.

On July 27, future Hall of Famers Sandy Koufax and Jim Bunning became embroiled in a dazzling pitchers' duel in front of 44,937 fans at Dodger Stadium. Through 11 innings they were tied, 1–1, Koufax with 16 strikeouts, Bunning with 12. Phil Regan replaced Koufax in the top of the 12th to retire the Phillies in order. Darold Knowles came in for

Bunning to pitch the bottom of the 12th. Knowles walked the leadoff batter, Nate Oliver, on four pitches. Oliver advanced to second on a passed ball charged to catcher Bob Uecker. After pinch-hitter Lou Johnson twice failed to get a bunt down, he won the game with a line drive walk-off single. Ominously, Sandy Koufax had to throw another 163 pitches.[43] And it was Regan who ended up with the victory. It was on that night that Koufax, who labored for 11 innings to a no-decision, nicknamed Regan "the Vulture."[44]

Things were looking up for the Dodgers when they arrived in St. Louis on July 29 for a three-game weekend series to close out July. They had won their last six games in a row and were only a half-game out of first place. In fact, only .004 percentage points separated the Pirates, Giants, and Dodgers at the top of the NL standings. Drysdale was scheduled to pitch the Friday night opener, having won three of his last four decisions. He came through with a solid, complete-game performance. The only problem was that the Cardinals' remarkable rookie left-hander, Larry Jaster, shut out the Dodgers for the third straight time—4–0 on five hits. Jaster had a no-hitter until Drysdale broke it up with a single in the sixth inning.

The next day, Saturday July 30, the streaking Cardinals beat the Dodgers, 3–1, on Al Jackson's complete-game six-hitter. With their sixth straight win, the Cardinals had now won 12 of their last 13 games, moving up from sixth place into fourth.[45] Don Sutton, who lasted just five innings, suffered his eighth loss. Lou Brock feasted on him with a home run and two singles.

For the Sunday series finale on July 31, Osteen took on another Cardinals rookie left-hander, Steve Carlton. The 6'4" Carlton was making his first major league start, having just been called up from the Cardinals' Triple-A farm team in Tulsa. The game was played in front of 48,085 fans, the largest regular season turnout to date at the new Busch Memorial Stadium.[46] Carlton lasted four innings and Osteen lasted four and two-thirds. Neither starter figured in the outcome. Down 4–3, the Dodgers rallied for three runs in the top off the ninth inning off St. Louis reliever Joe Hoerner to win it, 6–4. Dick Stuart, who had already driven in two runs with a single and a homer earlier in the game, tied the game with a two-out double and scored the go-ahead run on John Roseboro's single. Stuart was now hitting .400 (14-for-35) since signing with the Dodgers after the Mets released him. Phil Regan, who pitched the last two scoreless innings, picked up his ninth victory.

July Ends in a Virtual 3-Way Tie for First Place

Despite having just lost two out of three to the Cardinals, at the end of play on Sunday, July 31, the Dodgers found themselves in a virtual tie with the Giants (who that same weekend lost three out of four in Atlanta) and Pittsburgh (who lost three in a row in Philadelphia) for the top spot in the National League. In fact, they actually led by a single (.001) percentage point.

	W	L	Pct.	GB
Los Angeles	59	42	.584	—
Pittsburgh	60	43	.583	—
San Francisco	61	44	.581	—

For the next two months, the 1966 Los Angeles Dodgers would play musical chairs with the Giants and the Pirates in a historic three-team dogfight for the pennant.

Three-Team NL Dogfight
Round 1—August

I don't think Drysdale is as fast as he was two or three year ago, but neither is Koufax.[1]—Willie McCovey, Candlestick Park, August 27, 1966

A Case of Buc Fever in Pittsburgh

The month of August began with a crucial four-game series with the league's top-hitting Pirates in Pittsburgh. Sandy Koufax had his "A" game for the opener at Forbes Field on the first night of August. But one lapse and a bad hop in the first inning prevented him from pitching a shutout and picking up his 18th win. In the bottom of the first, Koufax made the mistake of walking the leadoff man, Gene Alley. With one out, Roberto Clemente lined what looked like an ordinary single to right field. But the ball took a kangaroo bounce over Ron Fairly's head and became a run-scoring triple.[2] Koufax settled into a rhythm and shut out the Pirates on four singles over the next six innings. With the Dodgers still trailing, 1–0, in the eighth inning, he was removed for a pinch-hitter. Before the inning was over, Maury Wills had tied the game with a two-out RBI single. Before the game, a weary Wills asked Alston to switch him from shortstop to third base for a few games to rest his aching right knee. In turn, third baseman John Kennedy agreed to take over the shortstop position.

The Dodgers won the game in the ninth inning on a pair of two-run homers by Roseboro and Gilliam. Phil Regan, who pitched the last two scoreless innings, scavenged his tenth victory. Koufax got a no-decision after pitching seven great innings with nine strikeouts. Bill Mazeroski, who first faced Koufax in 1957, told reporters after the game: "He was as good as I've ever seen him."[3]

The next night, August 2, the Dodgers lost a tough 6–5 game. Drysdale was staked to an early 3–1 lead on home runs by Lou Johnson and Jim Lefebvre off Pirates starter Woody Fryman, but could not hold it. He was knocked out of the game before he could retire anyone in the fourth inning on a two-run, opposite-field homer by Donn Clendenon that put the Pirates in front, 4–3. In the bottom of the eighth, Manny Mota broke a 5–5 tie with an RBI double off Perranoski. Mota's game-winning hit ended a four-game Pittsburgh losing streak. The Dodgers fell into a tie for second place with the Pirates, one game behind the Giants.[4]

On August 3, the Dodgers were dropped into third place on one swing of the great

Above: On August 3, 1966, Roberto Clemente dropped the Dodgers into third place with a devastating home run off Don Sutton at Forbes Field in Pittsburgh. *Below:* On August 4, 1966, an incendiary Manny Mota feasted on Dodgers pitching for two run-scoring triples and a single to complete a three-games-to-one series win for the Pirates at Forbes Field.

Roberto Clemente's bat. That Wednesday night, Don Sutton took on Bob Veale at Forbes Field. In the bottom of the first inning, Pirates leadoff man Matty Alou legged out an infield single. Sutton got Gene Alley to ground out, with Alou advancing to second. Clemente, the National League's batting champ for the last two years, and then hitting .332, was next. Sutton made a good pitch to Clemente, a low-inside fastball. But Clemente pulled in his hands and drove the ball over the right-field wall to put the Pirates up, 2–0. Clemente's 17th home run of the season proved decisive. Sutton retired the next 12 men in a row and permitted only two more singles before he was lifted for a pinch-hitter in the seventh inning with the Dodgers behind, 2–1.[5] The Pirates won, 3–1, as their 6'6" left-hander, Bob Veale, pitched a complete-game seven-hitter. Veale, who had been sidelined since July 18 with a bad back, mowed down 11 batters on strikes.[6] The Dodgers were now in third place, two games off the pace. The Pirates stayed in second, one game behind the Giants.

In the series finale on August 4, the Pirates pulverized Claude Osteen and four Dodgers relievers for 16 hits in an 8–1 thumping. Osteen lasted only an inning and a third. The incendiary Manny Mota had two run-scoring triples and a single to raise his batting average to .358. Thirty-six-year-old right-hander Vernon Law, who had not won a game in a month, pitched a complete-game six-hitter with no walks.[7]

That first August series set the tone for the month. When the Dodgers arrived in Pittsburgh, they were in a virtual three-way tie for first place. When they left four days later, after losing three out of four, they were in third, two games off the pace. Not one of the top four Dodgers starters could register a victory. The Pirates had climbed back on top of the heap, albeit by just two percentage points. The City of Pittsburgh was consumed by "Buc fever."

	W	L	Pct.	GB
Pittsburgh	63	44	.589	—
San Francisco	64	45	.587	—
Los Angeles	60	45	.571	2

The Dodgers were able to bounce back by scoring 30 runs in a three-game sweep of the hapless Astros in Houston. In the opener on August 5, Sandy Koufax breezed to his 18th win as the Dodgers exploded for 18 hits in a 12–1 cakewalk. With an 11-run lead, Koufax was able to take the rest of night off after six innings of five-hit baseball with ten strikeouts. His only mistake was a home run pitch to Dave Nicholson leading off the second inning.[8] Roseboro, batting cleanup, had three hits to raise his average to .305. After a four-game "vacation" at third base in Pittsburgh, a semi-mummified Maury Wills returned to shortstop with his ailing right knee so heavily bandaged that it looked like an old-fashioned football pad. He also had his entire upper torso and right thigh bandaged.[9]

The next night, Drysdale went six and two-thirds innings to beat the Astros, 4–3, in front of 49,003 fans at the Astrodome. Drysdale got his eighth win in 20 decisions. Lou Johnson and John Kennedy both hit two-run singles off Houston starter Mike Cuellar,[10] who mowed down ten Dodgers on strikes in seven innings with a wicked screwball.

In the series finale on August 7, Claude Osteen pitched only one inning and walked three batters. But no matter, the Dodgers pounded Houston starter Turk Farrell and five relievers for 20 hits and 14 runs.[11] Joe Moeller came in for Osteen in the second inning and pitched five three-hit innings for his second win. The 14–3 win moved the Dodgers back into first place by a single percentage point. It was the eighth straight loss for the Astros.

	W	L	Pct.	GB
Los Angeles	63	45	.583	—
Pittsburgh	64	46	.582	—
San Francisco	65	47	.580	—

The Dodgers closed out a 13-game road trip with three games with the seventh-place Braves in Atlanta. In the August 8 opener, the Braves jumped on Don Sutton for five runs on six hits and a walk in the first inning. He was removed with two out in the second after giving up a home run and two singles with the Dodgers down, 6–2. The game devolved into wild free-for-all. By the end of eight innings, the Dodgers had come back to tie the game, 6–6, on the strength of three home runs.

They went in front, 9–6, on Johnny Roseboro's three-run double in the top of the ninth, and had Phil Regan poised to pick up his 11th consecutive relief victory—provided he could get the final three outs. But Regan, who had shut out Atlanta in the seventh and eighth innings, stumbled in the bottom of the ninth. He could retire only one batter—Hank Aaron on a line drive out—before Alston removed him with one run in and two runners on base.[12] A hastily prepared Perranoski took over to cough up a run-scoring infield single to Joe Torre, a solid, game-tying single to Rico Carty, and Denis Menke's smash to left field that drove in the fourth and winning run.

The devastating 10–9 loss dropped the Dodgers into third place, .001 behind the Giants, and .004 behind the Pirates.[13]

	W	L	Pct.	GB
Pittsburgh	64	46	.582	—
San Francisco	66	48	.579	—
Los Angeles	63	46	.578	½

Koufax Goes Down in the Ninth Inning

Sandy Koufax and Denny Lemaster met the night of August 9. Despite the threat of rain, a record crowd of 52,270 turned out at Atlanta Stadium. This was the first game for new Braves manager Billy Hitchcock. The 50-year-old Hitchcock, Atlanta's first base coach for the first 111 games, was awakened at 7:40 a.m. to learn that he was to replace Bobby Bragan, who was fired the night before. Bragan had been at the helm since 1963.[14]

In the bottom of the first inning, before he was fully loose, Koufax was tagged for a leadoff home run by Felipe Alou. He retired the next 15 batters until Woody Woodward doubled off him in the sixth. With the Dodgers batting in the fourth, a rain deluge caused play to be halted. Remarkably, at least 40,000 fans were still there to see Sandy Koufax pitch when play was resumed two hours and five minutes later.[15]

Lemaster had a no-hitter until Jim Lefebvre led off the eighth inning with a home run on a high change-up to tie the game, 1–1.[16] The game was still tied as it moved to the bottom of the ninth. Koufax had better luck with leadoff batter Felipe Alou, inducing him to ground out to shortstop. The Braves' captain, Eddie Mathews, was next. Koufax had struck him out his first three times up, sending his batting average south of .220. The left-handed Mathews worked the count to 2–2 and then unloaded on a high fastball, driving it deep into the right-field seats for a walk-off home run. By the end of the season, Mathews would be dealt to the Astros after 15 years with the Braves. With Koufax's sixth loss, the Dodgers dropped to a game and a half behind Pittsburgh.

Still shell-shocked by the blow to Koufax, the Dodgers had to get ready to finish the series the next night, August 10. Don Drysdale was unable to stop the bleeding. He was beaten by rookie left-hander Dick Kelley, just up from Triple-A Richmond.[17] Just as he did to Koufax, Felipe Alou rocked Drysdale with a leadoff homer in the first inning. Lefebvre was able to tie the game with a solo home run off Kelley in the second.

An error by Jim Gilliam at third base led to Drysdale's demise in the fifth. Drysdale should have had Alou on a routine ground ball leading off the inning. Instead, Gilliam booted it, allowing Alou to end up on second base. Before Drysdale could get out of the inning, the Braves had scored two unearned runs on a sacrifice fly by Aaron and a run-scoring double by Carty to take a 3–1 lead.[18] That was the end of the scoring. Drysdale was pulled before he could get anyone out in the sixth inning and went down to his thirteenth defeat.

The three-game sweep in Atlanta brought to an end a rocky 13-game road trip during which the Dodgers won only five games. As they headed for home on August 10, they were in third place, two and a half games off the pace.

	W	L	Pct.	GB
Pittsburgh	66	46	.589	—
San Francisco	66	49	.574	1½
Los Angeles	63	48	.568	2½

Reeling from their sweep at the hands of the Braves in Atlanta, the Dodgers had an excellent opportunity to regain some ground when they opened their home stand with a four-game weekend series with the Cubs. After all, Leo Durocher's boys were already hopelessly buried in tenth place, 29½ games out of it. However, they proved to be a stubborn adversary. The Friday night opener on August 12 was a tight pitchers' duel between rookies Don Sutton and Ken Holtzman. The Dodgers got a gift run in the bottom of the first inning when the 20-year-old Holtzman wild pitched in a run with two out. After that, he was nearly unhittable.[19]

Sutton had a 1–0 shutout before the breaks went Chicago's way in the ninth inning. Leadoff batter Glenn Beckert beat out a harmless topper to Wills. Billy Williams hit a ground ball to second base, but he beat Wills' relay to first. Ron Santo followed with a double to right-center that scored Williams with the tying run and brought Alston out of the dugout.[20] Regan was brought in and walked Ernie Banks intentionally. Pinch-hitter George Altman hit a perfect double play ball toward Lefebvre at second base that should have ended the inning. But the ball took a bad hop and sailed over Lefebvre's head into right field to score Santo with the tie-breaking run.

Holtzman, who had given up just one single after the first inning, shut down the Dodgers in the bottom of the ninth for a come-from-behind 2–1 win. Hard-luck Sutton was charged with his tenth loss. It was his six straight start without a victory. The Dodgers fell to four games behind the Pirates.

The next day at Dodger Stadium, Saturday, August 13, Sandy Koufax stopped a four-game Dodgers losing streak and evened the series with a complete-game, 6–1 win. He had a two-hit shutout with 11 strikeouts through the first eight innings, but tired in the ninth. Billy Williams and Ron Santo opened the inning with back-to-back singles. Koufax was lucky to get Ernie Banks to line into a double play on a great catch by Tommy Davis in left field. Byron Browne singled home Williams to spoil the shutout. By having to labor in the ninth, Koufax ended up throwing 133 pitches in the game.[21] His record was now 19–6. Dodgers hitters pounded Cubs left-hander Dick Ellsworth for 13 hits. Tommy Davis was a perfect 4-for-4 with a home run and three runs batted in to raise his average to .309.

The series concluded on August 14 with a Sunday doubleheader. In the first game, Drysdale and 37-year-old Curt Simmons were locked in a 2–2 tie at the end of nine innings. Both starters were pulled for pinch-hitters: Drysdale in the tenth and Simmons in the 12th. With the game still tied, 2–2, in the top of the 14th, the Cubs scored an unearned run on a throwing error by Bob Miller to take the lead. The Dodgers came back to win it, 4–3, on a two-out, bases-loaded single by pinch-hitter Wes Covington at the four hour and 27-minute mark.[22]

The second game was a wild free-for-all that the Cubs pulled out, 12–10, with two runs off Don Sutton pitching in relief in the tenth inning. The marathon doubleheader ended in the dark and lasted for eight hours and five minutes.[23] With the split, the Dodgers slipped to three and a half games behind the Pirates, in third place.

	W	L	Pct.	GB
Pittsburgh	69	47	.595	—
San Francisco	69	50	.580	1½
Los Angeles	65	50	.565	3½

The Dodgers next took on the sixth-place Reds in a three-game series that saw Osteen and Sutton break out of personal winless streaks before a Koufax elbow flare-up cast doubt on the season.

Claude Osteen and Jim O'Toole met in the August 15 opener. Osteen had gone five straight starts without a victory. The Dodgers got to O'Toole for four runs in the fourth inning on Lou Johnson's two-run homer and RBI singles by Parker and Roseboro.[24] The Reds cuffed Osteen around for 11 hits and two runs before Bob Miller came in with two out in the seventh inning to retire Deron Johnson with the tying runs aboard to preserve a 4–2 lead. Miller hung on until Pete Rose cut the lead to 4–3 on an RBI single with two out in the ninth. Phil Regan had to come in to strike out the Reds' cleanup batter, Deron Johnson, on a 3–2 pitch with the potential tying and winning runs on base. Osteen (13–9) got credit for his first win since July 15.[25]

In the second game, 21-year-old Don Sutton went up against the Reds' 38-year-old left-hander, Joe Nuxhall. Nuxhall was in his 16th season with Cincinnati, having made his major league debut at the age of 15 in the player-depleted war year of 1944—the year before Sutton was born. Sutton, who had gone six straight starts without a victory, pitched a brilliant two-hit shutout. The game was settled in the first inning, when Tommy Davis singled home two runs off Nuxhall. Sutton allowed only three batters to reach base: Rose walked in the fourth, Johnny Edwards singled in the sixth, and Leo Cardenas hit a ground ball that caromed off Gilliam's glove for a double. After the game Gordy Coleman, who struck out twice against Sutton, told reporters, "I rate this kid with the top five right-handers in the league." With his tenth win, Sutton broke Stan Williams' record for most wins by a Los Angeles Dodgers rookie pitcher, set in the team's first year on the West Coast.[26] The Reds had now lost six games in a row.

The Koufax Elbow Flare-Up

In the series finale on August 17, a large Wednesday night crowd of 43,778 turned out to see Sandy Koufax go for his 20th win of the season. He was opposed by right-hander Sammy Ellis (10–14) for Cincinnati. Koufax began to feel considerable pain in his left elbow while striking out Don Pavletich in the second inning. He managed to strike out the side, but not before giving up a double to Tommy Helms and a walk to Leo Cardenas. The game was a scoreless tie at the end of three innings. In the top of the fourth, the pain had increased to the point where Koufax was no longer able to control the baseball. After he threw a wild pitch and walked the bases loaded, Cardenas cleared the bases with a double over the third base bag to put the Reds up, 3–0. Koufax gamely came out for the fifth inning, but the pain rendered him ineffective. Vada Pinson led off with a line drive right at Lou Johnson in right field for an out. When Pete Rose followed with a line single to center, Alston had seen enough. Koufax was removed after pitching only four and one-third innings.[27] The Dodgers went on to lose the game, 5–1, to stay three games off the pace in third place.

Koufax's elbow flare-up on the night of August 17 set off warning lights. After the game, he was given a cortisone injection directly into the elbow.[28] Dr. Robert Kerlan told reporters, "He's had this trouble before, but this is the first time he has had that much pain during a game. Usually it hurts him between starts."[29] In the clubhouse after the game, Koufax raised some eyebrows by disclosing that his elbow had been "getting worse and worse,"[30] but he said he was hopeful that he would be able to make his next start. With the loss to the Reds, his record was 19–7. A spooked Dodgers nation couldn't help but remember that Koufax was 19–5 when the elbow ended his season in August of 1964.

In the opening game of a four-game weekend series with the Cardinals that began the next night at Dodger Stadium, Drysdale beat Bob Gibson, 3–1, with a complete-game six-hitter. It was Drysdale's best performance to date. He struck out eight batters and walked none. "I held my stuff for nine innings, and hit the spots,"[31] he told reporters after the game. The Dodgers got to Gibson for a pair of run-scoring singles by Jim Lefebvre and a solo home run by Willie Davis. Wills returned to the starting lineup at shortstop after giving his right knee a three-day rest.

The Larry Jaster Enigma ver. 4.0

On Friday night, August 19, Claude Osteen tried to build on Drysdale's win. His only problem was having to go up against the Cardinals' amazing, 22-year-old, rookie left-hander, Larry Jaster. Back on April 25, he threw a seven-hit shutout to beat Osteen, 2–0. On this night at Dodger Stadium, Jaster shut out the Dodgers for the fourth consecutive time—this time 4–0 on five singles. The Cardinals disposed of Osteen in the seventh inning with three runs on three singles, all started by a sacrifice bunt by Jaster. By the time Bob Miller came in from the bullpen to get the last two outs, the Dodgers were down, 4–0.[32]

On Saturday, August 20, Don Sutton gave up only four hits over the first eight innings. But two of these were solo home runs hit by Julian Javier using a bat he borrowed from Orlando Cepeda. "I was only trying to hit line drives, but the ball jumped off the bat," an amazed Javier told reporters.[33] The Dodgers tied the game, 2–2, on Jim Lefebvre's run-scoring single in the bottom of the ninth to send it into extra innings. Cepeda, supplier of the offending bat, won it in the 13th with a line drive RBI single off Joe Moeller, the Dodgers' fifth pitcher of the game.[34]

A Hinge Point for Koufax and the 1966 Dodgers

The elbow flare-up of August 17 had cast the Dodgers' season, as well as Sandy Koufax's future, in doubt. Rumors began circulating in the out-of-town press that Koufax was contemplating retirement. *The Chicago Tribune* quoted him as saying, "It's a matter of how long I can stand the pain."[35] On Friday, August 19, he threw for ten minutes on the sidelines. After the session, he told reporters he still "hoped" to make his regular start against the Cardinals in two days.[36]

Sunday, August 21, was a hinge point in the season. The Dodgers were not sure what they would get that afternoon when Sandy Koufax took the mound against the Cardinals at Dodger Stadium. And he nearly didn't survive the first inning, unable to get loose. The Cardinals got to him for three hits, including a two-out, run-scoring single by Curt Flood. After Koufax walked Mike Shannon to load the bases, Tim McCarver followed with a bullet headed for right field. Parker made a diving stop of the ball and, from a sitting position, flipped it to Koufax, who barely beat McCarver to the first base bag to end the inning. Parker's play saved at least two runs and kept Koufax in the game. Alston later revealed, "If Wes hadn't come up with that ball, I probably would have taken Sandy out."[37]

After Koufax got past the first inning, he was able to loosen up and find a rhythm. He went on to pitch a complete game, scattering three hits over the last eight innings to pick up his 20th victory. He threw 122 pitches, 30 just to get out of the first inning. The Dodgers chased St. Louis starter Ray Washburn in the third inning on their way to a 4–1 win. This heroic performance by Koufax enabled them to salvage a split of the series and stay three games behind in third place. He would not miss a start for the remainder of the season.

The Dodgers closed out the home stand with a three-game sweep of the Atlanta Braves from August 22–24 with Maury Wills restored to the leadoff position in the batting order. All three games were walk-off, one-run wins credited to the Dodgers' bullpen, the first one by Bob Miller and the last two by Phil Regan. As the team prepared to go back out on the road, they had moved to within two games of the lead.

	W	L	Pct.	GB
Pittsburgh	74	51	.592	—
San Francisco	75	52	.591	—
Los Angeles	72	53	.576	2

The first stop was San Francisco. A new Candlestick Park record crowd of 42,647 turned out to see Koufax pitch the Friday night opener on August 26. Koufax and Giants right-hander Bobby Bolin were locked in a scoreless pitchers' duel for the first seven innings.[38] Bolin struck out seven of the first nine batters he faced and did not give up a hit until Maury Wills singled to lead off the sixth inning. Wills stole second—his first steal since July 22—but was left stranded on third when Bolin got Roseboro to fly out to Mays on the warning track in center field with the bases loaded.

Bolin's leadoff walk to Parker in the eighth inning touched off a rally in which the Dodgers batted around to score the only four runs of the game. In a flurry of run-scoring hits by Fairly, Roseboro, and Johnson, plus a sacrifice fly by Koufax, the Dodgers knocked out Bolin and went through Giants relievers Bill Henry and Lindy McDaniel.[39]

Koufax pitched a four-hit, 4–0 shutout, the last in his career against the Giants. He was now 21–7 with a 1.62 ERA. The fifth straight Dodgers win knocked the Giants out of first place, with the Dodgers moving to within a game and a half of the lead.

Juan Marichal and Don Drysdale squared off the next afternoon in a wind-blown affair at Candlestick Park. It was Marichal who had prevented a Dodgers sweep by beating Drysdale the last time they met here back on June 12.

Twice Drysdale had a one-run lead and couldn't hold it. It was Candlestick Park's defining characteristic, the wind, that decided the game in the bottom of the sixth. Drysdale started the inning with a 2–1 lead. Mays led off with a single and McCovey followed with a double to tie the game, 2–2. With two out and McCovey at third, Jesus Alou hit a pop fly into shallow right field. Second baseman Lefebvre and right fielder Fairly converged on the ball as the wind blew it farther into the outfield. At the last instant, Lefebvre tried to make a difficult over-the-shoulder catch but couldn't put his glove on the ball.[40] With Lefebvre sprawled on the grass in right field, McCovey walked in with the tie-breaking run. Roseboro got Drysdale out of the inning by throwing out Alou as he tried to steal second. Drysdale was removed for a pinch-hitter in the seventh inning.

Marichal went all the way to beat the Dodgers, 4–2, and even the series. He was now 19–5 for the season and an amazing 13–0 against the Dodgers at Candlestick Park. The Giants' win, coupled with the Pirates' loss to Bob Gibson in St. Louis, put San Francisco back in first place by a half-game.[41] The Dodgers were left two games behind in third place.

The rubber game of the series was played on Sunday afternoon, August 28. The assignment fell to Don Sutton, making his debut at Candlestick Park in front of a third straight turn-away crowd of 41,952. Gaylord Perry (20–3) went for the Giants. After winning eight games in a row, Perry had been bombed here four days before by the Reds.

Sutton came through with a clutch, complete-game, 5–2 win. The Dodgers pounded

Perry for 12 hits, including home runs by Willie Davis, Lefebvre, and Fairly. He had to pitch with runners on base in each of his eight innings.

A trouble-free series for the first two games nearly erupted in fireworks in this one. In the third inning, Sutton singled off Perry and then slid hard into Hal Lanier at second base to break up a double play. The next time up, Perry drilled Sutton in the left forearm with a fastball. In the fifth inning, Sutton sailed a fastball over Perry's head. A warning to both benches from plate umpire Augie Donatelli diffused the situation before it could get out of hand.[42]

After two straight no-decisions, Sutton squared his record at 11–11 with a six-hitter that clinched the series for the Dodgers and put them within one game of the lead. Gaylord Perry would win only one more game for the 1966 Giants.

	W	L	Pct.	GB
Pittsburgh	76	54	.585	—
San Francisco	76	54	.585	—
Los Angeles	74	54	.578	1

The crowds for the Dodgers-Giants series averaged 42,148. The next night at Candlestick Park, the Beatles made their last public appearance in front of approximately 25,000 fans. Attendance for the group's fourth U.S. tour had been depressed in the wake of John Lennon's incendiary remark that the Beatles were "now more popular than Jesus."[43]

Two-Day Debacle at Shea Stadium

On their way to a showdown with the Pirates in Pittsburgh, the Dodgers stopped in New York City for what should have been a combination breather/tune-up with a ninth-place Mets team that had lost five games in a row. Instead, in turned into a two-day debacle.

Claude Osteen pitched the August 29 opener against Bob Shaw. Osteen had gone ten straight starts without completing a game. The Dodgers hoped that he could reverse that trend against the worst-hitting team in the league and give the bullpen a rest. But he lasted for an inning and two thirds. Jim Hickman rocked him for a two-run double off the center field wall in the first inning. In the second, a two-out throwing error by Nate Oliver, playing his first major league game at third base for the injured John Kennedy, led to two unearned runs and Osteen's departure.[44] Bob Miller had to come in from the bullpen to get the last out. Down 4–0, the Dodgers never recovered.

The game, played on a humid night at Shea Stadium, nearly erupted in a brawl in the ninth inning. With the Dodgers down to their last out, Roseboro asked plate umpire Tom Gorman to examine the baseball after four straight pitches. Bob Shaw, who had a reputation for throwing a spitball, blew a fuse when a two-strike pitch was called a ball. He pushed his catcher, Jerry Grote, and sent him flying while trying to storm his way to home plate. Shaw was even further incensed when Roseboro rifled a single past him and into center field. Mets coach Whitey Herzog began to ride Roseboro unmercifully from the New York dugout. First base umpire Tony Venzon had to restrain Roseboro after he finally snapped and gestured to Herzog to come out and settle things on the field.[45] Shaw calmed down to strike out Lou Johnson to end the game without bloodshed. The 5–3 loss was a missed opportunity for the Dodgers. Since the Giants and Pirates both lost that night, a win would have put them back in first place by a single percentage point.

The next night, August 30, a crowd of 50,840 turned out to see what would be Sandy Koufax's last start at Shea Stadium. Tug McGraw drew the assignment for the Mets on his 22nd birthday. It was a year and four days since Koufax lost to the Mets for the first time in his career at the hands of the 21-year-old rookie McGraw. On this night, Wes Parker tagged McGraw for a two-run homer in the first inning, and Bob Friend had to relieve him before he could complete the second.

Koufax, with a 2–0 lead against the Mets, was usually a sure bet. But as he told reporters after the game, "I didn't have a thing."[46] Koufax lost his control in the second inning, walking three batters—including a bases-loaded walk to Eddie Bressoud that cut the Dodgers' lead to 2–1. Alston pulled him in the third inning after he gave up an RBI single to Ron Swoboda that put the Amazin's ahead, 4–2. Joe Moeller took over, only to give up a two-run double to Jerry Grote (both runs charged to Koufax) that increased the New York lead to 6–2. The Mets pummeled the Dodgers' bullpen for four more runs in a 10–4 route. Friend allowed four hits over the last 7⅔ innings—including a two-run pinch-hit homer by Wes Covington—for his sixth win.

Koufax's record was now 21–8. With five earned runs in two innings of work, his ERA jumped 15 points to 1.79. Before the Dodgers could get out of New York, they had slipped to two games behind the Giants and the Pirates.[47]

	W	L	Pct.	GB
Pittsburgh	77	55	.583	—
San Francisco	77	55	.583	—
Los Angeles	74	56	.569	2

Showdown at Forbes Field—Game 1

On the last day of August, the Dodgers began a crucial two-game series with the Pirates at Forbes Field. Drysdale (9–14) went up against 24-year-old right-hander Steve Blass (8–5). Drysdale held the Pirates scoreless for the first four innings and retired the first batter in the fifth before things began to unravel. Bob Bailey reached base on an infield single. Jim Pagliaroni blooped a single into left field. Blass hit a high chopper that died behind the mound. By the time Drysdale retrieved it, he had no play, and the bases were loaded. Matty Alou, the league's leading hitter, hit a shallow fly ball to left field that Lou Johnson caught for the second out. Drysdale was one strike away from getting out of the inning when Gene Alley hit a ground ball that glanced off Lefebvre's glove to score two runs. With many of the 31,036 Pirate fans waving "green weenies"[48] (rubber wieners painted green), the rally continued. Clemente bounced a ball up the middle to score the third run. After Stargell lined a single into right field to run to score the fourth Pittsburgh run, Drysdale was done. Bob Miller came in to strike out Donn Clendenon to end the inning.[49]

In the sixth inning, after Wills led off with a walk and Parker got on with an infield single, Willie Davis drove a Blass fastball into the upper deck in right field to cut the Pittsburgh lead to 4–3. Pittsburgh manager Harry Walker pulled Blass and brought in left-hander Billy O'Dell. Not only did O'Dell get the Pirates out of the sixth inning without any further damage, he held the Dodgers scoreless with the tying and winning runs on base in each of the last three innings.[50]

This 4–3 loss, in which the Dodgers blew so many chances, was a punch to the gut. At the end of play on August 31, the Dodgers were three games behind Pittsburgh and San Francisco. They were a flat 15–15 for the month. Sandy Koufax, after getting off to a 14–2 start through June, cooled off with a 3–3 July and a 4–3 August. When would the next elbow flare-up happen? Don Drysdale, with his 9–15 record compared to 18–11 a year ago at this stage, was still struggling with inconsistency. Claude Osteen had won only one game in his last nine starts. Hobbled by an injured right knee, Maury Wills hit .224 for the month and stole only two bases. Dodgers fans could not help but wonder whether it was over.

	W	L	Pct.	GB
Pittsburgh	78	55	.586	—
San Francisco	78	55	.586	—
Los Angeles	74	57	.565	3

The year after the Giants traded Matty Alou to Pittsburgh, he won the 1966 NL batting title with a .342 average.

That same day back in Los Angeles, an unusual jazz-rock-classical-blues band that called themselves The Doors finished recording their first album with Elektra Records. Ten days before, they had been fired as the house band at the Whiskey a Go Go on the Sunset Strip when singer Jim Morrison performed a profanity-laden version of their song, "The End."[51]

Three-Team NL Dog Fight
Round 2—September

Some days I can only throw fastballs without hurting, and then it's not as good a fast ball as before.[1]—Sandy Koufax, Dodger Stadium, September 14, 1966

Man, the Series is fun. It's the pennant race where the pressure is. You got to beat all those other teams.[2]—Jim Gilliam, Wrigley Field, September 23, 1966

Showdown at Forbes Field—Game 2

On September 1, the Dodgers played their last game of the season at Forbes Field. It was a must win. A loss would drop them four games behind Pittsburgh in the NL standings. Again, the responsibility fell on rookie Don Sutton, who was five years old when his opponent, Vernon Law, made his debut with the Pirates in 1950.

The game's first run was scored in the fourth inning when Jim Gilliam led off with a single and came around to score on a two-out triple into the left-center field gap by Jim Lefebvre. Sutton had a no-hitter until Law singled with one out in the sixth. Roberto Clemente, the league leader in runs batted in, drove in Law with a sharp single to center to tie the game at 1–1. Pitching against a background of oscillating green weenies, Sutton faced the minimum nine batters over the next three innings to keep the game deadlocked 1–1 at the end of regulation. The tenth inning would be a "game within a game."

Lou Johnson legged out an infield single to lead off the top of the tenth. Law, who had gone the first nine innings without walking a batter, walked both Jim Barbieri (pinch-hitting for Sutton) and Wes Parker to load the bases with one out. Pittsburgh manager Harry Walker brought in Pete Mikkelsen, who promptly walked Gilliam to force in the tie-breaking run. Willie Davis hit a blooper into right field in front of Clemente, who cut down Barbieri at home plate for the second out. A line shot up the middle by Ron Fairly scored two more runs to make it 4–1.

Walter Alston brought in Phil Regan to get the last three outs in the bottom of the tenth. But Regan was ripped for a single by Donn Clendenon and a two-run homer by Bob Bailey that cut the lead to 4–3. Ron Perranoski had to be rushed in to retire the .349-batting Manny Mota to close it out.

September 1 was a turning point. Instead of falling four games behind, the split at

Forbes Field kept the Dodgers within two games of the lead. They were able to win the second game without using Maury Wills, who began a much-needed four-game hiatus to rest his right knee. John Kennedy took over at shortstop; Gilliam back-filled at third base. The 37-year-old Devil came through with a 3-for-4 performance. He scored two of the team's four runs and drove one in himself.

That afternoon, the Mets beat Gaylord Perry and the Giants, 2–1, at Shea Stadium. For the fifth straight day, Pittsburgh and San Francisco remained deadlocked in a tie for first place.

	W	L	Pct.	GB
Pittsburgh	78	56	.582	—
San Francisco	78	56	.582	—
Los Angeles	75	57	.568	2

The ten-game road trip concluded with a weekend series in Cincinnati. In the Friday night opener on September 2, Claude Osteen and Bob Miller beat the Reds, 6–1 on a combined three-hitter. Osteen pitched six innings of three-hit ball before a groin pull forced him out of the game with a 4–1 lead. Bob Miller took over in the seventh inning and retired the last nine batters in a row to save Osteen's 14th win.[3] Fairly rocked Cincinnati starter Jim Maloney with a two-run homer in the first inning and drove in the Dodgers' sixth run on a fielder's choice in the eighth. The groin pull would cause Osteen to miss his next start. The win kept the Dodgers within two games of the lead.

Koufax's 22nd Victory Moves the Dodgers into Second Place

The next night Sandy Koufax, with help from Regan, beat the Reds, 7–3, to send the Dodgers back into second place after being stuck for 26 days in third. Laboring in the extreme humidity, Koufax narrowly survived the sixth inning. Lou Johnson threw out a runner at home plate for the third out to preserve a 5–3 lead.[4] Regan took over in the seventh and blanked the Reds on three hits for the last three innings to save Koufax's 22nd win. Reds starter Joe Nuxhall took the loss. It was the first time since 1960 that the Dodgers had beaten the 38-year-old left-hander at Crosley Field.

The Dodgers moved one percentage point ahead of the Giants, who lost that afternoon by one run to Larry Jaster and the Cardinals in St. Louis.[5]

	W	L	Pct.	GB
Pittsburgh	80	56	.588	—
Los Angeles	77	57	.575	2
San Francisco	78	58	.574	2

Don Drysdale pitched the final game of the series on Sunday afternoon, September 4. He gave up a two-run homer to Deron Johnson in the first inning and had to leave after completing the second inning when his "trick" left knee popped out again.[6] The game devolved into an offensive free-for-all. The Dodgers pounded Reds starter Sammy Ellis for five earned runs in the first three innings to get Drysdale off the hook with a no-decision. Four Dodgers pitchers gave up a total of 15 hits. Five Cincinnati pitchers gave up 13 hits and walked seven batters.

Poor Joe Nuxhall had to come in to pitch the eighth inning. After he walked Fairly,

Lefebvre, batting right-handed, hit a towering two-run homer over the left field wall to put the Dodgers in front, 8–3. In the bottom of the inning, Art Shamsky hit a three-run homer off Bob Miller to cut the lead to two runs. The Dodgers went on to win the game, 8–6, but not before Phil Regan struck out Chico Ruiz with the bases loaded in the bottom of the ninth to save it.

With the sweep in Cincinnati, the Dodgers completed a 6–4 road trip. As they headed for a final showdown with the Giants in Los Angeles, they were still only one percentage point ahead of San Francisco. That weekend, the Pirates swept the Cubs at Forbes Field to stay two games ahead of the pack.

	W	L	Pct.	GB
Pittsburgh	81	56	.591	—
Los Angeles	78	57	.578	2
San Francisco	79	58	.577	2

The Final Dodgers-Giants Series of the Koufax Era

The last Dodgers-Giants series of the Koufax Era began on Labor Day, September 5, before 54,769 fans at Dodger Stadium and a national television audience. Don Sutton (12–11) got the start against Gaylord Perry (20–5). Maury Wills was back at shortstop in the leadoff position after his four-day break. Alston kept the red-hot Devil, Jim Gilliam (9 for his last 18), at third base, batting second.

Hal Lanier's two-out solo home run off Sutton in the second inning put the Giants up, 1–0. In the top of the third, after getting the leadoff batter, Tito Fuentes, to fly out, Sutton had to leave the game with a strained muscle in his right forearm. Joe Moeller came in to retire the next two batters and blanked the Giants over the next three innings. Willie Davis tied the game, 1–1, with a solo homer off Perry in the fifth.

Bob Miller teamed with Phil Regan to form an outstanding right-hander duo in the Dodgers bullpen. Miller beat the Giants in the key Labor Day win of September 5, 1966.

In the bottom of the seventh inning, veteran left-hander Billy Hoeft, just activated after being signed five days before as the Giants' batting practice pitcher, walked three batters—including Parker on a 3–2 pitch to force in the deciding run. With two out in the bottom of the eighth, Willie Davis drove in the Dodgers' third run with a single and scored on Tommy Davis' double to make it 4–1.[7]

The Dodgers won the opener, 4–1. Bob Miller picked up his fourth victory in relief, and Phil Regan got his 17th save. Their fifth consecutive win left them a game and a half behind the Pirates, who split a Labor Day doubleheader with the Braves at Forbes Field. More ominously, this was the fourth consecutive game that a Dodgers starter had to leave prematurely due to a physical problem. After the game, Sutton's right arm was packed in ice and injected with cortisone. It would be 48 hours before the extent of his injury could be determined. A worried Alston told reporters, "This is the worst shape a pitching staff of mine has been in since 1955."[8]

	W	L	Pct.	GB
Pittsburgh	82	57	.590	—
Los Angeles	79	57	.581	1½
San Francisco	79	59	.572	2½

Claude Osteen was scheduled to go against Ray Sadecki the next night. But Osteen was scratched from the lineup 20 minutes before game-time when his pulled groin muscle prevented him from warming up sufficiently. Drysdale would have to make an emergency start with only one full day of rest. And the Giants shelled him unmercifully for 11 hits. Tito Fuentes put Drysdale in a 3–0 hole with a bases-loaded double off the left field wall in the second inning. He left with one out in the sixth to a chorus of angry boos from the crowd of 52,360.[9]

Sadecki came through with a three-hit, 6–0 shutout to even the series. It was his first shutout in two years. The Dodgers could manage just three singles and did not advance a runner beyond first base. The loss made Drysdale 9–16 for the year—0–4 against the Giants. The Dodgers remained a game and a half behind the Pirates, a single percentage point ahead of the Giants in second place.

	W	L	Pct.	GB
Pittsburgh	82	58	.586	—
Los Angeles	79	58	.577	1½
San Francisco	80	59	.576	1½

The Dodgers had a golden opportunity to win the series with Koufax on the mound for the September 7 finale. They had a record crowd of 54,993 at Dodger Stadium. They didn't have to face Juan Marichal (21–5). By a gift of the Giants' rotation, Marichal did not make an appearance in the series. Instead, Bob Bolin (8–10) would go for San Francisco. The stars were aligned for the Dodgers. But it didn't happen.

Koufax struck out the first two batters he faced and then walked Willie Mays on a 3–2 pitch. Jim Ray Hart exploited the opening with a tremendous blast over the back fence of the Dodgers' bullpen to put the Giants ahead, 2–0. It was the first ball to clear the bullpen in the six-year history of Dodger Stadium. Koufax settled down and held the Giants to four singles over the next six innings before leaving the game for a pinch-hitter in the seventh inning with the Dodgers behind, 2–1.

In the bottom of the eighth, Willie Davis led off with a pop fly to short center field that fell in between

On September 7, 1966, a prodigious home run by Jim Ray Hart off Sandy Koufax at Dodger Stadium dropped the Dodgers into third place.

Fuentes, Ollie Brown, and Jesus Alou. Still the fastest man in baseball, the "3-Dog" converted a bloop into a triple. Tommy Davis tied the game, 2–2, with a pinch-hit sacrifice fly.[10]

The game went to the 12th inning tied, 2–2. After Joe Moeller retired the first two batters, Alston ordered him to walk Mays intentionally to prevent him from beating them with a home run. Rookie outfielder Frank Johnson, who was called up from Phoenix only the day before, lined a hit into right-center. Mays advanced to third base and made a wide turn. When second baseman Lefebvre hesitated after taking the relay throw from the outfield, Mays (still limping from a strained groin muscle he sustained in the opener) surprised everyone by breaking for the plate. Lefebvre's throw beat Mays, but his aggressive slide jarred the ball loose from Roseboro. Mays was called safe by plate umpire Tony Venzon, despite an irate Roseboro's contention that Mays had intentionally kicked the ball out of his mitt. The Giants were now ahead, 3–2, and Roseboro was charged with an error on the play.[11]

Roseboro had a chance to atone for his "error" in the bottom of the 12th. With a walk and two singles, the Dodgers loaded the bases with two out against Frank Linzy. But Linzy got Roseboro on a comebacker to end it.

But for his one mistake to Hart in the first inning, Koufax could have clinched the series two games to one with his 23rd victory. Instead, the Dodgers fell back into third place—albeit by a single percentage point behind the Giants. However, they remained a game and a half behind as the Pirates lost their third straight game to the Braves that night in Pittsburgh. With a no-decision, Koufax's record stayed at 22–8. The Dodgers and Giants ended their 18-game season series deadlocked at nine wins apiece. The Koufax Era (1955–1966) ended with the Giants clinging to a one game advantage, 124–123.

	W	L	Pct.	GB
Pittsburgh	82	59	.582	—
San Francisco	81	59	.579	½
Los Angeles	79	59	.572	1½

Dodgers Shut Out the Astros Four Games in a Row to Retake First Place

The Dodgers' pitching staff shut out the Astros in all four games of a weekend series at Dodger Stadium to take over sole possession of first place.

On Friday night, September 9, Claude Osteen came within three infield singles of a perfect game in his 7–0 shutout of the Astros. It was a hopeful sign, since Osteen had to skip his last start after being forced out of the September 2 game in Cincinnati with a strained groin muscle. He was masterful on this night, throwing only 89 pitches—62 for strikes. He was behind in the count on only one batter. The Dodgers pounded Houston starter Bob Bruce and four relievers for 14 hits, including four run-producing doubles.[12]

The next afternoon, Don Drysdale, with his left leg wrapped from ankle to thigh to keep his knee from popping out, blanked the Astros for the first eight innings on three singles. Houston left-hander Mike Cuellar matched him with his own six-hitter. Drysdale was relieved by Phil Regan with one out in the top of the ninth after walking Joe Morgan and Rusty Staub. It took Regan one pitch to get Chuck Harrison to hit into an inning-ending double play.

The game went to extra innings as a scoreless tie. With Cuellar still pitching for the Astros, Wills led off the bottom of the tenth with a single. Gilliam sacrificed him to second. Willie Davis advanced Wills to third with a ground out. Al Ferrara, who had been swinging a bat in the tunnel since Wills got on board, pinch-hit for Regan. Ferrara ended it with a walk-off single to left field.[13] The Vulture, Regan, picked up his 13th victory. Hard-luck Drysdale got a no-decision after throwing eight and one-third scoreless innings.[14]

Up at Candlestick Park, the Cubs trounced Gaylord Perry and the Giants, 12–3.[15] In Pittsburgh, the Pirates blew a three-run lead in the ninth inning in a 6–5 loss to Bob Gibson and the Cardinals.[16] The Dodgers thus closed to within a half-game of the lead.

Koufax Lifts the Dodgers into First Place with a Six-Hit Shutout

The four-game series concluded on September 11 with a Sunday doubleheader in front of 42,978 fans at Dodger Stadium. In the first game, Sandy Koufax had a rematch with Houston's 19-year-old phenom, Larry Dierker, who beat him here back on June 14. Koufax came through with a six-hit, 4–0 shutout to send the Dodgers into first place. Two walks and two errors led to three unearned Dodgers runs in the fifth inning, giving Koufax an insurmountable 4–0 lead. Dierker was gone after six innings.

In the second game, Joe Moeller got the start against 22-year-old left-hander Chris Zachary. Moeller had a two-hit shutout through five innings before his back stiffened. Bob Miller took over in the sixth. With two out in the seventh, Roseboro broke up a scoreless tie with a pinch-hit, RBI single to finish off Zachary. Regan struck out Bob Aspromonte with the tying run on second in the ninth inning to close it out. With the combined 1–0 shutout, the Dodgers completed a four-game shutout sweep of the Astros.[17]

That day at Forbes Field, the Cardinals came from behind to beat Bob Veale, 4–3, on Tim McCarver's two-run single in the eighth inning. It was Pittsburgh's fifth loss in its last six games.[18] Though Bob Bolin shut out the Cubs, 2–0, in the second game of a doubleheader at Candlestick Park to give the Giants a split, they still lost a half-game in the standings.[19] For the first time since August 7—when they led Pittsburgh for 24 hours by a single percentage point—the Dodgers took over sole possession of first place.

	W	L	Pct.	GB
Los Angeles	83	59	.585	—
Pittsburgh	83	61	.576	1
San Francisco	82	62	.569	2

The Dodgers had two games with the Mets before a crucial three-game showdown with the Pirates. Twenty-one-year-old Don Sutton and 22-year-old Tug McGraw met in the September 12 opener. Sutton had skipped his last start after straining a flexor muscle in his forearm in Cincinnati on September 5. On this Monday night at Dodger Stadium, he pitched four so-so innings before leaving for a pinch-hitter in the fifth with the Dodgers behind, 2–1. Ron Perranoski took over and shut out the Mets over the next four innings with seven strikeouts—including six in a row in the fifth and sixth innings to tie an NL record for a relief pitcher. Tommy Davis knocked McGraw out of the game with a two-run single in the bottom of the fifth inning that put the Dodgers ahead, 3–2. It was the last run of the game. Regan came in with one out in the ninth to save the win for Perranoski. With the Giants and Pirates idle, the Dodgers picked up a half-game on both teams.[20]

	W	L	Pct.	GB
Los Angeles	84	59	.587	—
Pittsburgh	83	61	.576	1½
San Francisco	82	62	.569	2½

The Sutton Bombshell

When Don Sutton woke up the next morning, his right arm was so stiff he could hardly move it. Upon informing the team, he was sent immediately to Dr. Robert Kerlan, the team's orthopedic specialist. Dr. Kerlan determined that Sutton had suffered a second strain to his flexor muscle and ordered him to not touch a baseball for at least ten days. Dr. Kerlan warned that it would be difficult for Sutton—who already had 12 wins and 202 strikeouts in 33 starts—to get back in good enough shape to pitch again that season.[21] Kerlan delivered the news to Buzzie Bavasi minutes before the Dodgers took the field that evening for the concluding game of the series with the Mets.[22]

Jolted by the Sutton bombshell, the Dodgers pulled together for an 8–3 win over New York, their sixth in a row. Sweet Lou Johnson stepped up to deliver two home runs: a solo homer off Mets starter Bob Friend that tied the game, 2–2, in the fourth inning and a three-run homer off Jack Hamilton that broke the game open in the fifth.[23] Claude Osteen gave Alston six solid innings before giving way to Bob Miller, who held the Mets hitless for the last three innings to save Osteen's 16th victory. Dick Schofield, who joined the team two days before to become the Dodgers' fifth switch-hitter, played third base, contributed four hits.

Since the Pirates and Giants had already posted wins before the game at Dodger Stadium concluded, the NL standings remained unchanged.

With 18 games to go and Sutton's future availability in doubt, Alston would have to find a right-hander to fill the gap in the rotation. His choices were limited: Joe Moeller, with his unpredictable back, or 22-year-old Bill Singer. Moeller, who had to have his back heavily taped every time he pitched, had made only six starts so far in the season.[24] Singer, recently called up from Spokane, had made two major league starts—both in the last week of the 1964 season.

September 14 was an off-day for both the Dodgers and Pirates. At Candlestick Park, the Phillies' premier right-hander, Jim Bunning, shut out the Giants, 2–0, to put them three games behind. Hard-luck Gaylord Perry went down to his fifth straight defeat despite pitching eight innings of four-hit ball with 11 strikeouts.

A Missed Chance to Bury the Pirates

The final three-game series with the Pirates began September 15 before 50,559 fans at Dodger Stadium, Don Drysdale against Vernon Law. The Pirates were the top-hitting team in baseball with five regulars batting over .300: Matty Alou .350; Roberto Clemente .327; Willie Stargell .318; Gene Alley .303; and Donn Clendenon .302. And if that wasn't enough, super reserve Manny Mota was batting .342, though he didn't have enough at-bats to qualify for the batting title.[25]

Law never made it out of the first inning as the Dodgers exploded for five runs. Drysdale, who had not won in his last six starts, retired the first nine batters he faced. In fielding Gene Michael's comebacker to end the third inning, he fell so hard on his trick left knee that the impact split the rubberized bandage the trainers had devised to protect it. A single by Alou and a double by Stargell gave the Pirates a run in the fourth.

With his left knee almost completely numb from the fall in the third inning, Drysdale took a 5–1 lead to the ninth.[26] He got the first two batters to ground out and then hit a wall. Clemente hit a slow curve ball into the left field pavilion. Stargell followed that by hitting a high changeup into the right field pavilion to cut the Dodgers' lead to 5–3. Phil Regan had to be brought in from the bullpen to get the final out. Drysdale finally got his tenth win, an 8⅔-inning five-hitter with no walks. The Dodgers increased their lead to 2½ games.

	W	L	Pct.	GB
Los Angeles	86	59	.593	—
Pittsburgh	84	62	.575	2½
San Francisco	84	63	.571	3

Sandy Koufax beat Bob Veale and the Pirates, 5–1, the next night before a capacity crowd of 54,510. Lou Johnson gave Koufax all the runs he needed with a towering three-run home run that landed in the lower box seats in left field in the third inning. The home run finished off Veale.

Koufax appeared to be laboring at times. With one out in the seventh, he found himself with the bases loaded after he walked two batters and gave up a bunt single to Jose Pagan. The next batter, Gene Alley, got the Pirates on the board with a sacrifice fly—a solid line drive caught by Wes Parker in center field. With runners at first and third, Ron Fairly got Koufax out of the inning with a tumbling one-hand catch of Mota's line shot in right field. The play saved two runs and kept Koufax in the game.[27]

Koufax retired the last six batters, but uncharacteristically without striking out anyone: four on fly outs and two on groundouts. For the game, he had to make 131 pitches—44 were out of the strike zone.[28] It was becoming more and more apparent that his strikeouts were declining. He struck out only five on this night and had averaged 4.8 in his last six starts.

The win extended the Dodgers' winning streak to eight straight—their longest of 1966—and their lead to 3½ games. The Pirates had now lost seven of their last nine. That night at Candlestick Park, the Giants' bullpen coughed up three runs in the ninth inning in a 5–4 loss to the Mets that dropped San Francisco four games behind.

	W	L	Pct.	GB
Los Angeles	87	59	.596	—
Pittsburgh	84	63	.571	3½
San Francisco	84	64	.568	4

The Dodgers had a chance to bury the Pirates by winning the series finale on Saturday afternoon, September 17. A series sweep in Los Angeles could prove fatal to Pittsburgh's chances, since it would put them 4½ games behind with 14 games left in the season.

With Sutton on the shelf, Alston had to go with Joe Moeller (2–3) against Tommie

Sisk (10–3). In addition to his six spot starts, Moeller had made 22 relief appearances and came into the game with a 2.42 earned run average. But Moeller couldn't come through for Alston on this day. He left after four innings with the score tied, 2–2. He walked three batters and was tagged for a solo home run by Willie Stargell. After that, the Dodgers' bullpen—considered the best in the league—disintegrated. The Pirates pounded Miller, Regan, and Perranoski for seven more runs. The deciding blow was a three-run homer by Donn Clendenon off Regan in the seventh inning that erased a 3–2 Dodgers lead and put the Pirates in front, 5–3. The Pirates destroyed Perranoski with four runs in the eighth on their way to a 9–5 victory, thus ending the Dodgers' eight-game win streak. Vern Law, the losing pitcher in the series opener, came back to pick up a win in an inning and a third of relief.

By salvaging the final game of the series, Pittsburgh was able to stay 2½ games behind the Dodgers in second place. Just as they did with the Giants, the Dodgers ended their 18-game season series with the Pirates dead even at 9–9. In San Francisco, the Giants beat the Mets, 6–4, on Willie McCovey's third home run of the game—a two-run walk-off in the tenth inning to move back to within three games of the lead.

	W	L	Pct.	GB
Los Angeles	87	60	.592	—
Pittsburgh	85	63	.574	2½
San Francisco	85	64	.570	3

The last homestand of the season concluded with a four-game series against the Phillies. At the same time in San Francisco, the Pirates and Giants locked horns in what the Dodgers hoped would be a mutually destructive battle for second place.

On September 18, 1966, at Candlestick Park, the Giants' struggling right-hander, Gaylord Perry, lost his sixth straight game, 3–1, to the Pirates. Perry was 12–1 at the All-Star break and 20–2 on August 20.

Larry Jackson shut out the Dodgers, 4–0, in the opening game of the series on Sunday, September 18. Philadelphia snapped Claude Osteen's three-game winning streak. He was knocked out of the game in the third inning before he could get a single out. Young Bill Singer took over and balked in the fourth Phillies run. Rain halted the game for seven minutes at the start of the ninth inning. But play was resumed and Jackson completed his shutout. The Dodgers continued their perfect record of 726 consecutive games without a rainout in nine years on the West Coast.[29]

Meanwhile, in front of a sellout crowd of 41,981 at Candlestick, Gaylord Perry lost his sixth straight game, 3–1, to Woody Fryman and the Pirates. Fryman pitched a complete-game four-hitter. Only a leadoff home run by Tito Fuentes in the bottom of the ninth prevented a shutout. The Pirates closed to within a game and a half of the Dodgers.[30]

	W	L	Pct.	GB
Los Angeles	87	61	.588	—
Pittsburgh	86	63	.577	1½
San Francisco	85	65	.567	3

On Monday night, September 19, Don Drysdale pitched a complete-game five-hitter to beat Jim Bunning, 6–1. Again, Drysdale was sharp. He allowed only five singles, walked no one, and retired the last 12 batters in succession. Lou Johnson hit two home runs and drove in three runs against the great Bunning. Johnson had now hit five home runs in his last six games.[31]

That day at Candlestick Park, the Pirates broke open a 1–1 tie with five runs in 11th inning on a solo home by Clemente and a grand slam by Bob Bailey—both off Giants reliever Frank Linzy. Willie Mays had sent the game into extra innings with a pinch-hit RBI single with two out in the bottom of the ninth.[32] As the Dodgers and Pirates stayed a game and half apart, San Francisco fell four games behind.

	W	L	Pct.	GB
Los Angeles	88	61	.591	—
Pittsburgh	87	63	.580	1½
San Francisco	85	66	.563	4

The next night, Koufax won his 25th game in an 11–1 laugher against Chris Short. But Koufax was not overpowering. He scattered five singles, walked three batters, and struck out a modest six. Still, only a tainted run in the fourth inning kept him from pitching a shutout. Johnny Callison singled, stole second, and came all the way home when Torborg's throw hit the second base bag and skidded into shallow left-center field. The Dodgers broke the game open with six runs in the fifth inning to knock out Short. The big blow was a three-run double by Fairly off 38-year-old Philadelphia reliever Bob Buhl.[33] When asked by reporters after the game how his arm felt, Koufax told them, "With a 10-run lead a dead man's arm feels good."[34]

That night at Candlestick Park, the Giants lost their third straight game to the Pirates as Vern Law shut them out, 6–0, to drop them five games behind.[35]

	W	L	Pct.	GB
Los Angeles	89	61	.593	—
Pittsburgh	88	63	.583	1½
San Francisco	85	67	.559	5

After beating Bunning and Short, the Dodgers had a chance to win the series and expand their lead by beating 21-year-old Rick Wise in the concluding game on September 21. Instead, young Wise beat Claude Osteen, 3–2, to give the Phillies a split. An unearned run in the sixth inning cost Osteen his 17th victory. With one out and Dick Groat on first, Dick Schofield fielded Harvey Kuenn's grounder but threw it away trying to force Groat at second. Groat subsequently scored on Tony Taylor's squeeze bunt to break a 2–2 tie. The Dodgers finished their 16-game home stand at 11–5.[36]

That afternoon at Candlestick Park, the Giants were about to fall six games behind with eight games to play when they entered the bottom of the ninth down, 5–3, with Juan Marichal on the hook for the loss. But Tom Haller tied the game with a two-run homer, and Marichal hit a walk-off solo homer—both off Elroy Face. It was just the second home run of Marichal's career.[37] As a result, the Dodgers and Pirates stood pat, and the Giants climbed back to within four games of the lead.

	W	L	Pct.	GB
Los Angeles	89	62	.589	—
Pittsburgh	88	64	.579	1½
San Francisco	86	67	.562	4

The Dodgers closed out their home season with a record of 53–28 (.654) at Dodger Stadium. They would have to play the final 11 games on the road, beginning with a four-game weekend series with Leo Durocher's tenth-place Cubs in Wrigley Field.

Thursday, September 22, was an off-day for both the Dodgers and the Giants. In Atlanta, the Braves pounded Woody Fryman and the Pirates, 14–1. As a result, the idle Dodgers picked up a half-game on the Pirates. They now led Pittsburgh by two games and the Giants by four going into the weekend series in Chicago.

	W	L	Pct.	GB
Los Angeles	89	62	.589	—
Pittsburgh	88	65	.575	2
San Francisco	86	67	.562	4

The Orioles Clinch the American League Pennant

That day at Municipal Stadium in Kansas City, the Orioles clinched the American League pennant by beating the Athletics, 6–1. Baltimore's 20-year-old, ace right-hander, Jim Palmer, pitched a five-hit complete game for his 15th victory. Frank Robinson, closing in on a Triple Crown, accounted for four of the Orioles' runs with two doubles and a single. The win gave Baltimore a ten-game lead over the Detroit Tigers with nine games to go, thereby eliminating the Tigers. The Orioles moved into first place on June 14 and were never displaced. The Orioles were now 29 games ahead of the tenth-place New York Yankees, who would finish in the cellar for the first time since 1912.

It was the first pennant for a Baltimore franchise since an Orioles team won three consecutive National League flags in 1894, 1895, and 1896. The 1966 Orioles had been in existence since 1954, when the St. Louis Browns were moved to Baltimore. The Browns won their only pennant in 1944, but lost an all-St. Louis World Series to the Cardinals in six games.[38]

The Final Road Trip

Friday, September 23—
Drysdale and the Vulture Sweep a Double Header

The weekend series in Chicago began with a Friday afternoon doubleheader on September 23. Don Drysdale went up against 37-year-old Curt Simmons in the opener. Drysdale, who was 0–3 against the Cubs for the season, threw a brilliant, eight-hit, 4–0 shutout for his third straight victory. It was a dominating performance with only one Chicago runner advancing past second base. The Dodgers disposed of Simmons in the third inning. Drysdale's RBI single against reliever Bill Hands made it 4–0.

In the second game, Don Sutton made his first start since re-injuring his arm on September 12. He gave up one unearned run on Don Kessinger's two-out RBI single in the second inning. Alston took him out after four innings with the score tied, 1–1. With three walks, it was evident that his control was off. After the game, Roseboro observed that his fastball lacked its usual velocity.[39] The Dodgers won the game, 4–2, on Roseboro's 425-foot, two-run homer onto Sheffield Avenue in the ninth inning. Vulture Regan held the Cubs hitless over the last 2⅔ innings to pick up his 13th consecutive victory, all in relief. Regan's record was now 14–1, his earned run average 1.62.

That day in Atlanta, Bob Veale shut out the Braves, 3–0, with 12 strikeouts.[40] But with the doubleheader sweep, the Dodgers increased their lead to 2½ games over Pittsburgh and to five over San Francisco. The magic number was now seven.

	W	L	Pct.	GB
Los Angeles	91	62	.595	—
Pittsburgh	89	65	.578	2½
San Francisco	86	67	.562	5

Saturday, September 24—
Ferguson Arthur Jenkins, Ace

The next afternoon, Joe Moeller pitched the third game of the series against Fergie Jenkins. By now Durocher had made the rookie, Jenkins, a regular member of the starting rotation, after spending the first five months in the bullpen. And Ferguson Arthur Jenkins, from Chatham, Ontario, was magnificent on this day at Wrigley Field. He shut out the Dodgers, 4–0, on four hits—the first of 49 shutouts in a storied 19-year career. Moeller was charged with the loss after lasting only four innings.[41]

In Atlanta, the Pirates came from behind with five runs in the seventh inning to beat the Braves, 8–6. Roberto Clemente's two-run homer was the dagger that broke a 6–6 tie in the seventh. The Pirates cut the Dodgers' lead to a game and a half.[42] At the Astrodome in Houston, the Giants beat the Astros, 9–5, with their own five-run outburst in the 13th inning to stay four games back with seven games to play.[43]

	W	L	Pct.	GB
Los Angeles	91	63	.591	—
Pittsburgh	90	65	.581	1½
San Francisco	87	67	.565	4

Sunday, September 25—
Koufax and the 20-Year-Old College Kid

In the Sunday afternoon finale, the Dodgers expected to clinch the series with Sandy Koufax (25–8) on the mound against the Cubs' 20-year-old college student/pitcher, Ken Holtzman (10–15). However, Koufax again had trouble getting loose in the first inning. He walked the leadoff batter, Don Kessinger, on four pitches. Glenn Beckert followed with a line drive over third base that skidded off the brick wall next to the Cubs bullpen and into the left field corner. By the time Tommy Davis pulled the baseball out of the ivy, Kessinger had scored on a triple by Beckert. Koufax settled down to strike out Billy Williams and got Ron Santo on a comebacker. It looked like he was out of the inning when Ernie Banks lofted a routine pop fly behind second base. But it was evident to everyone in the ballpark that Lefebvre was having trouble with the wind blowing off

The Cubs' 20-year-old college student/pitcher, Ken Holtzman, beat Sandy Koufax, 2–1, on September 25, 1966, at Wrigley Field. Dick Schofield broke up Holtzman's no-hitter with a single in the ninth inning.

Lake Michigan, as he kept drifting and drifting to his left. When the ball came down, it struck the heel of his glove and popped out for an error as Beckert scored to make it 2–0.

Holtzman was brilliant, pitching against his idol, Sandy Koufax, in front of a crowd of 21,659 that included several members of his family from St. Louis.[44] He had a no-hitter as he took the 2–0 lead to the ninth inning. If not for a walk to Dick Schofield in the second, it would have been an eight-inning perfect game. And it was Schofield who broke up the no-hitter with a leadoff single—a bouncer over the mound that ticked off Beckert's glove as it rolled into center field. Al Ferrara drew a walk pinch-hitting for Roseboro. Alston sent in Willie Crawford to run for Ferrara and Jim Gilliam to hit for Koufax, with instructions to bunt both runners into scoring position. Gilliam was one of the best bunters on the team. He fouled off two attempts and then looked at a called third strike on a pitch that he argued vehemently with plate umpire Tony Venzon was above the strike zone. Wills kept it going with a sharp single up the middle to score Schofield and send Crawford to third. With Holtzman on the ropes, and Bob Hendley and Bill Hands warming up in earnest in the bullpen, Willie Davis tied into a 0–2 fast ball and lined it right at Beckert. Beckert ran the ball over to first base to easily double up Wills, who was attempting to steal second on the pitch. The game ended so suddenly that the crowd was stunned for a moment before giving Holtzman a thunderous standing ovation.[45]

It was a bitter defeat for the Dodgers, as they could only split the four games with a tenth-place team—the first team to finish below the New York Mets. Koufax lost his ninth game despite giving up only four hits in eight innings. The unearned run on Lefebvre's error in the first inning proved decisive. The amazing Holtzman pitched a complete-game two-hitter for his 11th victory. The next day he returned to the University of Illinois at Urbana-Champaign to begin his senior year as an English Literature major.

Since the Pirates and Giants both lost, the Dodgers lost no ground. They left Chicago in the same position they were in when they arrived: a game and a half ahead of the Pirates. These were three days in the Windy City full of sound and fury, signifying nothing.

	W	L	Pct.	GB
Los Angeles	91	64	.587	—
Pittsburgh	90	66	.577	1½
San Francisco	87	68	.561	4

Monday, September 26—
Osteen Beats Bob Gibson

The next night in St. Louis, the Dodgers opened a four-game series with the Cardinals by beating Bob Gibson for the fourth straight time, 6–3, to expand their lead to two and a half games. Claude Osteen won his 17th game with help from Phil Regan, who shut out the Cardinals over the last three and one-third innings for his 21st save.

Ron Fairly rocked Gibson with a two-run homer in the first inning. Alston got a scare in the seventh with the Dodgers trying to hold onto 5–3 lead. With two out and the tying runs on, Orlando Cepeda hit a Regan pitch 430 feet into the upper deck in left field—just foul. On the next pitch, Regan got Cepeda to ground into a force play to end the threat.[46] Lou Johnson hit his 17th home run in the eighth inning off Cardinals reliever Ron Piche to make it 6–3, Los Angeles.

In the clubhouse after the game, the Dodgers huddled around the radio and heard the Phillies beat the Pirates, 5–4, in Philadelphia on a two-out, bases-loaded single by John Briggs in the bottom of the 11th inning. Jim Bunning, who came in from the bullpen to pitch the top of the 11th, got credit for his 19th victory. It was his first win as a relief pitcher since 1957 as a member of the Detroit Tigers.[47]

	W	L	Pct.	GB
Los Angeles	92	64	.590	—
Pittsburgh	90	67	.573	2½
San Francisco	88	68	.564	4

Tuesday, September 27—
Drysdale Shuts Out Cardinals on Four Hits

Don Drysdale and Ray Washburn pitched the second game of the series on Tuesday night, September 27. Drysdale came into the game seeking his fourth win in a row after a drought of three losses and three no-decisions in six starts from August 22 to September 10 that had sunk his record to a dismal 9–16. On this night in St. Louis–in the home stretch of the pennant race–he came through with his second straight shutout, a four-hit, 2–0 masterpiece in which he had to make only 82 pitches. Ron Fairly's solo homer off Ray Washburn in the second inning decided it. The win increased the Dodgers' lead to three games over the idle Pirates with five games to go.

In Atlanta, the Giants' captain, Willie Mays, hit his 36th homer and drove in four runs to keep them alive with a 6–3, come-from-behind win. San Francisco remained four games behind with four games to go. But if, by winning a makeup game in Cincinnati on Monday, October 3, they ended the season tied with the Dodgers, they could force a third Dodgers-Giants playoff series.

The magic numbers for the Dodgers were now three against the Pirates and two against the Giants.

	W	L	Pct.	GB
Los Angeles	93	64	.592	—
Pittsburgh	90	67	.573	3
San Francisco	89	68	.567	4

Wednesday, September 28—
The Larry Jaster Enigma ver. 5.0

The evening of September 28, Walter Alston gave Don Sutton another try in the third game against a reeling Cardinals team that had now lost eight games in a row.[48] Unfortunately, Sutton had to go up against Larry Jaster. Sutton held the Cardinals scoreless for the first three innings on one hit—a double by Curt Flood in the first. In the fourth inning, Flood led off with a ground ball to third base that Dick Schofield booted for an error. Sutton issued his only walk of the game to Tim McCarver but steadied himself to strike out the dangerous Cepeda, and got Mike Shannon to ground into a force play. When Sutton got ahead in the count, 1–2, to Ed Spiezio, it looked like he would get out of the inning. But the .224-hitting Spiezio lined the next pitch into the left field corner to score both Flood and McCarver with the only runs of the game.[49]

Sutton left the game for a pinch-hitter in the fifth inning. Bob Miller and Ron Perranoski held the Cardinals scoreless the rest of the way on two hits. But it wasn't good enough. The remarkable Jaster shut out the Dodgers for the fifth consecutive time: 2–0, on four hits. The last pitcher to shut out a team five times in one year was Grover Cleveland Alexander of the Phillies, who shut out Cincinnati five times in 1916. Larry Jaster had now shut out the Dodgers for 46 consecutive innings on 24 hits, going back to September 17, 1965. All 24 hits were singles.

This was Don Sutton's last appearance of his rookie year. He finished with a record of 12–12, 209 strikeouts, and a 2.99 earned run average.

In the seventh inning, Lou Brock stole his 73rd base of the season. He would end Maury Wills' run of six straight years as the major league leader in stolen bases. Hobbled by his bad right knee, Wills had stolen only two bases in his last 25 games.

Jaster's historic performance threw the NL pennant race into a scramble with four days left. Coupled with a doubleheader sweep by the Pirates in Philadelphia, the Dodgers' lead was cut in half: from three games to a game and a half.[50] The magic numbers were still three against the Pirates and two against the Giants who beat the Braves in Atlanta.

	W	L	Pct.	GB
Los Angeles	93	65	.589	—
Pittsburgh	92	67	.579	1½
San Francisco	90	68	.570	3

September 29 was a travel day for the Pirates and Giants. Those two teams would meet in Pittsburgh for a do-or-die, three-game weekend series to close out the season. That night, it would be up to Sandy Koufax to win the series in St. Louis.

Thursday, September 29—
Koufax Wins His 26th to Clinch the Series in St. Louis

Koufax (25–9) and Al Jackson (13–14) met in the series finale at Busch Stadium the night of September 29. The Dodgers pecked away at Jackson for runs in the second and fifth innings on RBI singles by Parker and Willie Davis. With his elusive curveball working again,[51] Koufax had a two-hit, 2–0 shutout with ten strikeouts through the first six innings. Curt Flood led off the seventh with a home run to cut the lead to 2–1.

Koufax took the 2–1 lead to the bottom of the ninth inning. He struck out the first two batters to give him a total of 13 in the game. After the pesky Flood doubled, Alston came out to the mound and told Koufax to put the winning run on base by walking Cepeda and pitch instead to Mike Shannon. The gamble paid off. Koufax got Shannon to fly out to Willie Davis in center field on a 2–1 pitch to end the game.[52]

Sandy Koufax's 26th win was of immense importance. A loss would have cut the Dodgers' lead to one game with three left to play, setting up the possibility of an emergency start by Koufax on less than two days' rest.[53] Instead, the Dodgers were able to take two-game lead to Philadelphia for the final weekend series. The win reduced the Dodgers' magic numbers to two against the Pirates and one against the Giants. With 13 strikeouts, Koufax raised his season total to 307. He thus became the first pitcher in major league history to record 300 strikeouts in three seasons.

	W	L	Pct.	GB
Los Angeles	94	65	.591	—
Pittsburgh	92	67	.579	2
San Francisco	90	68	.570	3½

17

The Last Weekend

Who cares about Baltimore? It's going to take us a few days to get over this.[1]—Jim Lefebvre, post-game clubhouse, Connie Mack Stadium, October 2, 1966

Friday, September 30—Bill White Delivers a Dagger

Claude Osteen (17–13) opened the series at Connie Mack Stadium in Philadelphia against the Phillies' big left-hander, Chris Short (18–10). While the Dodgers had been beaten twice in the last week by left-handers, Holtzman and Jaster, and they had lost five out of six to Short in 1965, they had beaten him three out of four times so far this season.[2] The scoreboard showed that the game between the Giants and the Pirates had been rained out in Pittsburgh. The Dodgers could thus increase their lead to two and a half games with a win.

After battling Short to a scoreless tie for the first three innings, Osteen began to fall apart in the fourth. The first three batters singled to put the Phillies up, 1–0. With one out, Callison lined out to Lou Johnson in right field to score a second run. Bob Uecker and Short followed with line-drive singles, but Willie Davis bailed out Osteen by gunning down 36-year-old Harvey Kuenn at the plate to end the rally.

Osteen was on a short leash, having pitched only one complete game in his last ten starts. Already down, 2–0, after four innings, Alston took him out for a pinch-hitter in the fifth. In that inning, the Dodgers got a run back on a run-scoring groundout by Lou Johnson. Bob Miller took over for Osteen and held the Phillies scoreless for the next two innings.

Perranoski came in to pitch the bottom of the seventh with Philadelphia still leading, 2–1. He made the mistake of walking the leadoff batter, John Briggs.[3] Cookie Rojas sacrificed him to second, and a groundout to the right side by Groat moved him to third. The dangerous Richie Allen, with 40 home runs and 118 runs batted in, was next. Perranoski walked Allen intentionally to pitch to the left-handed-batting Bill White, who had entered the game as a pinch-hitter in the sixth inning. Alston conferred at length at the mound with Perranoski about what to do if Allen tried to steal second. Alston returned to the dugout, and White bombed Perranoski's next pitch 425 feet into the right field seats for a devastating three-run homer to open up a 5–1 Philadelphia lead. It was only the fourth home run Perranoski had given up against a left-handed batter in his six-year career. William DeKova White would never hit another home run against Ron Perranoski.

Short went to the ninth with the 5–1 lead. He walked the first two batters, Schofield and Parker—his fifth and sixth walks of the game. Both runners moved up on a groundout by Roseboro. Short got pinch-hitter Al Ferrara to ground out, with Schofield scoring on the play. Wills singled in Parker to cut the lead to 5–3. Willie Davis doubled to put the tying runs on second and third. Acting Phillies manager Peanuts Lowry (Gene Mauch had been ejected in the sixth inning by home plate umpire Shag Crawford), rushed to the mound to ask Short how he felt. When Short told him, "I feel real strong,"[4] Lowry kept him in to pitch to Lou Johnson. Short staggered in by getting Johnson on a pop fly to Tony Taylor behind second base on a 3–1 pitch to end it. In the clubhouse after the game, Short told Gene Mauch he would be ready for relief duty in the last two games if needed.

The Dodgers finished with a 20–9 record for the month of September. The loss cut their lead to a game and a

On September 30, 1966, Bill White's decisive three-run homer off Ron Perranoski at Connie Mack Stadium in Philadelphia cost the Dodgers the game. It increased the chances that they would have to use Koufax on short rest on the last day of the season.

half over the Pirates. The Giants stayed alive at three games back. The Giants and Pirates would play a makeup doubleheader the next day in Pittsburgh.

	W	L	Pct.	GB
Los Angeles	94	66	.588	—
Pittsburgh	92	67	.579	1½
San Francisco	90	68	.570	3

Saturday, October 1—Dodgers Are Rained Out; the Giants Eliminate the Pirates

It was Don Drysdale's turn to start that night in Philadelphia. With rain coming down all day, Drysdale spent the entire afternoon cooped up in his room at the Warwick Hotel with teammates Ron Fairly and Bob Miller, watching the Giants and Pirates play a nationally televised doubleheader at Forbes Field on a raw, rainy day across the state in Pittsburgh.[5] In the opener, the Pirates got 13 hits off Juan Marichal and still lost the game, 5–4. The Giants' rookie outfielder, Ollie Brown, came through with his best performance of the season. In the fourth inning, Brown broke a 1–1 tie with a two-run homer off Pittsburgh starter Woody Fryman. The Pirates went back in front, 4–3, in the fifth on a double by Clemente and a single by Clendenon—both off Marichal with two out. In the eighth, Brown tied the game, 4–4, with a double and scored the winning run on a single by Jim Davenport. Marichal went all the way for his 25th win. On the final play of the game, Brown made a leaping catch of Gene Alley's drive against the right field wall with the .334-hitting Manny Mota on deck.[6]

In the nightcap, Giants right-hander Bobby Bolin eliminated the Pirates by pitching a brilliant one-hit, 2–0 shutout, in one hour and 52 minutes. The only Pittsburgh hit was Bill Mazeroski's two-out bloop single to right field in the second inning on a pitch that was at least a foot outside. Bolin faced only 28 batters—one over the minimum. The only other Pirates base runner was starting pitcher Tommie Sisk, who walked in the sixth inning and was promptly erased on a double play.

Early that evening in Philadelphia, after an inspection of the rain-sodden field at Connie Mack Stadium, the umpires called off the Dodgers-Phillies game scheduled for 8 p.m.[7] The two teams would make it up as part of a doubleheader the next day.

	W	L	Pct.	GB
Los Angeles	94	66	.588	—
San Francisco	92	68	.575	2
Pittsburgh	92	69	.571	2½

The Pirates were gone, but the Giants were still alive. For the third time in the last five years, the outcome of the National League pennant race was undecided going into the final day of the season.[8] If the Dodgers won either game of their doubleheader in Philadelphia, they would clinch the pennant. If they lost both games and the Giants won in Pittsburgh, the Dodgers lead would be reduced to a half-game. In that case, the Giants would play a makeup game the next day in Cincinnati for a game that was rained out on August 10. If the Giants won that game, it would result in a nightmare scenario for the Dodgers. The two teams would end the season in a tie for first, forcing a third Dodgers-Giants playoff series beginning on October 5 at Candlestick Park—the same setup as the catastrophic 1962 playoff. The World Series, scheduled to begin on Wednesday, October 5, would have to be delayed.

Sunday, October 2—Koufax Clinches After Drysdale Falls Short

Drysdale (13–16) went up against Larry Jackson (15–13) in the first game of the Sunday doubleheader. Drysdale came into the game with four straight victories. But confined to his hotel room, he did not pick up a baseball on Saturday. Big D was programmed to pitch every fourth day. In 13 starts that season in which he had *more* than three days' rest, he was 2–7 with four no-decisions. His record was 11–8 on his normal three days' rest.

The disruption to Drysdale's routine from the rainout was evident early. In the first inning, Phillies leadoff batter John Briggs hit Drysdale's third pitch 400 feet into the left field seats for a home run that ended his 25-inning scoreless streak. Drysdale walked Tony Gonzalez on a 3–2 pitch and gave up a line single to Johnny Callison. After he got

Richie Allen to pop up, Bill White drove in Gonzalez with a line single to make it 2–0. Lefebvre got Drysdale out of the inning with a leaping catch of a Dick Goat line drive that he converted into a double play.

Drysdale made it to the third inning. But after Briggs led off with a single and Gonzalez walked on four pitches, he was replaced by Perranoski. A three-run home run by Ron Fairly on a 2–1 Jackson pitch put the Dodgers ahead, 3–2, in the sixth.

Bob Miller took the 3–2 lead to the bottom of the eighth. Richie Allen opened with a bad-hop infield single off Lefebvre's glove. After Bill White's sacrifice bunt attempt was fielded by Miller and thrown over the head of Wills into center field to put runners on second and third,[9] Alston brought in "The Vulture" Regan—with 14 wins and 17 saves to his credit—with instructions to walk Groat intentionally to load the bases for Cookie Rojas. Rojas grounded Regan's first pitch to third baseman Schofield, who threw wide to the plate, allowing Allen to score the tying run. Clay Dalrymple, the Phillies' .240-hitting catcher, looped a single into center field, scoring White with an unearned run to make it 4–3, Philadelphia.

Chris Short, who came in from the bullpen to pitch the eighth inning, set down the Dodgers in order in the ninth to close it out. Short got credit for his 20th victory—the first 20-game winner for the Phillies since Robin Roberts in 1955. One bad inning by Phil Regan proved disastrous for the Dodgers.

In the clubhouse between games, the Dodgers learned that the Giants had come from behind to beat the Pirates, 7–3, in 11 innings to melt their lead to one game.[10] That made it necessary for Koufax to pitch the second game of the doubleheader with less than three days' rest against Jim Bunning, who would be gunning for his 20th win. The second game—and the season—would be decided by two future Hall of Fame pitchers with perfect games in the record book.

In the nightcap, the Dodgers scored three runs off Bunning after two were out in the third inning on an RBI single by Schofield and a two-run homer by Willie Davis. They scored a fourth run on Roseboro's sacrifice fly in the fourth.

Bunning was removed for a pinch-hitter, Gary Sutherland, in the fifth with the Phillies behind, 4–0. Koufax snapped off a curveball to get Sutherland to fly out to left field.[11] On that pitch, he said he felt something "pop"[12] behind his left shoulder at the base of the neck. After completing the inning, Koufax was rushed into the clubhouse, where trainers Bill Buhler and Wayne Anderson popped a slipped vertebra back into place while Don Newcombe held onto his feet. After a rubdown with Capsolin, Koufax was able to continue, but he would have to rely exclusively on his fastball the rest of the way.[13]

The 1966 NL pennant was decided on the last day of the season in the second game of a doubleheader at Connie Mack Stadium in Philadelphia on October 2, 1966. Sandy Koufax, pitching on less than three days' rest, beat fellow future Hall of Famer Jim Bunning to clinch it.

The Dodgers added an unearned run off Rick Wise in the eighth inning and an earned run off Darold Knowles in the ninth on a two-out RBI single by Ron Fairly.

Koufax gave up only three infield singles and a double to Bill White through the first eight innings.[14] He went to the bottom of the ninth with a commanding 6–0 lead. An error by Lefebvre on Richie Allen's leadoff grounder opened the door for the Phillies. In rapid succession, Kuenn singled (in his last major league at-bat), Taylor singled, and the irrepressible Bill White doubled off the right field scoreboard to cut the Dodgers' lead to 6–3. Koufax was on the ropes with nobody out. Alston told reporters after the game, "Sandy would have been taken out if one more man got on base."[15] But Koufax steadied himself to strike out Bob Uecker, retire pinch-hitter Bobby Wine on a groundout, and blow away Jackie Brandt on three pitches to close it out. Exactly one year to the day after he clinched the 1965 pennant on two days' rest, Koufax had done it again.

Ron Fairly's clutch hitting down the stretch was essential to the Dodgers' 1966 pennant success. "The Redhead" hit .472 in the last two weeks of the season.

Ron Fairly drove in four runs with four hits in the doubleheader. Down the stretch—in the last two weeks of the season—he hit .472 (17-for-36) with four home runs and 15 runs batted in.

The Giants were waiting in the passenger lounge at the airport in Pittsburgh when they got the news at 7:12 p.m. that evening. There would be no trip to Cincinnati. After being five games behind and buried on September 20, the Giants had won eight of their last nine games—including four in a row against the Pirates—only to have Koufax end their season before they could get to game no. 162. That day at Forbes Field, Willie Mays hit his 37th home run of the season in the third inning off Bob Veale. He would never hit thirty again.

Final National League Standings

	W	L	Pct.	GB
Los Angeles	95	67	.586	—
San Francisco	93	68	.578	1½
Pittsburgh	92	70	.568	3

In the visitors' clubhouse at Connie Mack Stadium after the pennant-clinching game, a reporter asked Jim Lefebvre, "What about Baltimore?" "Who cares about Baltimore," he answered, "It's going to take us a few days to get over this."[16] The big question for the Dodgers: would they have anything left?

By September the swelling and the pain had grown so severe for Koufax that the team doctors were making frequent cortisone injections directly into the elbow joint to control it. In addition to Butazolidine pills, he was taking Empirin with codeine. He fought through the pain to make all eight of his last regularly scheduled starts, completing the last six and winning six of seven decisions.

By September the swelling and the pain had grown so severe for Koufax that the team doctors were making frequent cortisone injections directly into the elbow joint to control it.[17] In addition to Butazolidine pills, he was taking Empirin with codeine.[18] He fought through the pain to make all eight of his last regularly scheduled starts, completing the last six and winning six of seven decisions.

18

The World Series with the Orioles

If I can see them, I can catch them.[1]—Willie Davis, Dodger Stadium, October 6, 1966

They out-hit us, out-fielded us, and out-pitched us.[2]—Sandy Koufax, Memorial Stadium, October 9, 1966

An exhausted Dodgers team arrived at 4:10 a.m. on Monday, October 3, at Los Angeles International Airport. They slept all day. Eight thousand bleacher seats for the four scheduled games at Dodger Stadium went on sale at 10:00 a.m. They were gone in 45 minutes. That night the well-rested and confident Orioles landed at LAX and took up residence at Gene Autry's Continental Hotel on the Sunset Strip. Though they had slipped into town virtually unnoticed, a brass band and scores of Orioles fans greeted them when their bus arrived at the hotel.[3]

The Quiet Man and the Marine

Walter Alston, the quiet man from Darrtown, Ohio, was appearing in his sixth World Series, his fourth on the West Coast. He had already won four championships: one in Brooklyn (1955), and three in Los Angeles (1959, 1963, and 1965). Over the weekend in Philadelphia, Buzzie Bavasi told the press that Alston would be back for his 14th year as manager of the Dodgers in 1967—no matter the outcome of the current season.

While this was Hank Bauer's first World Series as a manager, he was no stranger to the Fall Classic. A winner of two Bronze Stars and two Purple Hearts as a lieutenant in the U.S. Marine Corps in the South Pacific during World War II, Bauer was signed by the New York Yankees as an amateur free agent before the 1946 season. After three years in the Yankees' farm system, Bauer was called up to the big club at

The 1966 World Series was the sixth for Walter Alston at the helm of the Dodgers. He was given a vote of confidence over the weekend in Philadelphia when Buzzie Bavasi announced that the quiet man from Darrtown would be back for his 14th year as Dodgers manager in 1967.

the end of 1948, when the Yankees finished third behind the Indians and the Red Sox. In 1949, new Yankees manager Casey Stengel gave the 26-year-old rookie his big chance to play as a regular. From 1949 through 1958, Bauer played in nine World Series with Stengel's Yankees. He hit seven home runs—including four in the 1958 Series with the Milwaukee Braves. After the 1959 season—an "off year" for the Yankees in which they finished third behind Chicago's Go-Go Sox and the Cleveland Indians—37-year-old Bauer was traded to the Kansas City Athletics in a seven-player deal that sent a promising young outfielder named Roger Maris to New York. Bauer spent a year and half in Kansas City as a part-time right-fielder. In June 1961, the Athletics' new owner, Charles O. Finley, fired manager Joe Gordon and made Bauer player-manager. Bauer played his last game on July 21, 1961, and continued to manage the club from the dugout to a ninth-place tie with the expansion Washington Senators. After a 90-loss season in 1962, Bauer resigned before Finley could fire him.

Baltimore Orioles general manager Lee MacPhail, who had been a Yankees executive and the boss of Bauer's wife in the 1950s, hired Bauer as a coach for the 1963 season. After finishing 18½ games behind the Yankees in fourth place, MacPhail fired his manager, Billy Hitchcock, and signed Bauer to a one-year contract for the 1964 season. The Orioles added shortstop Luis Aparicio and young pitchers Wally Bunker and Dave McNally to make a run at the Yankees in 1964. They held first place for 111 days. But with a 15–4 run, the Yankees caught them on September 17 and went on to win their 14th pennant in 16 years. With 97 wins, the Orioles finished third, and Bauer was named Manager of the Year.

Bauer's 1965 Orioles again finished third, behind the Twins and the White Sox. MacPhail resigned after the 1965 season to take a position with the new baseball commissioner, William Eckert. Under his successor, Harry Dalton, the Orioles rolled the dice and traded their ace right-hander, Milt Pappas, to Cincinnati for Frank Robinson. Bauer was initially opposed to the trade due to Robinson's reputation as a troublemaker.[4] But Frank Robinson led the Orioles to their first pennant in 1966 with 49 home runs, 122 runs batted in, and a .316 batting average—baseball's first Triple Crown season since Mickey Mantle in 1956.

The first two games of World Series would be played in Los Angeles. For the last two years, the Dodgers were a combined 103–59 at Dodger Stadium. With Drysdale and Koufax scheduled to start Games 1 and 2, the oddsmakers in Las Vegas made the Dodgers 8–5 picks to win the Series. There was talk in Dodgers Nation of another sweep, à la 1963.

Baltimore Orioles manager Hank Bauer. The 1966 World Series was his first as a manager. From 1949 to 1958 the gritty ex–Marine played in nine Fall Classics as an outfielder with Casey Stengel's Yankees, hitting a total of seven Series home runs.

Power Imbalance

The Orioles scored 755 runs, tops in the American League. The Dodgers scored 606 and were shut out 17 times that season. Only the Mets hit fewer home runs than the Dodgers' 108. Lefebvre led the team with 24. Tommy Davis, by now a part-time player, was their only .300 hitter, batting .313 in 100 games. The Orioles hit 175 home runs, with four players producing over 20: Frank Robinson 49, Boog Powell 34, Brooks Robinson 23, and Curt Blefary 23.

Baby Birds

Only three Orioles had ever played in a World Series: Luis Aparicio with the 1959 White Sox, Frank Robinson with the 1961 Reds, and Stu Miller with the 1962 Giants. Eighteen Dodgers had World Series experience. In the Baltimore starting rotation, Dave McNally was 23, Wally Bunker was 22, and Jim Palmer was 20. Their principal catcher, Andy Etchebarren, was 23. Center fielder Paul Blair was 22.

Game 1—Wednesday, October 5 at Dodger Stadium— Moe's Finest Hour

The opening game was played in front of a record crowd of 55,941 at Dodger Stadium. Baseball Commissioner William D. Eckert threw out the first pitch. Danish opera star Lauritz Melchior sang the national anthem from center field. A Hollywood contingent, led by Cary Grant, watched from their exclusive dugout-level boxes.[5]

The choice of a starting pitcher was problematic for both clubs. Forced to use Koufax to clinch the pennant in the final game of the season, and with Sutton done for the year, Walter Alston had to go with Drysdale on two days' rest. Since left-hander Steve Barber, the ace of the Orioles staff for the first half of the season, was unavailable due to tendonitis in his elbow, Hank Bauer had to go with his number two left-hander, the stocky, 5'11", 185-pound Dave McNally.

McNally attended Central Catholic High School in Billings, Montana. The winters were so long in Montana that the school did not have a baseball team. Instead, he starred on the powerhouse Billings Post 4 American Legion team that won 14 consecutive state championships. In his last year, 1960, he was 18–1 and struck out 27 batters in a single game. That September, the Orioles won a bidding war with the Dodgers for McNally and signed the 17-year-old for $80,000. He spent two years in the Orioles' farm system before being called up at the end of the 1962 season. He made a dazzling major league debut on September 26, 1962, in a start in Memorial Stadium against the Kansas City Athletics: a two-hit shutout in which he retired the last 17 batters.[6] He was still only 19 year old. He won 27 games over the next three years with Baltimore as a spot starter. While McNally finished the 1966 season with a respectable 13–6 record, he had won only one of his last eight starts. In his last outing of September 30, the Twins routed him for ten runs on 12 hits, including three home runs.

Drysdale had good stuff warming up but struggled with his command from the start. In the top of the first inning, after walking Russ Snyder, he had to face Frank Robinson for the first time in a Baltimore uniform. Drysdale and Robinson had a long history.

In a game with the Cincinnati Reds at the Coliseum in July of 1961, Drysdale threw three pitches behind the plate-hugging Robinson and then hit him on the arm. The incident cost Drysdale a three-game suspension.[7] Robinson tied into an errant 1–0 pitch—a fastball up in his eyes—and drove it deep into the lower left field stands for a two-run homer. The next batter, Brooks Robinson, took a ball and then hit another mislocated high fastball 30 feet deeper into the same section to make it 3–0.[8] Maury Wills led off the bottom of the first with a walk and stole second, but was left stranded when Tommy Davis made the mistake of hitting a ground ball within range of Brooks Robinson. The Dodgers thus wasted the only hit and the only stolen base by Wills in the Series.

In the top of the second, Drysdale's last inning, he gave up a two-out RBI single to Russ Snyder that put the Orioles up, 4–0. In the bottom half of the inning, Lefebvre led off with a 400-foot home run into the left field pavilion to cut the lead to 4–1.

McNally was having problems adjusting to the steepness of the Dodger Stadium mound. It threw off his control. He walked five batters in two and one-third innings. After McNally walked the bases loaded in the bottom of the third, Bauer removed him and brought in the 31-year-old, Polish-born right-hander, Myron "Moe" Drabowsky. Before he could get the Orioles out of the inning, Drabowky walked in the Dodgers' second run. The Orioles increased their lead to 5–2 on Luis Aparicio's run-scoring groundout against Joe Moeller in the fourth inning.

The Dodgers had seen Drabowky for years as a journeyman starter in the National League. Pitching for the Cubs, Braves, and Reds from 1956 to 1962, he was an unremarkable 5–8 with a 4.00 earned run average against them. They were not prepared for the Moe Drabowsky they would see on this day. Drabowsky, who was 6–0 in the regular season, shut them out over the last six and two-thirds innings. He struck out 11 batters—all swinging—including six in a row in the fourth and fifth innings to tie a Series record.[9] The Dodgers could manage only one hit off him, a harmless single by Willie Davis in the seventh inning.

The Orioles won it, 5–2, to take a one-game lead in the Series. Drabowsky was credited with the victory. It was the first time the Dodgers had lost a World Series game in Dodger Stadium. Commenting on Drabowsky afterward in the clubhouse, Alston told reporters,

The Dodgers had seen Myron "Moe" Drabowsky for years as a journeyman starter in the NL. They were not prepared for his career performance out of the bullpen in Game 1 of the 1966 World Series at Dodger Stadium.

"I never saw him with such stuff, or control of it." In his two innings of work, Drysdale gave up four earned runs on four hits—including the two home runs by the Robinson boys—and walked two batters. Bauer was not concerned about McNally's poor performance: "It's just one game. McNally will start again on Sunday."[10]

Veteran Baltimore scouts Jim Russo and Al Kubski had scouted the Dodgers during the month of September. Their scouting report contained a recommendation relating to the Dodgers hitters' vulnerability to a good fastball: "Throw the ball hard. Challenge them."[11] After seeing Drabowsky blow away 11 Dodgers with hard stuff, a brash 20-year-old Jim Palmer told reporters, "You can beat the Dodgers with a fast ball."[12]

That evening the Las Vegas oddsmakers changed the Series odds to *even money*.

Game 2—Thursday, October 6 at Dodger Stadium— Meltdown in Center Field

The Dodgers expected to tie the Series with Koufax on the mound in the second game in front of a new Dodger Stadium record crowd of 55,947 (six more than the day before). In six previous World Series starts, he had a 4–2 record with a 0.88 earned run average. He came into the game with 19 consecutive scoreless innings in Series competition. But he was also making his third start in eight days. His opponent, Jim Palmer, was nine days shy of his 21st birthday. As a middle school kid in Beverly Hills, Palmer used to watch an unformed Koufax pitch in the Coliseum in 1958 and 1959.[13] Joking with reporters in the locker room before the game, Palmer told them he would probably have to throw a shutout to beat Koufax.[14] Never mind that he had never pitched a shutout at the major league level.

The game was a scoreless tie through four innings, with Koufax and Palmer throwing matching one-hitters. Koufax threw 25 strikes in his first 28 pitches. The game, as well as the Dodgers' chances to repeat as world champions, changed dramatically in the top of the fifth. Boog Powell, the mammoth, 6'4", 250-pound offensive tackle masquerading as a first baseman, led off with a sharp single to left field. The Orioles' 23-year-old, rookie second baseman, Davey Johnson, attempting a sacrifice bunt, popped out on a running one-hand catch by Roseboro in foul territory. Twenty-two-year-old center fielder Paul Blair lofted a routine fly into the cloudless sky over center field. Willie Davis appeared to have the ball all the way, when at the last split-second the glare from the sun caused him to turn his head away. He lunged for the ball, but it glanced off his glove. Blair ended up on second and Powell on third. Davis was charged with a two-base error. After a conference at the mound between Alston and Koufax, it was decided to pitch to the weak-hitting Andy Etchebarren with first base open. Etchebarren hit another seemingly harmless fly into shallow center field—clearly not deep enough to score a run. Settled under the ball, Davis suddenly began to gesture helplessly with his arms to signal he had again lost the ball in the sun. He got a glove on it chest-high, but the ball popped out for his second error, allowing Powell to score from third. Blair was heading for third base when a flustered Davis picked up the ball and unleashed a wild throw that sailed 20 feet over Jim Gilliam's head, skipped past Koufax backing up the play, and went into the Dodgers' dugout. Blair walked home with the Orioles' second run, and Willie Davis was charged with his third error of the inning.[15] After Koufax struck out Palmer, Aparicio lined a double down the left field line to score Etchebarren with the Orioles' third unearned run. Koufax got Curt Blefary to fly out to Fairly in right field to end the nightmare inning.

Thunderous boos rocked the stadium as the Dodgers left the field. Minutes later in the dugout, Koufax threw his arm around Davis to comfort him.

Willie Davis committed three errors in the disastrous fifth inning of Game 2 of the 1966 World Series, putting Koufax and the Dodgers in a hole from which they would never recover.

Frank Robinson led off the top of the sixth inning with a long drive to deep right-center. Davis and Fairly both had a chance to make a play on the ball, but they shied away from each other at the last instant, and the ball fell to the turf between them. While no error was charged on the play, Robinson ended up with a gift triple.[16] The boos erupted anew from the stands. After Koufax got Brooks Robinson to foul out, Powell punched a soft single into right-center to score Robinson to make it 4–0. Davey Johnson singled to right field. Ron Fairly's relay throw overshot the cutoff man (the Dodgers' fifth error) enabling both runners to advance, Powell to third and Johnson to second. Blair was walked intentionally to load the bases. Koufax got Etchebarren to ground into a double play to end what no one realized was the last inning of his career. Koufax was done after six. During the regular season, he had completed 27 games—four more than the entire Baltimore pitching staff. Only one of the four runs he gave up on this day at Dodger Stadium went into the record book as "earned." And that was because official scorers did not assign errors when one outfielder spooked another off a fly ball, as happened on Frank Robinson's tainted "triple."[17]

The tragi-comedy continued in the top of the eighth inning. With Perranoski pitching, Frank Robinson led off with a walk. Brooks Robinson followed with a single to left. Powell's perfect sacrifice bunt advanced the runners to second and third. Davey Johnson hit a bullet off Perranoski's shin to score Robby from third. Perranoski retrieved the ball pathetically on his hands and knees and, even though Johnson had the play beaten, he made a desperate flip to first base beyond the reach of Wes Parker, allowing Brooks to score. The boos grew louder. Perranoski was charged with the Dodgers' sixth error of the game.[18]

An increasingly confident Palmer took the 6–0 lead to the ninth inning. After Palmer struck out Fairly, Lefebvre managed to draw a walk. But Palmer promptly retired Johnson and Roseboro to complete a brilliant four-hit shutout. At age 20, he became the youngest player to pitch a shutout in the World Series. And he relied almost exclusively on one pitch. Of the 115 pitches he threw, 100 were fastballs.[19]

The Orioles had beaten both Drysdale and Koufax and were going home with a 2–0 lead. In the 1965 Series, Claude Osteen was able to right the ship after Drysdale and Koufax lost the first two games in Minnesota. But he did it in front of a home crowd in Dodger Stadium. The odds in Las Vegas shifted to 3–1 in favor of the Orioles to win the World Series.

Series fever enveloped Baltimore. In the early morning of October 7, a howling mob of 10,000 swarmed over Friendship Airport to welcome their Orioles. A brass band serenaded the players as they deplaned onto a red carpet. Scalpers were getting as much as $50 for an $8 ticket.[20]

After a lifeless Dodgers team completed their Friday workout, a member of the organization confided to Charles Maher of the *Los Angeles Times*, "These guys won their 95 games. They won the pennant. They could care less about this thing."[21]

Game 3—Saturday, October 8 at Memorial Stadium— The Revenge of Paul Blair

In a shocking upset, 20-year-old Baltimore right-hander Jim Palmer beat Sandy Koufax with a four-hit shutout in Game 2 of the 1966 World Series at Dodger Stadium.

Claude Osteen and Wally Bunker were the starting pitchers for Game 3 in Baltimore. It had been eight days since Osteen last pitched—a four-inning, losing effort in Philadelphia. A crowd of 54,445 packed Memorial Stadium. The stadium, built in 1950, was named in honor of the soldiers who died in World Wars I and II. The Baltimore Colts were the first residents. The Orioles played their first game there on April 15, 1954.[22] For Game 3 of the 1966 World Series, a huge replica of the 15-star American flag that flew over Fort McHenry during the siege in the War of 1812, which inspired Francis Scott Key to write "The Star Spangled Banner," was hung on the flagpole in center field.[23]

Bunker was considered doubtful to participate in the Series until he pitched five scoreless innings against the Twins on the last day of the regular season. Tendinitis in his elbow had caused him to go on the disabled list for seven weeks in the summer. The rangy, 6'2" right-hander was signed by Baltimore after graduating from Capuchino High School in San Bruno— seven miles from Candlestick Park. He won 19 games with a 2.69 ERA as a 19-year-old rookie phenom for Bauer's 1964 Orioles. Plagued by arm problems, he slipped to 10–8 the next year. He was 10–6 in 24 starts for 1966. Warming up before the game, Bunker didn't like his stuff. His

Sore-armed Orioles right-hander Wally Bunker shut out the Dodgers on six hits in Game 3 of the 1966 World Series at Memorial Stadium. He would win only five more games for Baltimore and be out of baseball by age 27.

arm hurt. But once the bell rung, he began making one perfect pitch after another. He struck out the first two batters, Wills and Parker, on six pitches. The third batter, Willie Davis, hit Bunker's first pitch—a curveball—in the air toward the left field corner. Curt Blefary chased the ball from his position in left-center field as it sliced away from him. Just before crashing into the retaining wall, he made a lunging, two-handed catch. The sore-armed Bunker had just disposed of the Dodgers on seven pitches in the first inning.

Bunker blanked the Dodgers in the second and third as well, facing the minimum six batters. Osteen, despite his eight-day layoff, matched Bunker with his own one-hit shutout through the third inning. Bad luck prevented the Dodgers from taking the lead in the fourth. With one out, Wes Parker lined an 0–2 pitch deep into the gap in right-center field—a sure triple for the fleet Parker. But the ball landed on the hard cinder warning track and took a high bounce into the bleachers for a ground rule double. With Parker sent back to second base, Willie Davis lifted a fly to Blair in medium-deep center for the second out. Parker would have scored easily on the play had he been on third. After Bunker walked Fairly to put runners on first and second, he struck out Lefebvre on a wicked sinker to get out of the inning. Bunker would call it "the best pitch I ever threw in my life."[24] The Dodgers had not scored a run in 19 innings.

Osteen retired the first two batters the bottom of the fifth inning before Paul Blair, batting seventh in the order, stepped into the batter's box. Nineteen sixty-six was Blair's

second season as a platoon center fielder for the Orioles. He hit .277 with a modest seven home runs in 133 games. Blair had been a standout athlete in baseball, track, and basketball at Manual Arts High School in Los Angeles. At age 17, he got a tryout with the Dodger Juniors at the Coliseum, but was rejected despite hitting two singles and a home run in one of the games. The Dodgers scouts thought he was too small to make it in the major leagues.[25] The Mets signed him in the summer of 1961 as a shortstop and converted him to an outfielder. After one year in the Mets' farm system, the Orioles drafted the unprotected Blair in the November 1962, first-year draft. He worked to improve his hitting and cut down on his strikeouts for the next two seasons in the Orioles' system before being called up to the big club in September of 1964. Still classified as a rookie in 1965, he hit .234 with five home runs in 119 games.

A tape-measure fifth-inning homer by Dodgers reject Paul Blair off Claude Osteen gave the Orioles an insurmountable 1–0 lead in Game 3 of the 1966 World Series at Memorial Stadium.

Though Blair was not perceived as a longball threat, he drove Osteen's first pitch 430 feet into the back of the left field bleachers. Lou Johnson took two steps back and just watched the ball sail over his head. Osteen said he made a good pitch—a low fastball on the outside corner. Blair characterized it as a "fat fast ball, a trifle inside." No matter whose version was true, the Orioles were up, 1–0, after five innings. Blair would tell reporters in the clubhouse after the game, "I never hit a ball that far in my whole life."[26]

Blair's home run was the Orioles' third and last hit in the game. Osteen held Baltimore scoreless in the sixth and seventh innings before being removed for a pinch hitter in the eighth.

Bunker continued to baffle the Dodgers, using only two pitches: a fastball and a sinker. Since his last complete game on June 10, he had lasted an average of five innings in his final 13 starts. Perhaps the stars were aligned for him on this day. With the aid of massive amounts of Capsolin applied to his aching right arm by the Baltimore trainer between innings,[27] he took the 1–0 lead to the ninth inning. The Dodgers went down meekly in order. It took Wally Bunker only 91 pitches and an hour and 55 minutes to pitch a six-hit shutout that put the Orioles up, 3–0, in the Series. He would win only five more games for the Baltimore Orioles and was out of baseball by age 27.

The Dodgers had not scored a run since the third inning of Game 1—24⅓ consecutive innings. Smoking a cigarette in the visitors' clubhouse, 34-year-old Maury Wills, in denial, tried to convince reporters that the Dodgers could still win the next four straight games. If they survived tomorrow, he argued, Sandy Koufax would be ready to go on his normal three days' rest for Game 5. No one was buying it.[28]

Game 4—Sunday, October 9 at Memorial Stadium— Robby Was the Difference

The fourth game, a rematch between Don Drysdale and Dave McNally, was a 180-degree turnaround from the first game, in which both pitchers were chased early. Today they both pitched four-hitters. Neither deserved to lose. The crowd of 54,458 was the largest ever to see a baseball game in Baltimore. In the stands, a crude bedsheet banner read, "Support the Dodgers. Give blood!"[29] With President Johnson back at his Johnson City, Texas, ranch preparing for a meeting with Soviet Foreign Minister Andrei Gromyko, Vice President Hubert Humphrey threw out the first ball from a box behind the Orioles' dugout.[30] While he was officially neutral, the former Senator from Minnesota was still smarting over his Twins' defeat at the hands of the Dodgers in the 1965 Series.

Drysdale breezed through the first three innings. He retired Russ Snyder leading off the fourth before Frank Robinson hurt him again with a tremendous home run to the back of the left field bleachers. The ball came within ten rows of going out of Memorial Stadium. It was the eighth home run Drysdale had given up in World Series competition, a new record. As Robinson circled the bases, he thought to himself, "That may be enough."[31] With two out, Boog Powell hit what looked like a second home run—a towering drive headed for the flagpole in center. But Willie Davis, the goat of the second game, made the play of the Series to save Drysdale. Looking over his right shoulder, Davis tracked the ball as he glided back across the warning track to the center field fence. The ball was hit so high that Davis was able to turn completely around and regain sight of the ball. A sudden gust of wind started to blow the ball away from him. He took five lateral steps to his right, leapt high over the fence at the 410-foot sign, and brought the ball back after it had actually gone over the seven-foot railing.[32] From the NBC radio booth, Vin Scully told a national audience, "One nice thing, it's the same man who was called a little league outfielder for dropping two fly balls. From one human being to another, I'm sure glad he got off the hook."

Lefebvre ripped a single into center field on McNally's hanging curve, leading off the top of the fifth inning. Parker followed with a sharp ground ball into the hole, headed for left field. Brooks Robinson moved to his left like a cat to stop it on one hop, stumbled, and made a perfect throw to Davey Johnson to start a crippling 5–4–3 double play.[33] McNally struck out Roseboro, looking, to end the inning. Drysdale set down the Orioles in order in the bottom half of the inning.

Frank Robinson's solo homer off Don Drysdale in the fourth inning of Game 4 was all the Orioles needed to complete a four-game sweep of the Dodgers at Memorial Stadium.

John Kennedy led off the top of the sixth with a line single to left field on another hanging McNally curve. With the count full to Drysdale after two unsuccessful bunt attempts, Alston started Kennedy on the 3–2 pitch. But Drysdale struck out on a foul tip, and Etchebarren threw out Kennedy for another rally-killing double play. Wills hit McNally's next pitch on the ground to Brooks Robinson—the definition of an automatic out. In the bottom of the sixth, Drysdale gave up a one-out single to Aparicio. But Roseboro threw out "Looie" attempting to steal second. With Frank Robinson lurking on deck, Drysdale got Snyder to ground back to him for the third out.

After McNally retired the Dodgers in order on seven pitches in the top of the seventh inning, they were down to their last six outs. Drysdale had to face Frank Robinson one last time in the bottom of the inning. He and Roseboro were determined not to let Robby see another fastball after he had already turned around two for home runs in the Series. Roseboro called for nothing but curves. Robinson swung and missed three of them. With two out, Boog Powell hit Drysdale' first pitch off his fists into center field for a single. But Drysdale got Curt Blefary to fly out to Lou Johnson in right field to get out of the inning.

Before the eighth inning began, Bauer removed Blefary, moved Russ Snyder over to left, and brought in Paul Blair to play center field. At this point in the game, McNally appeared to be tiring. The right-hand-batting Lefebvre, who homered off him in the first game, led off with a long drive to the deepest part of the park in straightaway center field. After taking off from his customary position in shallow center, Blair raced all the way back to the chain-link fence and made a leaping, two-handed catch of the ball with his glove three feet above the barrier. In an instant, a game-tying home run was converted into a loud out.[34] McNally got Parker and Roseboro on groundouts to retire the side in order. Drysdale, in turn, retired the Orioles in order in bottom of the inning.

McNally took the 1–0 lead to the ninth inning. The game was slipping away. Down to his last three outs, Alston tried to tie the game with one swing by sending up longball threat Dick Stuart as a pinch-hitter for John Kennedy to lead off the ninth. Stuart had hit three home runs at Memorial Stadium as a member of the Boston Red Sox. But today he was caught looking at a 1–2 pitch for a called third strike. Al Ferrara, pinch-hitting for Drysdale, lined McNally's first pitch into center field for a single. As the speedy Nate Oliver ran for Ferrara, Stu Miller and Moe Drabowsky began to warm up in the Baltimore bullpen. Wills worked McNally for a walk to put the tying run on second base and the winning run on first. Willie Davis followed with a solid line drive to right field, but right at Frank Robinson for the second out. With Lou Johnson (who won the seventh game of the 1965 World Series with a home run) heading to the plate, Bauer sent Orioles pitching coach Harry Brecheen out to the mound to talk to McNally. Brecheen would recall, "I reminded him that Johnson was a first ball, fast ball hitter. But mostly I just wanted him to catch his breath."[35] It had been

It took Dave McNally one hour and 45 minutes to finish off the Dodgers with a four-hit 1–0 shutout in Game 4 of the 1966 World Series at Memorial Stadium.

overcast all day. But as Brecheen trotted back to the Orioles' dugout, the sun suddenly came out. On McNally's first pitch, Johnson swung at and missed a curveball. After he missed a second curve, the Dodgers were down to their last strike. Johnson later said that he was up there with one goal: to hit the ball out of the park.[36] He made solid contact on the third pitch—an 0–2 curve—and thought it might go out. But Blair was able to haul it in in medium-deep center field for the final out. At 3:47 p.m., it was over in Baltimore. It took McNally just one hour and 45 minutes to shut out the Dodgers, 1–0, on four hits. He got halfway to the third base line before his teammates pummeled him for nearly a minute and then carried him into the clubhouse as thousands of fans poured out onto the field. Bauer told reporters after the game that had Lou Johnson gotten on base, he would have removed McNally and brought in Stu Miller to pitch to Tommy Davis. After beating the likes of Bob Gibson and Jim Maloney in the regular season, the Dodgers were shut out three games in a row by Orioles pitchers whose average age was 22.

Game 4 was a devastating loss for Don Drysdale after he had come through with a big-time performance with the Dodgers' backs to the wall. Aside from Frank Robinson's deciding home run, he gave up three singles in eight innings. He had to make only 78 pitches. Commenting after the game on his one mistake to Robby, a laconic Drysdale, smoking a cigarette, told reporters, "It was a fast ball up high. I knew the moment he hit the ball, it would take a guy with a ticket to catch it."[37] Frank Robinson was named Most Valuable Player of the Series.

After elbowing his way into the visitors' clubhouse, an effervescent Vice President Humphrey announced with a laugh, "I remember you from last year when you beat my Minnesota Twins." He then switched to Consoler-in-Chief: "I've lost a couple myself, and I've come back." The unconsoled Walter Alston told him, "I'm not going to jump off any bridges, I'll tell you that." When he asked Sandy Koufax if he were going on the Dodgers' tour of Japan, Koufax replied, "No, I'm going to take a slow airplane home and see my doctor."[38]

A Celebration or a Riot?

Outside Memorial Stadium, the city of Baltimore erupted in celebration. By the early evening, it had escalated to near-riot proportions. Police and fire units were called out to quell a victory celebration that had deteriorated into mob violence. Vehicles had their roofs caved in as the crowds swarmed over them. Signs were ripped from their poles. Crowds estimated at 10,000 jammed the streets from curb to curb for blocks. Revelers opened a fire hydrant and turned its stream into crowds roaring their approval. Beer cans were hurled at random, and bar patrons took their drinks outside to join the action.[39] Drivers abandoned their vehicles at traffic lights to join others snake-dancing through the streets. By early evening, vendors still hawked their Orioles banners and World Series souvenirs which had suddenly become more valuable than tickets to the non-existent fifth game.[40]

A New Record for World Series Futility

The Dodgers were shut out over the last 33⅓ innings to set a new Series record for futility that had lasted for 61 years. In 1905, the New York Giants' pitching staff, led by Christy Mathewson, and Iron Man McGinnity, blanked the Philadelphia Athletics for 28 consecutive innings.

Dodgers hitters set new Series records for fewest runs scored, 2; fewest hits, 17; lowest team batting average, .142; lowest slugging percentage, .192; and fewest total bases, 24 (14 singles, 3 doubles, 1 home run). Ron Fairly, who carried the team with his bat in September, was 1-for-7 with no runs batted in for the Series. Willie Davis was 1-for-16. John Roseboro was 1-for-14. Maury Wills, the man who made the Dodgers go, was 1-for-13 with one stolen base. In four games, the Dodgers left 24 runners on base.

The maligned Baltimore pitching staff gave up only two earned runs and had a combined earned run average of 0.50. The Orioles had to use only one relief pitcher in the Series: Moe Drabowsky with his career performance in Game 1. The Orioles defense did not make a single error. The Orioles never used a pinch-hitter.

Coming Apart in Japan

As captain of the team a higher degree of devotion to duty was expected of Maury Wills.[1]—Walter O'Malley, Tokyo, October 28, 1966

I felt I'd earned a rest after the season I went through.[2]—Maury Wills, Los Angeles, November 11, 1966

Four hundred of the most diehard Dodgers fans greeted the team when they arrived at LAX early in the morning of October 10. Some waived signs such as "Willie Davis for Governor in '66" and "So What?!" Sandy Koufax, flanked by two security guards, was met by a contingent of screaming women, some declaring, "We love you, Sandy!"

The next day the Dodgers announced that Don Sutton had been scratched from the upcoming tour of Japan after their medical department advised not letting him throw a baseball until next spring.[3] Sandy Koufax, Don Drysdale, and Wes Parker had already announced that they would not be making the trip. The five-week trip would begin with two games in Honolulu and conclude with 18 games in Japan. In 1956, the Dodgers made a highly successful tour of Japan after losing the World Series in seven games to the Yankees. In the intervening ten years the host, Yomiuri Newspapers, had repeatedly invited Walter O'Malley to return with his team.

On October 12, Walter Alston was voted National League Manager of the Year in an *Associated Press* poll of 380 baseball writers. Alston got 206 votes. Pittsburgh's Harry Walker was second with 130. It was the fourth time in 13 seasons—and second year in a row—that Alston had won the award. At a Los Angeles press conference he told reporters, "While we had our problems in 1966, our eventual success in the NL race is an indication of what a good spirited club this is."[4] That spirit had vanished after the humiliation in the World Series. Many of the Dodgers resented having to make the trip to Japan.

While in Los Angeles after the Series, Maury Wills was examined to determine whether he would require surgery to correct the injury to his right knee he sustained back on July 15. On that day at Shea Stadium, he strained the knee trying to beat out a bunt. It was feared that he had suffered a cartilage tear. The exam showed no tear; no surgery was needed. Instead, the 34-year-old Wills would be put on a weight-training program to strengthen the knee.

The morning of October 14, when the Dodger entourage left LAX on a Japan Air Lines DC-8 bound for Honolulu, Wills was not on the plane. The team played two games without him in a stopover in Honolulu against all-star teams with name major leaguers such as Bo Belinsky and Don Larsen, who had pitched a perfect game against them in Game 5 of the 1956 World Series. After breaking his commitment to play in the first two exhibition games, Wills joined the team at the Honolulu airport in time for the October 19 flight to Tokyo. The 80-member delegation included Walter and Mrs. O'Malley, various Dodgers executives and their wives, Commissioner William Eckert, Walter Alston, his coaching staff, and 25 players. Hours later, the team was enthusiastically received by the baseball-rabid Japanese in Tokyo.

The 18-game Japanese tour began the weekend of October 22 in Tokyo with two games against the Yomiuri Giants, perennial champions of Japanese baseball. The Giants featured slugging first baseman Sadaharu Oh, "The Japanese Babe Ruth." Wills understood that he would be asked to play only two or three innings per game on the tour, allowing him to rest his knee. But in the first game, he played 8½ innings and even stole a base to the delight of the Japanese fans. In the second game, he played eight innings.

On October 25, in the third game in Sapporo, Wills aggravated the injury to his knee running the bases. As he rounded third base, the turf gave way under his right leg, causing the knee to buckle. He was immediately replaced by a pinch-runner.

The next day, Wills told Alston he wanted to go home. Alston said it was out of his hands and referred him to Walter O'Malley. Wills called O'Malley and asked to meet with him in person to discuss his situation. When Wills was told by O'Malley that he had guests and could not meet with him, Wills made his request to leave the tour—and his reasons for it—over the phone. O'Malley was unmoved. His answer was short and unequivocal: "I will not permit it!"[5] O'Malley went into a stern lecture about how more was expected of Wills, who exemplified the spirit of the team. Taken aback, Wills' last words were, "I guess I'd better go."[6] Communications had clearly broken down. On the off-day of October 27, the team moved on to Osaka without Wills, who was on his way back to Tokyo.

Schism

The morning of October 28 in Tokyo, Wills got on a Japanese Airlines flight bound for Los Angeles. When O'Malley learned that Wills had left the team, he was furious: "It is a breach of contract!" he told reporters. "I thought this particular *boy* showed evidence of executive ability. That was why he was made captain."[7] Instead of proceeding to Los Angeles for treatment, Wills got off his flight in Honolulu for some R&R. He stayed there for ten days.

The Japanese were offended. On November 4, O'Malley had to make a personal call on Japanese Premier Sato to apologize to the Japanese government for Wills leaving the tour. He told the press, "The United States was embarrassed by the Wills defection."[8] That night in Honolulu, a local sportscaster spotted Wills playing his banjo at a night club on the stage with Sammy Davis, Jr. Honolulu became a soap opera when Buzzie Bavasi, on a 15-day cruise with his wife, landed there on a stopover. When reporters tracked him down to ask him about Wills, he told them, "If he hurt his leg, he should see Dr. Kerlan. But if he is off playing his banjo somewhere, he must think the banjo is more important than baseball."[9] Back in Los Angeles, Dr. Kerlan said he still hadn't heard from Wills.

Wills slipped back into L.A. unnoticed. He finally went to see Dr. Kerlan on November 11, two weeks after he left Japan. After examining Wills, Kerlan told the press, "His knee is definitely no worse than it was at the end of the season, for which I am thankful."[10]

The Dodgers ended the Japanese tour on November 16 with a fourth straight loss to the Yomiuri Giants, a humiliating 7–3 pounding in Tokyo. Sadaharu Oh saw them off with his fifth home run in seven games against the Dodgers. Their record in Japan of nine wins, eight losses, and one tie was the poorest showing of any visiting major league team.[11]

By Thursday, November 17, things were coming to a head. The consensus in the L.A. press was that Wills had effectively ended his career when he walked out on the team in Tokyo. For O'Malley, the nightclub episode in Honolulu was the last straw. And this was after Wills had already been paid a $3,000 guarantee to accompany the team on the Japan tour and had pocketed $750 in expense money. Rumors swirled in the media that Wills would be on the trading block at the winter meetings. What could the Dodgers get for a 34-year-old shortstop with a bad knee? As the game's highest-paid shortstop, who could afford him? The Wills matter thus became an all-consuming crisis for the Los Angeles Dodgers. In 24 hours' time, it would be downgraded to a minor distraction.

20

Black Friday

I don't regret one minute of the last twelve years. But I think I would regret one year that was too many.[1]—Sandy Koufax, Los Angeles November 18, 1966

On Wednesday, November 16, Sandy Koufax called Dodgers general manager Buzzie Bavasi and dropped a nuclear bomb: "I've made up my mind. I think it's best that I retire."[2] After a moment of silence, Bavasi recovered enough to respond, "Whatever you do is perfectly agreeable to me." When Koufax asked Bavasi to call a press conference for Friday, November 18, Bavasi told him, "No, I think we owe Walter O'Malley the courtesy of waiting until he and the team return from Japan on Sunday." Koufax acquiesced and agreed to postpone the press conference until Wednesday, November 23.

On November 17, it was announced that Roberto Clemente had narrowly edged Koufax for the National League Most Valuable Player Award. Twenty writers from the Baseball Writers' Association of America—two from each franchise in the league—cast votes totaling 218 points for Clemente and 210 for Koufax. Koufax actually received more first place votes: nine versus eight for Clemente. In a strange twist, Koufax was completely shut out on one of the 20 ballots.

That night, Koufax called Bavasi again to tell him that he had reconsidered and wanted to go through with the announcement right away. Instead of waiting for O'Malley to return, he would make the announcement the next day. Bavasi reacted by telling Koufax he could have no part in it and wished him luck. With Bavasi out of the picture, Koufax contacted his attorney and advisor, William Hayes, who set up a hastily-arranged press conference for the following day, November 18, at the Beverly Wilshire Hotel.[3]

The Press Conference

A few minutes after 12:00 noon, Sandy Koufax, dressed in a blue sports coat and dark slacks, walked into the Sans Souci Room of the Beverly Wilshire Hotel. "Here I am," the greatest pitcher on the planet sheepishly announced to an overflow crowd of over 100 representatives of the news media, city officials, and a contingent of female fans without press passes. No one from the Los Angeles Dodgers management was in attendance. Looking uncomfortable, as he usually did at public functions, Koufax posed for photographers for about five minutes in front of a table packed with 15 microphones. Then he sat down and said, "I don't have much to say, just one short statement: A few minutes ago I sent Buzzie Bavasi a letter asking him to put me on the voluntarily retired list."[4]

After a moment of silence, the questions began.

"The question is why, Sandy?" one reporter called out.

"The question is why," Koufax began as he formulated a response in his head. "I don't know if cortisone is good for you or not," he continued. "But to take a shot every other ball game is more than I wanted to do. And to walk around with a constant upset stomach because of the pills; and to be high half the time during the ball game because you're taking pain killers. I don't want to have to do that."[5]

"What is your thought about the loss of income?" another reporter posed.

"Well, the loss of income," Koufax again began by restating the question. "Let's put it this way: If there was a man who did not have the use of one of his arms, and you told him it would cost a lot of money and he could buy back that use. He'd give 'em every dime he had, I believe. In a sense, maybe this is what I'm doing."[6]

Koufax disclosed that he had made up his mind to quit even before the end of the season, and that he felt guilty having to obfuscate when the media relentlessly asked him about his plans: "In my own mind, I was being devious. People would come up and ask me, and I'd say I didn't know—when I had actually made up my mind."[7] For the first time, the media was made aware that his arthritic condition had progressed to the point that he had to have the left sleeves of his coats shortened.

As the press conference was winding down, someone asked, "What regrets do you have?"

Koufax's enigmatic response to this one must have produced some false hopes: "My only regret is leaving."[8]

Koufax concluded by saying, "I've got a lot of years to live after baseball. And I would like to live them with the complete use of my body."[9] He stood up and began to make his way out of the room, graciously shaking hands and signing autographs. Some of the women appeared to be wiping away tears. This day, November 18, 1966, would be forever known in Dodgers Nation as *Black Friday*.[10] Don Drysdale and John Roseboro were now the last of the old Brooklyn Dodgers on the roster.

The Aftermath

The reaction from the Dodger management was stark. "Sandy is the greatest pitcher I have ever seen," said his only manager, Walter Alston. "I hate to lose him, but it's his decision. Everybody has his own life to lead."[11] General Manager Buzzie Bavasi, in his mind subtracting the 53 wins Koufax had contributed over the past two seasons, commented, "We've had crises before, but never a challenge like this. You just don't replace a Koufax."[12]

His teammates were devastated. "It's a real shock. We are very close friends, and I didn't know it was coming. It's a tragedy for baseball," said Ron Perranoski. "There is no way to replace him," said Ron Fairly. "I only wish his arm was better so he could continue awhile and break every record in the book." Don Drysdale, a close friend of Koufax since their time together in the U.S. Army Reserve, commented from his Hidden Valley ranch, "It surprised me. It leaves you with kind of an empty feeling."[13]

The news caused an earthquake across the broader baseball world. Leo Durocher called Koufax "the best pitcher I've ever seen" and added, "There's no way the Dodgers can win the pennant now." Durocher's boss, Cubs General Manager John Holland, summed it up: "Koufax was the greatest pitcher of our age."[14]

At the age of 30, after 12 years as a major league baseball player and one year of college, Sandy Koufax had no concrete post-retirement plans beyond a vacation to the Bahamas after Thanksgiving.

Epilogue

The End of the Koufax Era

On November 2, 1966, Sandy Koufax won his second straight unanimous Cy Young Award, the third of his career. As documented in *Finding the Left Arm of God*, he was considering leaving the game after the end of the 1960 season—his sixth year in the majors. At that point, he had a career losing record of 36–40. But he decided to give it one more year and turned his career around in 1961 with 18 wins and a new National League-record 269 strikeouts. "One more year" became six more years of historic proportions in which he won 129 games and lost 47.

In his final three seasons, he was 72–22. As we have seen, the freak injury to his elbow on August 8, 1964, in Milwaukee caused a likely fourth Cy Young Award season to be cut short eight days later after he shut out the Cardinals at Dodger Stadium. Pitching every fourth day in increasing pain from traumatic arthritis in 1965 and 1966, he completed a remarkable 54 games, winning 53 while striking out an average of 350 batters over those last two years—all without missing a single turn.

Year	W	L	W-L%	GS	CG	IP	SO	ERA	SHO	WHIP
1964	19	5	.792	28	15	223	223	1.74	7	0.928
1965	26	8	.765	41	27	335.2	382	2.04	8	0.855
1966	27	9	.750	41	27	323	317	1.73	5	0.985
Total	72	22	.766	110	69	881.2	922	1.85	20	0.921

In the last five years of the Koufax Era, a period in which he won 111 games, lost only 34, and won five straight ERA titles, the Los Angeles Dodgers won three pennants and two World Championships.

Year	W	L	W-L%	Finish	Post-Season
1962	102	63	.618	2nd	Lost a three-game playoff series to the Giants
1963	99	63	.611	1st	Won the World Series from the Yankees, 4–0
1964	80	82	.494	6th	Koufax missed the last 45 games.
1965	97	65	.599	1st	Won the World Series from the Twins, 4–3
1966	95	67	.586	1st	Lost the World Series to the Orioles, 0–4
Total	473	340	.582		

The Axe Falls at the Winter Meetings

Buzzie Bavasi knew he would be going into the winter meetings at the end of November 1966, in Columbus, Ohio, in a vulnerable position. On the day Koufax retired, he told reporters, "Now that I have to go into the meetings without Koufax, the other clubs will have us right where they want us."[1] On November 29, the Dodgers traded Tommy Davis to the Mets for Ron Hunt and outfielder Jim Hickman. It was expected that Hunt would take over second base, allowing Jim Lefebvre to move over to third. Parting with Tommy Davis, a top run producer who hit .304 in seven seasons with the Dodgers, was bittersweet. He won consecutive NL batting titles in 1962 and 1963. In 1964, he led the team in runs batted in for the third straight season, but he had been a platoon player after breaking his ankle in May of 1965.[2]

Rumors had been swirling for days that Maury Wills would be unloaded as punishment for abandoning the team in Japan. On December 1, he was traded to the Pirates for third baseman Bob Bailey and shortstop Gene Michael.[3] Thus ended his eight-year role as the man who made the Dodgers Go-Go! Wills was brought up in June of 1959 after spending nine years in

Following the World Series and the Japan tour, Dodgers General Manager Buzzie Bavasi took action at the winter meetings. He traded Tommy Davis to the Mets and Maury Wills to the Pirates.

the minor leagues. He wrested the shortstop position away from Don Zimmer and sparked the Dodgers to their first pennant on the West Coast with his inspiring play, capped by a sensational performance in the late-September showdown series with the Giants at Seals Stadium in San Francisco. In 1960, Wills took over the leadoff position—held by Jim Gilliam since 1953—and led the league in stolen bases for the first of six straight seasons. In 1962, he stole a new major league record 104 bases and won the Most Valuable Player Award. A leader on the field, Wills was named team captain before the 1965 season. Dodgers trainer Bill Buhler contended that Wills' injury-laden 1966 season was caused by his trying to "play his way into shape" after holding out and arriving late to spring training.[4] The loss to the Dodgers would be immeasurable for his two and a half years in exile in Pittsburgh and Montreal. He returned to Los Angeles in mid–1969 and finished his career with the Dodgers in 1972.

Koufax at 31

Sandy Koufax turned 31 on December 30, 1966. On that day, it was reported that he had signed a ten-year, $1 million contract with NBC.[5] The network had big plans for him. In addition to his principal duties as a baseball commentator on radio and television, he would be asked to help develop new talent, initiate programs of his own creation, and develop special projects. In the words of the NBC vice president in charge of sports, Carl Lindemann, Koufax "will have the widest latitude with the network, and give us the benefit of his wisdom in any manner we may require."[6] After six weeks adrift with no plans for his future, Koufax now had a chance to make a fresh start in broadcasting. But the question was: given his introverted nature, would this be a fit?

1967 Collapse and Beyond

The 1967 season was the Dodgers' first in Los Angeles without Sandy Koufax. They finished eighth, 16 games below .500, 28½ games back. Their .451 winning percentage was the team's lowest since 1944. Attendance at Dodger Stadium fell from 2,617,029 with Koufax to 1,664,362 without him. Drysdale was again 13–16, Sutton was 11–15, and Osteen 17–17. Phil Regan went from 14–1 in 1966 to 6–9 with only six saves.

In Pittsburgh, Maury Wills hit .302, the highest average of his career. His replacement, Gene Michael, hit .202, playing only 83 games for the Dodgers at shortstop. Restored to a full-time player in New York, Tommy Davis hit .302 in 154 games for the Mets, leading the team in home runs and runs batted in.

The St. Louis Cardinals won the National League pennant by 10½ games over the Giants. Giants castoff Orlando Cepeda was voted the league's Most Valuable Player. The Cardinals won their second World Championship in four years by beating the Boston Red Sox in seven games. A dazzling three-win performance by Bob Gibson earned him his second Series MVP award.

Frank Howard blossomed in 1967, hitting 36 home runs for the Washington Senators under Gil Hodges. For the next three seasons (1968–1970) he would be one of the game's premier power hitters, averaging 45 home runs and 114 runs batted in.

Don Drysdale threw a career-best eight shutouts in 1968, the "Year of the Pitcher." His 58⅔ consecutive scoreless innings from May 10 to June 8 set a major league record. Shoulder problems forced him to retire in mid-season 1969 at the age of 33.[7] The next year, he began a broadcasting career that included stints with the Expos (1970–1971), Rangers, (1972), Angels (1973–1981), White Sox (1982–1987), and finally back home with the Dodgers (1988–1993). Tragically, he died alone in a hotel room in Montreal on July 3, 1993, at the age of 56. Vin Scully broke the news to Dodgers Nation during the intro to the broadcast of a Dodgers-Expos game from Olympic Stadium.[8]

On February 23, 1973, NBC announced that their ten-year contract with Sandy Koufax was ended by mutual consent. A baseball commentator for NBC sports for six years, Koufax said he never felt comfortable before the camera.[9] The Dodgers would not return to the World Series until 1974. The next year the reserve clause was struck down, opening the door to salary arbitration and free agency. The Koufax-Drysdale joint holdout of 1966 had set in motion a chain of events that led to the eventual demise of the reserve clause.

This concludes the third and final volume in my trilogy on the Los Angeles Dodgers in the Koufax era seen through the eyes of a Dodger fan who lived with the team growing up in Southern California during this period. Sandy Koufax is still the greatest pitcher I have ever seen. And he is one of the finest people.

Appendix:
Sandy Koufax Statistics

• 1964 •

Date	Loc	Opp	Rslt	Innings	Decision	IP	H	R	ER	BB	SO	HBP	ERA	Batters	AB	1B	2B	3B	HR	AVG
Apr 14		STL	W,4-0	SHO	W(1-0)	9	6	0	0	0	5	0	0.00	32	32	6	0	0	0	.188
Apr 18		CIN	L,0-3	GS-8	L(1-1)	8	3	3	3	3	6	0	1.59	29	26	2	0	0	1	.115
Apr 22	@	STL	L,6-7	GS-1	L(1-2)	1	2	3	3	1	1	0	3.00	7	6	1	0	0	1	.333
April					**1-2**	**18**	**11**	**6**	**4**		**12**	**0**	**3.00**	**68**	**64**	**9**	**0**	**0**	**2**	**.172**
May 4		CHC	W,2-1	CG(10)	W(2-2)	10	3	1	1	3	13	0	2.25	34	31	1	1	0	1	.097
May 9	@	SFG	L,2-3	GS-6	L(2-3)	6	4	3	3	3	4	0	2.65	25	20	3	1	0	0	.200
May 14	@	CHC	W,6-4	GS-4	W(3-3)	4	6	4	4	2	4	0	3.32	20	17	5	0	0	1	.353
May 17(1)		PIT	W,3-2	GS-8	W(3-3)	7.667	10	2	2	0	8	0	3.15	32	32	7	2	1	0	.313
May 21		NYM	W,6-1	CG	W(4-3)	9	7	1	1	2	11	0	2.8	35	33	7	0	0	0	.212
May 24		PHI	W,3-0	7-GF	S(1)	3	1	0	0	1	2	0	2.65	10	10	1	0	0	0	.100
May 27	@	CIN	L,0-1	GS-7	L(4-4)	7	3	1	1	5	7	0	2.51	27	22	3	0	0	0	.136
May 31	@	PIT	W,6-4	GS-8	W(5-4)	7	8	4	3	4	8	0	2.64	33	29	6	1	0	1	.276
May					**4-2**	**53.667**	**42**	**16**	**15**	**19**	**57**	**0**	**2.52**	**216**	**194**	**33**	**5**	**1**	**3**	**.216**
Jun 4	@	PHI	W,3-0	SHO	W(6-4)	9	0	0	0	1	12	0	2.34	27	26	0	0	0	0	.000
Jun 8		CIN	W,2-1	CG	W(7-4)	9	4	1	0	3	5	0	2.21	32	32	3	0	0	1	.125
Jun 12		STL	W,3-0	SHO	W(8-4)	9	4	0	0	3	6	0	2.01	34	31	2	2	0	0	.129
Jun 17		MLN	W,5-0	SHO	W(9-4)	9	3	0	0	0	8	0	1.84	33	32	3	0	0	0	.094
Jun 21(1)	@	CIN	W,4-2	GS-6	W(10-4)	6	7	2	2	1	6	0	1.9	26	25	3	4	0	0	.280
Jun 25	@	SFG	L,1-2	GS-9		9	6	1	1	5	10	0	1.83	37	31	5	1	0	1	.194
June					**5-0**	**51**	**24**	**4**	**4**	**11**	**47**	**0**	**0.71**	**189**	**177**	**16**	**7**	**0**	**1**	**.136**
Jul 1		PHI	W,3-2	CG	W(11-4)	9	5	2	2	1	10	0	1.85	32	31	3	0	1	1	.161
Jul 5		NYM	W,5-0	SHO	W(12-4)	9	6	0	0	1	5	0	1.73	32	31	4	2	0	0	.194
Jul 10	@	HOU	W,4-3	GS-6	W(13-4)	5.333	5	2	2	3	8	0	1.79	24	21	5	0	0	0	.238
Jul 14	@	STL	L,7-8	GS-8		7.667	8	4	4	2	7	0	1.93	35	32	6	0	0	2	.250
Jul 18		CHC	W,3-1	CG	W(14-4)	9	8	1	1	1	10	0	1.88	36	34	6	2	0	0	.235
Jul 22		HOU	W,1-0	SHO	W(15-4)	9	4	0	0	0	12	0	1.78	31	31	3	1	0	0	.129
Jul 26		SFG	L,2-5	CG	L(15-5)	9	11	5	5	2	10	0	1.74	41	37	9	1	0	1	.297
Jul 30	@	NYM	W,5-3	GS-7		7	5	3	3	1	7	0	1.82	27	25	4	0	0	1	.200
July					**5-1**	**65**	**52**	**17**	**13**	**11**	**69**	**0**	**1.80**	**258**	**242**	**40**	**6**	**1**	**5**	**.215**
Aug 4(1)	@	PIT	W,5-1	GS-9	W(16-5)	8.333	6	1	1	5	6	0	1.79	36	30	4	2	0	0	.200
Aug 8	@	MLN	W,5-4	CG	W(17-5)	9	7	4	3	1	9	0	1.84	34	33	4	2	0	1	.212
Aug 12	@	CIN	W,4-1	CG	W(18-5)	9	5	1	1	1	10	0	1.81	34	32	3	1	0	1	.156
Aug 16(1)		STL	W,3-0	SHO	W(19-5)	9	7	0	0	1	13	0	1.74	35	34	5	2	0	0	.206
August					**4-0**	**35.333**	**25**	**6**	**5**	**8**	**38**	**0**	**1.27**	**139**	**129**	**16**	**7**	**0**	**2**	**.194**
Year					**19-5**	**223**	**154**	**49**	**43**	**53**	**223**	**0**	**1.74**	**870**	**806**	**114**	**25**	**2**	**13**	**.191**

• 1965 •

Date	Loc	Opp	Rslt	Innings	Decision	IP	H	R	ER	BB	SO	HBP	ERA	Batters	AB	1B	2B	3B	HR	AVG
Apr 18	@	PHI	W,6–2	CG	W(1–0)	9	6	2	2	5	7	0	2	37	32	5	0	0	1	.188
Apr 22	@	NYM	W,2–1	CG	W(2–0)	9	4	1	0	1	9	0	1	32	31	4	0	0	0	.129
Apr 26		PHI	L,3–4	GS-6	L(2–1)	6	7	3	3	1	6	1	1.88	25	23	3	2	1	1	.304
Apr 30		SFG	W,6–3	GS-6		5	6	3	2	0	7	0	2.17	22	21	4	1	0	1	.286
April					**2–1**	**29**	**23**	**9**	**7**	**7**	**29**	**1**	**2.17**	**116**	**107**	**16**	**3**	**1**	**3**	**.215**
May 5		CIN	W,4–2	CG	W(3–1)	9	9	2	1	1	8	1	1.89	37	35	8	1	0	0	.257
May 9	@	SFG	L,3–6	GS-8	L(3–2)	7	6	5	5	4	11	0	2.6	32	27	3	2	0	1	.222
May 13		HOU	W,3–0	SHO	W(4–2)	9	3	0	0	0	13	0	2.17	30	30	2	1	0	0	.100
May 17	@	HOU	W,5–3	GS-11	W(5–2)	10.333	5	3	3	3	13	1	2.24	40	36	4	0	1	0	.139
May 22	@	CHC	W,3–1	CG	W(6–2)	9	6	1	1	1	12	0	2.09	34	33	4	0	0	1	.182
May 26		STL	L,1–2	GS-8	L(6–3)	8	7	2	2	1	6	1	2.1	33	30	5	2	0	0	.233
May 30		CIN	W,12–5	CG	W(7–3)	9	5	5	2	2	13	0	2.09	36	34	3	1	1	0	.147
May					**5–2**	**61.333**	**41**	**18**	**14**	**12**	**76**	**3**	**2.05**	**242**	**225**	**29**	**7**	**3**	**2**	**.182**
Jun 3	@	STL	W,11–1	GS-3		2	6	7	2	1	1	0	2.24	15	14	4	1	0	1	.429
Jun 7	@	PHI	W,14–3	CG	W(8–3)	9	9	3	3	2	13	0	2.31	38	36	6	0	0	2	.250
Jun 12	@	NYM	W,5–0	SHO	W(9–3)	9	5	0	0	1	8	0	2.12	33	32	5	0	0	0	.156
Jun 16		SFG	W,2–1	CG	W(10–3)	9	6	1	1	1	8	0	2.04	32	30	5	0	1	0	.200
Jun 20(1)		NYM	W,2–1	CG	W(11–3)	9	1	1	1	2	12	0	1.96	30	28	0	0	0	0	.036
Jun 25		PIT	W,4–1	CG	W(12–3)	9	6	1	1	1	12	0	1.9	34	33	5	1	0	0	.182
Jun 29	@	SFG	W,9–3	CG	W(13–3)	9	8	3	3	1	10	0	1.97	36	35	6	1	0	1	.229
June					**6–0**	**56**	**41**	**16**	**11**	**9**	**64**	**0**	**1.77**	**218**	**208**	**31**	**3**	**2**	**5**	**.197**
Jul 3	@	HOU	W,3–1	CG	W(14–3)	9	5	1	1	1	10	0	1.91	33	32	4	0	0	1	.156
Jul 7	@	CIN	L,6–7	GS-5		4.667	9	5	5	3	6	0	2.14	25	22	6	2	0	1	.409
Jul 11(1)	@	PIT	W,4–2	CG	W(15–3)	9	5	2	2	2	10	0	2.13	36	33	3	0	0	2	.152
Jul 16		CHC	W,3–0	SHO	W(16–3)	9	4	0	0	2	9	0	2.02	33	31	3	1	0	0	.129
Jul 20		HOU	W,3–2	CG	W(17–3)	9	3	2	2	2	10	0	2.02	32	30	1	1	0	1	.100
Jul 24		STL	L,2–3	GS-9		9	4	2	2	3	8	0	2.02	34	28	3	0	0	1	.143
Jul 28		CIN	L,1–4	GS-8	L(17–4)	8	5	4	3	1	8	0	2.07	30	29	4	0	0	1	.172
July					**4–1**	**57.667**	**35**	**16**	**15**	**14**	**61**	**0**	**2.34**	**223**	**205**	**24**	**4**	**0**	**7**	**.171**
Aug 1	@	STL	W,3–2	CG	W(18–4)	9	5	2	2	0	11	0	2.07	32	32	2	3	0	0	.156
Aug 5	@	MLN	W,6–3	CG	W(19–4)	9	7	3	3	2	12	0	2.11	35	33	5	0	0	2	.212
Aug 10		NYM	W,4–3	CG	W(20–4)	9	7	3	3	2	14	0	2.14	36	33	4	2	0	1	.212
Aug 14		PIT	W,1–0	SHO(10)	W(21–4)	10	5	0	0	0	12	0	2.05	36	36	5	0	0	0	.139
Aug 18		PHI	L,3–6	GS-8		7	5	3	3	4	9	0	2.1	29	23	5	0	0	0	.217

Date	Loc	Opp	Rslt	Innings	Decision	IP	H	R	ER	BB	SO	HBP	ERA	Batters	AB	1B	2B	3B	HR	AVG
Aug 22	@	SFG	L,3–4	CG(8)	L(21–5)	8	4	4	4	4	8	0	2.18	33	28	2	0	0	2	.143
Aug 26	@	NYM	L,2–5	GS-7	L(21–6)	7	4	3	2	2	5	0	2.19	28	25	2	2	0	0	.160
Aug 28	@	PHI	W,8–4	9-GF	S(1)	1	1	0	0	0	2	0	2.18	4	4	1	0	0	0	.250
August					**4–2**	**60**	**38**	**18**	**17**	**14**	**73**	**0**	**2.55**	**233**	**214**	**26**	**7**	**0**	**5**	**.178**
Sep 1(1)	@	PIT	L,2–3	CG(11)	L(21–7)	10.667	8	3	3	3	10	0	2.2	43	40	4	3	1	0	.200
Sep 5	@	HOU	W,4–2	GS-7		7	4	2	2	3	5	1	2.2	28	23	4	0	0	0	.174
Sep 9		CHC	W,1–0	SHO	W(22–7)	9	0	0	0	0	14	0	2.14	27	27	0	0	0	0	.000
Sep 14	@	CHC	L,1–2	GS-6	L(22–8)	6	5	2	1	0	3	0	2.12	23	23	2	2	0	1	.217
Sep 16	@	CHC	W,2–0	9-GF	S(2)	1	0	0	0	0	0	0	2.12	3	3	0	0	0	0	.000
Sep 18	@	STL	W,1–0	SHO	W(23–8)	9	4	0	0	0	6	0	2.05	32	30	4	0	0	0	.133
Sep 22	@	MLN	W,7–6	GS-3		2	6	5	5	0	3	0	2.19	12	12	4	0	0	2	.500
Sep 25		STL	W,2–0	SHO	W(24–8)	9	5	0	0	3	12	0	2.12	32	29	5	0	0	0	.172
Sep 29		CIN	W,5–0	SHO	W(25–8)	9	2	0	0	1	13	0	2.07	30	29	2	0	0	0	.069
September					**4–2**	**62.667**	**34**	**12**	**11**	**11**	**66**	**1**	**1.58**	**230**	**216**	**25**	**5**	**1**	**3**	**.157**
Oct 2		MLN	W,3–1	CG	W(26–8)	9	4	1	1	4	13	0	2.04	35	30	3	0	0	1	.133
October					**1–0**	**9**	**4**	**1**	**1**	**4**	**13**	**0**	**1.00**	**35**	**30**	**3**	**0**	**0**	**1**	**.133**
Year					**26–8**	**335.667**	**216**	**90**	**76**	**71**	**382**	**5**	**2.04**	**1297**	**1205**	**154**	**29**	**7**	**26**	**.179**

• 1966 •

Date	Loc	Opp	Rslt	Innings	Decision	IP	H	R	ER	BB	SO	HBP	ERA	Batters	AB	1B	2B	3B	HR	AVG
Apr 13		HOU	L,6–7	GS-4		3	5	5	1	2	2	0	3	17	14	3	0	1	1	.357
Apr 17		CHC	W,5–0	GS-6	W(1–0)	6	5	0	0	1	6	0	1	24	23	3	2	0	0	.217
Apr 22	@	CHC	W,2–1	CG	W(2–0)	9	6	1	1	3	11	0	1	36	33	5	1	0	0	.182
Apr 26		STL	W,4–2	CG	W(3–0)	9	13	2	2	1	8	0	1.33	41	39	12	1	0	0	.333
Apr 30		CIN	L,1–3	CG	L(3–1)	9	6	3	3	2	9	0	1.75	35	33	5	0	0	1	.182
Apr					**3–1**	**36**	**35**	**11**	**7**	**9**	**36**	**0**	**1.75**	**153**	**142**	**28**	**4**	**1**	**2**	**.246**
May 5	@	SFG	L,8–9	GS-2		1.333	4	4	4	1	0	0	2.65	9	8	3	1	0	0	.500
May 10	@	PHI	W,6–1	CG	W(4–1)	9	6	1	1	3	10	0	2.33	35	32	4	2	0	0	.188
May 14	@	PIT	W,4–1	CG	W(5–1)	9	7	1	1	0	9	0	2.11	33	33	2	3	1	1	.212
May 19		SFG	W,4–0	SHO	W(6–1)	9	3	0	0	2	10	0	1.82	31	29	3	0	0	0	.103
May 23		PIT	W,3–2	CG	W(7–1)	9	8	2	2	1	7	0	1.84	36	34	7	1	0	0	.235
May 28		NYM	W,7–1	CG	W(8–1)	9	3	1	0	2	10	0	1.64	29	27	2	1	0	0	.111
May					**5–0**	**46.333**	**31**	**9**	**8**	**9**	**46**	**0**	**1.55**	**173**	**163**	**21**	**8**	**1**	**1**	**.190**
Jun 1	@	STL	W,1–0	SHO	W(9–1)	9	7	0	0	1	9	0	1.48	35	34	6	1	0	0	.206
Jun 5(1)	@	NYM	W,16–3	CG	W(10–1)	9	5	3	1	2	9	0	1.44	34	32	3	1	0	1	.156

Date	Loc	Opp	Rslt	Innings	Decision	IP	H	R	ER	BB	SO	HBP	ERA	Batters	AB	1B	2B	3B	HR	AVG
Jun 10	@	SFG	W,6-1	CG	W(11-1)	9	4	1	1	2	11	0	1.4	32	30	4	0	0	0	.133
Jun 14		HOU	L,0-3	GS-8	L(11-2)	8	7	3	3	1	6	0	1.53	31	30	6	0	0	1	.233
Jun 18		SFG	W,3-2	CG	W(12-2)	9	4	2	2	2	10	0	1.57	34	31	3	0	0	1	.129
Jun 22	@	HOU	W,5-2	CG	W(13-2)	9	10	2	2	0	6	0	1.6	36	36	5	4	0	1	.278
Jun 26	@	ATL	W,2-1	CG	W(14-2)	9	7	1	1	2	11	0	1.56	35	33	7	0	0	0	.212
June					**6-1**	**62**	**44**	**12**	**10**	**10**	**62**	**0**	**1.45**	**237**	**226**	**34**	**6**	**0**	**4**	**.195**
Jul 1		STL	L,0-2	GS-8	L(14-3)	8	5	2	2	1	10	0	1.6	28	27	4	0	0	1	.185
Jul 5		CIN	W,1-0	SHO	W(15-3)	9	10	0	0	1	8	0	1.51	36	35	9	1	0	0	.286
Jul 9		ATL	L,2-5	GS-7	L(15-4)	7	6	4	3	1	3	0	1.6	29	27	2	1	0	3	.222
Jul 14	@	NYM	W,4-2	CG	W(16-4)	9	8	2	2	3	11	0	1.62	39	36	6	1	0	1	.222
Jul 18	@	PHI	L,0-4	GS-5	L(16-5)	5	8	3	3	2	2	0	1.73	25	22	7	1	0	0	.364
Jul 23		NYM	W,6-2	CG	W(17-5)	9	8	2	1	5	7	0	1.69	40	33	7	1	0	0	.242
Jul 27		PHI	W,2-1	GS-11		11	4	1	1	3	16	0	1.65	39	35	3	0	0	1	.114
July					**3-3**	**58**	**49**	**14**	**12**	**16**	**57**	**0**	**1.86**	**236**	**215**	**38**	**5**	**0**	**6**	**.228**
Aug 1	@	PIT	W,5-1	GS-7	W(18-5)	7	5	1	1	2	9	0	1.63	27	25	4	0	1	0	.200
Aug 5	@	HOU	W,12-1	GS-6		6	5	1	1	1	10	0	1.63	24	23	2	2	0	1	.217
Aug 9	@	ATL	L,1-2	CG	L(18-6)	8.333	4	2	2	1	9	0	1.65	29	27	1	1	0	2	.148
Aug 13		CHC	W,6-1	CG	W(19-6)	9	5	1	1	3	11	0	1.62	34	30	5	0	0	0	.167
Aug 17		CIN	L,1-5	GS-5	L(19-7)	4.333	5	3	3	4	4	0	1.71	21	16	3	2	0	0	.313
Aug 21		STL	W,4-1	CG	W(20-7)	9	6	1	0	1	10	0	1.68	35	33	4	1	1	0	.182
Aug 26	@	SFG	W,4-0	SHO	W(21-7)	9	4	0	0	2	7	0	1.62	32	31	3	1	0	0	.129
Aug 30	@	NYM	L,4-10	GS-3	L(21-8)	2	4	6	5	3	1	0	1.79	15	12	3	1	0	0	.333
August					**4-3**	**54.666**	**38**	**15**	**14**	**17**	**61**	**0**	**2.30**	**217**	**197**	**25**	**8**	**2**	**3**	**.193**
Sep 3	@	CIN	W,7-3	GS-6	W(22-8)	6	8	3	3	1	4	0	1.85	27	25	5	2	0	1	.320
Sep 7		SFG	L,2-3	GS-7		7	5	2	2	3	6	0	1.87	28	25	4	0	0	1	.200
Sep 11(1)		HOU	W,4-0	SHO	W(23-8)	9	6	0	0	2	6	0	1.81	34	32	4	2	0	0	.188
Sep 16		PIT	W,5-1	CG	W(24-8)	9	5	1	1	3	5	0	1.78	35	29	5	0	0	0	.172
Sep 20		PHI	W,11-1	CG	W(25-8)	9	5	1	1	2	6	0	1.76	34	31	5	0	0	0	.161
Sep 25	@	CHC	L,1-2	CG(8)	L(25-9)	8	4	2	1	3	5	0	1.74	31	27	3	0	1	1	.148
Sep 29	@	STL	W,2-1	CG	W(26-9)	9	4	1	1	1	13	0	1.72	32	31	2	1	0	1	.129
September					**5-1**	**57**	**37**	**10**	**9**	**15**	**45**	**0**	**1.42**	**221**	**200**	**28**	**5**	**2**	**3**	**.185**
Oct 2(2)	@	PHI	W,6-3	CG	W(27-9)	9	7	3	2	2	10	0	1.73	37	35	5	2	0	0	.200
October					**1-0**	**9**	**7**	**3**	**2**	**1**	**10**	**0**	**2.00**	**37**	**35**	**5**	**2**	**0**	**0**	**.200**
Year					**27-9**	**323**	**241**	**74**	**62**	**77**	**317**	**0**	**1.73**	**1274**	**1178**	**179**	**38**	**5**	**19**	**.205**

• Career Statistics •

Year	W	L	PCT	ERA	G	GS	GF	CG	SHO	SV	IP	H	R	ER	HR	BB	IBB	SO	HBP	BK	WP	Batters	AVG	WHIP	H/9	HR/9	W/9	SO/9	SO/W
1955	2	2	.500	3.02	12	5	4	2	2	0	41.2	33	15	14	2	28	1	30	1	1	2	183	.216	1.464	7.1	0.4	6.0	6.5	1.07
1956	2	4	.333	4.91	16	10	1	0	0	0	58.2	66	37	32	10	29	0	30	0	2	1	261	.286	1.619	10.1	1.5	4.4	4.6	1.03
1957	5	4	.556	3.88	34	13	12	2	0	0	104.1	83	49	45	14	51	1	122	2	0	5	444	.216	1.284	7.2	1.2	4.4	10.5	2.39
1958	11	11	.500	4.48	40	26	7	5	0	1	158.2	132	89	79	19	105	6	131	1	0	17*	714	.220	1.494	7.5	1.1	6.0	7.4	1.25
1959	8	6	.571	4.05	35	23	6	6	1	2	153.1	136	74	69	23	92	4	173	0	1	5	679	.235	1.487	8.0	1.4	5.4	10.2	1.88
1960	8	13	.381	3.91	37	26	7	7	2	1	175	133	83	76	20	100	6	197	1	0	9	753	.207	1.331	6.8	1.0	5.1	10.1*	1.97
1961	18	13	.581	3.52	42	35	2	15	2	1	255.2	212	117	100	27	96	6	269*	3	2	12	1,068	.222	1.205	7.5*	1.0	3.4	9.5*	2.80*
1962	14	7	.667	2.54*	28	26	2	11	2	1	184.1	134	61	52	13	57	4	216	2	0	3	744	.197	1.036*	6.5*	0.6	2.8	10.5*	3.79
1963	25*	5	.833	1.88*	40	40	0	20	11*	0	311	214	68	65	18	58	7	306*	3	1	6	1,210	.189	0.875*	6.2*	0.5	1.7	8.9	5.28*
1964	19	5	.792*	1.74*	29	28	1	15	7*	1	223	154	49	43	13	53	5	223	0	0	9	870	.191	0.928*	6.2*	0.5	2.1	9.0*	4.21
1965	26*	8	.765*	2.04*	43	41	2	27*	8	2	335.2*	216	90	76	26	71	4	382*	5	0	11	1,297*	.179	0.855*	5.8*	0.7	1.9	10.2*	5.38*
1966	27*	9	.750	1.73*	41	41*	0	27*	5*	0	323*	241	74	62	19	77	4	317*	0	0	7	1,274*	.205	0.985	6.7	0.5	2.1	8.8*	4.12
12 Yrs	165	87	.655	2.76	397	314	44	137	40	9	2,324.1	1,754	806	713	204	817	48	2,396	18	7	87	9,497	.205	1.106	6.8	0.8	3.2	9.3	2.93

*League leader

	W	L	PCT	ERA	G	GS	GF	CG	SHO	SV	IP	H	R	ER	HR	BB	IBB	SO	HBP	BK	WP	Batters	AVG	WHIP	H/9	HR/9	W/9	SO/9	SO/W
1955–1960	36	40	.474	4.10	174	103	37	22	5	4	691.2	583	347	315	88	405	18	683	5	4	39	3,034	.224	1.429	7.6	1.1	5.3	8.9	1.69
6-YR AVG	6.0	6.7	.474	4.10	29.0	17.2	6.2	3.7	0.8	0.7	115.2	97.2	57.8	52.5	14.7	67.5	3.0	113.8	0.8	0.7	6.5	506	.224	1,429	7.6	1.1	5.3	8.9	1.69
1961–1966	129	47	.733	2.19	223	211	7	115	35	5	1,632.2	1,171	459	398	116	412	30	1713	13	3	48	6,463	.197	0.970	6.5	0.6	2.3	9.4	4.16
6-YR AVG	21.5	7.8	.733	2.19	37.2	35.2	1.2	19.2	5.8	0.8	272.1	195.2	76.5	66.3	19.3	68.7	5.0	285.5	2.2	0.5	8.0	1,077	.197	0.970	6.5	0.6	2.3	9.4	4.16
1964–1966	72	22	.766	1.85	113	110	3	69	20	3	881.2	611	213	181	58	201	13	922	5	0	27	3,441	.192	0.921	6.2	0.6	2.1	9.4	4.59
3-YR AVG	24	7.3	.766	1.85	37.7	36.7	1	23	6.7	1	293.7	203.7	71	60.3	19.3	67	4.3	307.3	1.7	0	9	1,147	.192	0.921	6.2	0.6	2.1	9.4	4.59

Source: Sports Reference LLC. "Players—Sandy Koufax." Baseball-Reference.com—Major League Statistics and Information. http://www.baseball-reference.com/players/k/koufasa01.shtml (Accessed August 2017).

Chapter Notes

Prologue

1. Bob Hunter, "No Rest for the Wicked," *The Sporting News*, December 14, 1963, 3.

Chapter 1

1. Bob Hunter, "Dodgers Heap Hopes Again on Top of Old Smokey," *The Sporting News*, October 10, 1964, 21.

2. Robert Lipsyte, "Clay Wins Title in Seventh-Round Upset," *New York Times*, February 26, 1964.

3. Drew Middleton, "French Doubtful War Can Be Won in South Vietnam," *New York Times*, February 28, 1964.

4. Frank Finch, "Howard Blasts Rumors He May Quit, Will Join Dodgers Soon," *Los Angeles Times*, March 3, 1964.

5. Frank Finch, "Howard Quits Dodgers—or Does He?" *Los Angeles Times*, March 13, 1964.

6. *Ibid.*

7. Frank Finch, "'Impossible to Play'—Frank Howard," *Los Angeles Times*, March 14, 1964.

8. Frank Finch, "Howard to Join the Dodgers Friday," *Los Angeles Times*, March 25, 1964.

9. Bob Hunter, "Howard Arrives, and All's Well in Dodgers' Family," *The Sporting News*, April 11, 1964, 3.

10. *Ibid.*

11. Frank Finch, "DODGERS MAY ADD BREWER TO ROSTER," *Los Angeles Times*, April 10, 1964.

12. Frank Finch, "Belinsky on Key, and Angels Sing, 5–0," *Los Angeles Times*, April 13, 1964.

13. Shirley Povich, "Buzzie Kept His Promise to Gil; That's How Nats Got Skowron," *The Sporting News*, December 21, 1963, 22.

Chapter 2

1. Frank Finch, "Koufax Probably Through for Year," *Los Angeles Times*, August 31, 1964.

2. Sandy Koufax and Ed Linn, *Koufax* (New York: Viking, 1966), 220.

3. Bob Hunter, "Koufax Leaves Fresh Hand Print on Sands of Time," *The Sporting News*, June 20, 1964, 4.

4. Frank Finch, "Nobody's Perfect—Sandy Walks One!" *Los Angeles Times*, June 5, 1964.

5. Koufax and Linn, *Koufax*, 221.

6. Allen Lewis, "Was Koufax Lucky? 'He's Great'—Mauch," *The Sporting News*, June 20, 1964, 6.

7. Bob Hunter, "Fast-Firing Podres Johnny-on-the-Spot as '65 Comebacker," *The Sporting News*, November 28, 1964, 13.

8. Bob Hunter, "Podres, Rushing Recovery, Told by Doc to 'Ease Up,'" *The Sporting News*, August 15, 1964, 17.

9. E.W. Kenworthy, "President Signs Civil Rights Bill," *New York Times*, July 3, 1964.

10. Bob Hunter, "Big D Approaching 10-Year Milestone in Peak Hill Form," *The Sporting News*, December 12, 1964, 18.

11. Bob Hunter, "Don, Thumb Healed, Rushes to Rescue of Hapless Dodgers," *The Sporting News*, August 8, 1964, 15.

12. Frank Finch, "Sandy Had it Locked up, but ... Two Errors Let Giants Win, 5–2," *Los Angeles Times*, July 27, 1964.

13. E.W. Kenworthy, "Congress Backs President on Southeast Asia Moves," *New York Times*, August 8, 1964.

14. Arnold H. Labasch, "Two Torpedo Vessels Believed Sunk in Gulf of Tonkin," *New York Times*, August 5, 1964.

15. Koufax and Linn, *Koufax*, 222.

16. Brian M. Endsley, *Finding the Left Arm of God: Sandy Koufax and the Los Angeles Dodgers, 1960–1963* (Jefferson, NC: McFarland, 2015), 123.

17. Koufax and Linn, *Koufax*, 223.

18. *Ibid.*

19. *Ibid.*

20. Frank Finch, "Sandy's 18th Ends Slump of Dodgers," *Los Angeles Times*, August 13, 1964.

21. Frank Finch, "Sandy, Simmons Fill in the Blanks, 3–0, 4–0; Dodgers Could Have Used Flood Control," *Los Angeles Times*, August 17, 1964.

22. Koufax and Linn, *Koufax*, 224.

23. *Ibid.*, 226.

24. Jane Leavy, *Sandy Koufax: A Lefty's Legacy* (New York: HarperCollins, 2002), 156.

25. Koufax and Linn, *Koufax*, 237.

26. Leavy, *Sandy Koufax*, 156; Steve Cady, "Trainers Unfazed by Medication Ban," *New York Times*, June 6, 1976.

27. Frank Finch, "Koufax Injures Elbow; to Miss Tonight's Game," *Los Angeles Times*, August 20, 1964.

28. Frank Finch, "Koufax Arm Test Proves Washout," *Los Angeles Times*, August 31, 1964.

29. Frank Finch, "Koufax Probably Through for Year," *Los Angeles Times*, August 31, 1964.

30. Bob Hunter, "'It's Time for a Change,' Buzzie Barks," *The Sporting News*, September 12, 1964, 9.

31. Bryan Soderholm-Difatte, "Beyond Bunning and Short Rest: An Analysis of Managerial Decisions That Led to the Phillies' Epic Collapse of 1964," *The Year of the Blue Snow: The 1964 Philadelphia Phillies* (Phoenix: SABR, 2013), 334.

32. Koufax and Linn, *Koufax*, 228.

Chapter 3

1. Allen Lewis, "Mauch Finds Hunk of Gold Among the Phillies' Rubble," *The Sporting News*, October 17, 1964, 6.

2. Bob Hunter, "Dodgers Heap Hopes Again on Top of Old Smokey," *The Sporting News*, October 10, 1964, 21.

3. Leonard Koppett, "Yanks Score 5 in 8th for 29th Pennant," *New York Times*, October 4, 1966.

4. Bryan Soderholm-Difatte, "Beyond Bunning and Short Rest: An Analysis of Managerial Decisions That Led to the Phillies' Epic Collapse of 1964," *The Year of the Blue Snow: The 1964 Philadelphia Phillies* (Phoenix: SABR, 2013), 342.

5. Bob Burnes, "Shannon's Shot Sends Ford Careening on Path to Defeat," *The Sporting News*, October 24, 1964, 23.

6. Bob Burnes, "Stottlemyer Stifles Cards, Gives Bombers Big Lift," *The Sporting News*, October 24, 1964, 24.

7. Bob Hunter, "'Dodgers Go to Market Seeking Help on the Hill, Three Other Spots," *The Sporting News*, October 24, 1964, 23.

8. Bob Hunter, "Coaching Box First to Feel Dodger Ax," *The Sporting News*, October 21, 1964, 21.

9. Bob Burnes, "Mick's Ninth-Inning Homer Sets Mark, Sinks Redbirds," *The Sporting News*, October 24, 1964, 26.

10. Bob Burnes, "Home Run Shocks Schultz," *The Sporting News*, October 24, 1964, 27.

11. Bob Burnes, "Ken Boyer's Grand-Slam HR Ties up Series for Cardinals," *The Sporting News*, October 24, 1964, 27.

12. Bob Burnes, "McCarver's Tenth-Inning Homer Grounds Bombers," *The Sporting News*, October 24, 1964, 29.

13. Bob Burnes, "Weary Gibson and Redbird Belters Finish Off Yankees," *The Sporting News*, October 24, 1964, 33.

14. Robert A. Rosenbaum, *The Penguin Encyclopedia of American History* (New York: Penguin Reference, 2003), 294.

Chapter 4

1. Bob Hunter, "Dodgers Heap Hopes Again on Top of Old Smokey," *The Sporting News*, October 10, 1964, 21.

2. Bob Hunter, "Deal Makes Dodgers Look Like Cat That Swallowed the Canary," *The Sporting News*, December 19, 1964, 17.

3. "Vietnam—Escalation of the War," http://www.globalsecurity.org/military/ops/vietnam2-escalation.htm.

Chapter 5

1. Sid Ziff, "No Sandy, No Flag," *Los Angeles Times*, April 9, 1965.

2. United Press International, "Koufax Is Sidelined with Arthritic Elbow and Likely to Miss Opening Day," *New York Times*, April 2, 1965.

3. Bob Hunter, "Captain Post Spurs Maury to Hike Goals," *The Sporting News*, April 17, 1965, 12.

4. Koufax and Linn, *Koufax*, 228.

5. *Ibid.*, 230.

6. Frank Finch, "'Sunday Hurler' Koufax to Rejoin Team," *Los Angeles Times*, April 6, 1965.

7. Frank Finch, "Sandy's Dandy," *Los Angeles Times*, April 13, 1965.

8. Oscar Kahan, "Ticket Sales Soar," *The Sporting News*, April 24, 1965, 1.

9. Leonard Koppett, "Koufax Is Sidelined with Arthritic Elbow and Likely to Miss Opening Day," *New York Times*, April 13, 1965.

10. Bob Hunter, "Coach Taught Wes to Play to Win, Accept Defeat, Too," *The Sporting News*, June 19, 1965, 3.

11. Bob Hunter, "Parker's Polish Makes Dodgers Glitter," *The Sporting News*, June 19, 1965, 3.

12. Frank Finch, "'T. Davis and Oliver Hurt in 1–0 Loss," *Los Angeles Times*, April 6, 1965.

13. Bob Hunter, "Lefebvre Tosses Wrench in Dodger Plan," *The Sporting News*, April 24, 1965, 5.

14. Bob Hunter, "Ex-Batboy Learned Great Players Shake Off Skids," *The Sporting News*, April 24, 1965, 5.

15. Bob Hunter, "Dodgers Proud of Own Big O, Osteen," *The Sporting News*, May 15, 1965, 7.

16. Frank Finch, "Osteen Baffles Bucs on Two Hits, 3–1," *Los Angeles Times*, April 15, 1965.

17. Frank Finch, "It's All the Way by Sandy K., 3–1," *Los Angeles Times*, April 19, 1965.

18. Koufax and Linn, *Koufax*, 233.

Chapter 6

1. Koufax and Linn, *Koufax*, 241.

2. United Press International, "Dodgers Rally to Beat Giants, 4–2; Tommy Davis Breaks Ankle," *New York Times*, May 2, 1965.

3. Frank Finch, "Dodgers Win ... but Tommy Davis May be Out for the Season," *Los Angeles Times*, May 3, 1965.

4. Paul Hirsch, "Al Ferrara," *Society for Baseball Research*, http://sabr.org/bioproj/person/2de64825.

5. Frank Finch, "Lou Johnson: Partner in 'Crime' of Wills," *Los Angeles Times*, May 30, 1965.

6. Billy Thompson, "Bluegrass Country Hails Lexington Lou," *The Sporting News*, November 6, 1965, 5.

7. United Press International, "Koufax of Dodgers Checks Astros, 3–0," *New York Times*, May 14, 1965.

8. Frank Finch, "Koufax Fans 13, Shuts Out Astros: Johnson Homers, Beaned Later," *Los Angeles Times*, May 14, 1965.

9. Bob Hunter, "Dodgers Post 'Disaster Area' in LF After John's Beaning," *The Sporting News*, May 29, 1965, 9.

10. Frank Finch, "Ferrara Breaks Up Ellsworth's No-Hitter, 3–1," *Los Angeles Times*, May 16, 1965.

11. Frank Finch, "KOUFAX, DODGERS GET SIMMONIZED, 2–1," *Los Angeles Times*, May 27, 1965.

12. Frank Finch, "DODGERS GO ALL WAY WITH 'LBJ'," *Los Angeles Times*, May 30, 1965.

Chapter 7

1. Bob Hunter, "'Running Wills' New Theme Song of Wills," *The Sporting News*, September 18, 1965, 11.

2. Clifford Katchline, "Free-Agent Draft Launched Without a Hitch," *The Sporting News*, June 19, 1965, 7.

3. Clifford Katchline, "Players Land a Real Bonanza—Pension Doubled," *The Sporting News*, December 17, 1966, 20.

4. John W. Finney, "Johnson Permits U.S. Units to Fight if Saigon Asks Aid," *New York Times*, June 9, 1965.

5. Frank Finch, "Podres' Fine Relief Job Helps Dodgers Bag 2," *Los Angeles Times*, June 14, 1965.

6. Bob Hunter, "'Running Wills' New Theme Song of Wills," *The Sporting News*, May 1, 1965, 13.

7. Koufax and Linn, *Koufax*, 237.

8. Frank Finch, "Dodger Rookie LeJohn Breaks in with a Boom," *Los Angeles Times*, July 1, 1965.

9. Bob Hunter, "Dodgers Ring Recall Bell; Presto, LeJohn Delivers Clutch Hits," *The Sporting News*, July 17, 1965, 16.

10. Bob Hunter, "Smokey Blows Up, Ignites Explosion at Dish," *The Sporting News*, July 24, 1965, 8.

11. Joseph Durso, "National League Wins All-Star Game, 6–5," *New York Times*, July 14, 1965.

12. Robert Shelton, *No Direction Home: The Life and Music of Bob Dylan* (Milwaukee: Backbeat Books, 2011), 210.

13. John D. Pomfret, "Johnson Orders 50,000 More Men to Vietnam and Doubles the Draft," *New York Times*, July 29, 1965.

14. David Halberstam, *The Best and the Brightest* (New York: Random House, 1969), 600.

15. *Ibid.*, 601.

16. Frank Finch, "Sammy (not Sandy) Fans 12—Reds Win," *Los Angeles Times*, July 29, 1965.

17. Frank Finch, "ELBOW TROUBLE? IT'S NEWS TO SANDY," *Los Angeles Times*, July 30, 1965.

18. John D. Morris, "President Signs Medicare Bill; Praises Truman," *New York Times*, July 31, 1965.

19. Frank Finch, "DODGERS LOSE NOD—DRYSDALE, TOO," *Los Angeles Times*, August 1, 1965.

20. Frank Finch, "Koufax Shows Elbow OK, Fans 11 Redbirds," *Los Angeles Times*, August 2, 1965.

21. E.W. Kenworthy, "Johnson Sign Voting Rights Bill," *New York Times*, August 7, 1965.

22. Frank Finch, "Reds Smash Four Homers, Then Win in 11th on Single," *Los Angeles Times*, August 7, 1965.

23. Frank Finch, "Bombs Away! Reds TKO L.A., 18–0," *Los Angeles Times*, August 9, 1965.

24. Bob Hunter, "Dodgers Teaching Rivals to Zip Lips, Stash Fold-up Talk," *The Sporting News*, August 28, 1965, 8.

25. *Ibid.*

26. Peter Bart, "New Negro Riots Erupt on Coast; 3 Reported Shot," *New York Times*, August 13, 1965.

27. Taylor Branch, *The King Years: Historic Moments in the Civil Rights Movement* (New York: Simon & Schuster, 2013), 132.

28. Peter Bart, "2,000 Troops Enter Los Angeles on Third Day of Negro Rioting," *New York Times*, August 14, 1965.

29. Frank Finch, "Osteen Throttles Buc Sluggers, 3–1," *Los Angeles Times*, August 14, 1965.

30. Peter Bart, "21 Dead in Los Angeles Riots; 600 Hurt; 20,000 Troops Called; President Condemns Violence," *New York Times*, August 15, 1965.

31. Frank Finch, "DODGERS WIN HARD WAY—ERROR IN 10TH," *Los Angeles Times*, August 15, 1965.

32. Frank Finch, "Drysdale's Story: No Hit, No Pitch," *Los Angeles Times*, August 16, 1965.

33. Peter Bart, "Calm Returning to Los Angeles," *New York Times*, August 17, 1965.

34. Frank Finch, "Dodgers' League Lead Short-Ended to 1/2 Game," *Los Angeles Times*, August 17, 1965.

35. Frank Finch, "Dodgers Beaten on Wills' Muff in 12th," *Los Angeles Times*, August 18, 1965.

36. Leonard Koppett, "LOS ANGELES WINS IN 15TH INNING, 8–5," *New York Times*, August 20, 1965.

37. Frank Finch, "Johnson's Homer Wins in 15th, 8–5," *Los Angeles Times*, August 20, 1965.

38. Bob Hunter, "Dedicated, Exciting: That's How Dodgers Strike Pilot Smokey," *The Sporting News*, September 4, 1965, 16.

39. Sid Ziff, "Giants Play a 'Dirty' Trick on Dodgers," *Los Angeles Times*, August 21, 1965.

40. James S. Hirsch, *Willie Mays: The Life, The Legend* (New York: Scribner's, 2010), 434.

41. Frank Finch, "BAY BOMBERS BLAST DODGERS OUT OF FIRST, 5–1," *Los Angeles Times*, August 21, 1965.

42. Frank Finch, "THE GREAT RACE: Today the Dodgers ... Then?" *Los Angeles Times*, August 22, 1965.

43. Leonard Koppett, "Los Angeles Regains First on Parker Homer in 11th," *New York Times*, August 22, 1965.

44. Leonard Koppett, "Marichal Hits Roseboro with Bat and Starts Brawl," *New York Times*, August 23, 1965.

45. Koufax and Linn, *Koufax*, 249.

46. Hirsch, *Willie Mays*, 436.

47. *Ibid.*

48. Bob Hunter, "Dodgers Seething Over Marichal Attack," *The Sporting News*, September 4, 1965, 8.

49. Leonard Koppett, "Marichal Hits Roseboro with Bat and Starts Brawl," *New York Times*, August 23, 1965.

50. Koufax and Linn, *Koufax*, 249.

51. Jack McDonald, "Team Taking a Heavy Rap, Giants Claim," *The Sporting News*, September 4, 1965, 20.

52. Frank Finch, "Mays Breaks Up the Fight—and the Ball Game, 4–3," *Los Angeles Times*, August 23, 1965.

53. Bob Hunter, "Dodgers Seething Over Marichal Attack," *The Sporting News*, September 4, 1965, 7.

54. Gerald Eskenazi, "PENALTY TO COST PITCHER 2 STARTS," *New York Times*, August 24, 1965.

55. C.C. Johnson Spink, "Too Soft a Sentence for Marichal," *The Sporting News*, September 4, 1965, 14.

56. Frank Finch, "DODGER REACTION: 'RIDICULOUS ... A JOKE,'" *Los Angeles Times*, August 24, 1965.

57. *Ibid.*

58. *Ibid.*

59. *Ibid.*

60. Frank Finch, "Giles Bans Marichal From L.A. Series," *Los Angeles Times*, September 1, 1965.

61. Joseph Durso, "Mets Top Dodgers 3rd Time in Row, 5–2," *New York Times*, August 27, 1965.

62. Frank Finch, "AHEAD OF RECORD PACE, BUT: MAURY FEELS AILING LEG WILL KEEP HIM FROM BREAKING MARK," *Los Angeles Times*, August 31, 1965.

Chapter 8

1. Bob Hunter, "Now Sandy Stands Alone on Summit," *The Sporting News*, September 25, 1965, 3.

2. Frank Finch, "Dodgers Fall Out of Lead, Drop Two," *Los Angeles Times*, September 2, 1965.

3. Associated Press, "Roseboro Sues Giants, Marichal for $110,000," *The Morning Record*, September 2, 1965.

4. Frank Finch, "Osteen Beats Bucs to Put Dodgers Back on Top," *Los Angeles Times*, September 3, 1965.

5. United Press International, "MARICHAL COMEBACK: BOOS AND BEATING," *Los Angeles Times*, September 3, 1965.

6. Frank Finch, "GILLIAM'S TRIPLE TOPPLES ASTROS, 4–2," *Los Angeles Times*, September 6, 1965.

7. Bill Becker, "HIT BY DAVENPORT OFF REED DECIDES," *New York Times*, September 7, 1965.

8. Hirsch, *Willie Mays*, 442.

9. Frank Finch, "Dodgers Refuse to Win—It's OK with Giants," *Los Angeles Times*, September 7, 1965.

10. Bill Becker, "HART'S HOME RUN PROVES DECISIVE," *New York Times*, September 8, 1965.

11. Frank Finch, "Jim Hart's Homer Wrecks Dodgers," *Los Angeles Times*, September 8, 1965.

12. Bob Hunter, "Fans Have Doubts—But Dodgers Refuse to Get Jitters," *The Sporting News*, September 25, 1965, 4.

13. Koufax and Linn, *Koufax*, 252.

14. Associated Press, "Koufax of Dodgers Hurls Perfect Game," *New York Times*, September 10, 1965.

15. Frank Finch, "It's a Perfect Night at Dodger Stadium," *Los Angeles Times*, September 10, 1965.

16. Bob Hunter, "Hendley Forgotten Hero in Hurrahs to Dodgers' Dandy," *The Sporting News*, September 25, 1965, 3.

17. Koufax and Linn, *Koufax*, 252.

18. Vin Scully, "Sandy Koufax perfect game," *You Tube* (2009): https://www.youtube.com/watch?v=9uozLFsEPu8.

19. Bob Hunter, "Now Sandy Stands Alone on Summit," *The Sporting News*, September 25, 1965, 4.

20. Frank Finch, "DODGERS 3½ BACK AS KOUFAX NIPPED," *Los Angeles Times*, September 15, 1965.

21. Bob Hunter, "Wills to Rest Occasionally, Wear Heavy Pads Next Year," *The Sporting News*, October 2, 1965, 8.

22. Edward Prell, "No Excuses by Koufax—Williams Hit Good Pitch," *Chicago Tribune*, September 15, 1965.

23. Edward Prell, "CUBS BEAT DODGERS, 8–6: WOE! WOE! WOE!" *Chicago Tribune*, September 16, 1965.

24. Frank Finch, "Dodgers Bloodied—but Spirits High," *Los Angeles Times*, September 16, 1965.

25. Gary Estwick, "Bill Faul Was a Baseball Classic," *Cincinnati Enquirer*, February 22, 2002.

26. Frank Finch, "'Big D' Wins 20th as Dodgers Gain," *Los Angeles Times*, September 18, 1965.

27. Frank Finch, "KOUFAX GETS HIS RUN, WINS NO. 23," *Los Angeles Times*, September 19, 1965.

28. Bob Hunter, "Dodgers Refuse Funeral Roles, There's Still Some Kick Left," *The Sporting News*, October 2, 1965, 8.

29. *Ibid.*

30. Frank Finch, "DODGERS BAG SWEEP, BUT FAIL TO GAIN," *Los Angeles Times*, September 20, 1965.

31. Edward Prell, "Dodgers Call on Two Aces," *Chicago Tribune*, September 21, 1965.

32. Frank Finch, "Dodgers Win, 3–1, Cut Giants' Lead to 3," *Los Angeles Times*, September 22, 1965.

33. Koufax and Linn, *Koufax*, 253.

34. Bob Hunter, "'Go-Go-Go!' Fans Chant—and Wills Keeps 'Em Happy," *The Sporting News*, October 9, 1965, 12.

35. Frank Finch, "L.A. Beats Milwaukee in 11th, 7–6," *Los Angeles Times*, September 23, 1965.

36. Frank Finch, "DODGERS HAVE PENNANT (LE)FEBVRE, 4–3," *Los Angeles Times*, September 25, 1965.

37. Frank Finch, "Koufax Cracks Feller Record," *Los Angeles Times*, September 26, 1965.

38. Bob Hunter, "Koufax New King of Ks, Tops Feller's Season Mark," *The Sporting News*, October 9, 1965, 12.

39. Frank Finch, "Drysdale Shuts Cardinals Out for 22nd Win, 1–0," *Los Angeles Times*, September 27, 1965.

40. Charles Maher, "IT'S NEW RACE—DODGERS

CATCH GIANTS," *Los Angeles Times*, September 27, 1965.

41. Frank Finch, "DODGERS' WILLIE KEEPS 'EM UP THERE," *Los Angeles Times*, September 28, 1965.

42. Frank Finch, "DESTINY'S DODGERS ON TOP— L.A. NIPS CINCY IN 12TH, 2–1," *Los Angeles Times*, September 29, 1965.

43. Edward Prell, "DODGERS WIN IN 12TH, TAKE OVER LEAD," *Chicago Tribune*, September 29, 1965.

44. Paul Zimmerman, "Dodgers Make 'Whoopee' Like Kings," *Los Angeles Times*, September 28, 1965.

45. Frank Finch, "SANDY MAKES IT TWO UP AND FOUR TO GO," *Los Angeles Times*, September 30, 1965.

46. Frank Finch, "DODGERS WON'T LET UP, BLANK BRAVES," *Los Angeles Times*, October 1, 1965.

47. Frank Finch, "DODGERS STALLED, 2–0 BY BRAVES," *Los Angeles Times*, October 2, 1965.

48. James Enright, "Willie Fights 'Delayed Fatigue' by Passing Up Swatting Drills," *The Sporting News*, October 9, 1965, 34.

49. Koufax and Linn, *Koufax*, 254.

50. *Ibid.*

51. Frank Finch, "IT'S ALL OVER! The Dodger Way: 2 Hits+Sandy=Flag," *Los Angeles Times*, October 3, 1965.

52. Frank Finch, "Everyone Gets in Dodgers' Finale," *Los Angeles Times*, October 4, 1965.

53. Robert B. Semple, Jr., "Johnson Signs New Immigration Bill," *New York Times*, October 1965.

54. Robert A. Rosenbaum, *The Penguin Encyclopedia of American History* (New York: Penguin Reference, 2003), 169.

Chapter 9

1. Bob Burnes, "Sandy, Lou, and Jim Crush Twins' Last, Desperate Bid," *The Sporting News*, October 23, 1965, 31.

2. *Ibid.*

3. Joseph Wancho, "Mudcat Grant," *Society for Baseball Research*, http://sabr.org/bioproj/person/ba7b1b4d.

4. Regis McAuley, "Mudcat Seeks New Pigeons Following Transfer to Twins," *The Sporting News*, June 27, 1964, 17.

5. Bob Burnes, "Twin Bats Bomb Drysdale," *The Sporting News*, October 23, 1965, 21.

6. Frank Finch, "GRANT SHOWS 'EM WITH BAT, TOO, 5–1," *Los Angeles Times*, October 14, 1965.

7. Frank Finch, "Koufax Out to Even Series Against Twins' Kaat Today," *Los Angeles Times*, October 7, 1965.

8. Joseph Durso, "Twins Beat Dodgers, 5–1, and Lead, 2–0, in Series," *New York Times*, October 8, 1965.

9. Bob Burnes, "Dodgers Shocked as Twins and Kaat Conquer Koufax," *The Sporting News*, October 23, 1965, 22.

10. Frank Finch, "No Joy in 'Mudville': Dodgers (Alias Mets) Strike Out," *Los Angeles Times*, October 8, 1965.

11. Joseph Durso, "Twins Beat Dodgers, 5–1, and Lead, 2–0, in Series," *New York Times*, October 8, 1965.

12. Shirley Povich, "Osteen's Five-Hitter Stops Twins, 4–0," *Washington Post*, October 10, 1965.

13. Max Nichols, "Camilio's Fastball Crackles— Back Surgery a Huge Success," *The Sporting News*, October 2, 1965, 9.

14. Bob Burnes, "Osteen Toys with Twins—Lefty's Long-Time Patsies," *The Sporting News*, October 23, 1965, 24.

15. Frank Finch, "HOME SWEET HOME—DODGERS WIN, 4–0," *Los Angeles Times*, October 10, 1965.

16. Bob Addie, "Experience with Senators Helps Osteen Fool Twins," *Washington Post*, October 10, 1965.

17. Joseph Durso, "Dodgers Beat Twins, 7–2, in 4th Game to Tie Series," *New York Times*, October 11, 1965.

18. Shirley Povich, "Dodgers Daze Twins, Even Series," *Washington Post*, October 11, 1965.

19. Shirley Povich, "Dodgers Win, 7–0, as Wills, Twins Collect 4 Hits," *Washington Post*, October 12, 1965.

20. Bob Burnes, "Koufax Slams the Door," *The Sporting News*, October 23, 1965, 27.

21. Arthur Daley, "It's Now a One-Game Series," *New York Times*, October 14, 1965.

22. Leonard Koppett, "TWINS TIE SERIES, BEAT DODGERS, 5–1," *New York Times*, October 14, 1965.

23. Frank Finch, "GRANT SHOWS 'EM WITH BAT, TOO, 5–1," *Los Angeles Times*, October 14, 1965.

24. Bob Burnes, "Ailing Mudcat Bad Medicine for Dodgers' Anemic Bats," *The Sporting News*, October 23, 1965, 28.

25. Paul Zimmerman, "Rain May Be Key to Alston's Choice," *Los Angeles Times*, October 14, 1965.

26. Koufax and Linn, *Koufax*, 262.

27. *Ibid.*

28. Frank Finch, "JOHNSON HOMERS, SANDY DOES REST," *Los Angeles Times*, October 15, 1965.

29. Leonard Koppett, "DODGERS TRIUMPH OVER TWINS, 2–0, AND TAKE SERIES," *New York Times*, October 15, 1965.

30. Koufax and Linn, *Koufax*, 265.

31. *Ibid.*, 267.

32. Frank Finch, "L.A. HAILS DODGERS," *Los Angeles Times*, October 15, 1965.

33. Billy Thompson, "Bluegrass Country Hails Lexington Lou," *The Sporting News*, November 6, 1965, 5.

Chapter 10

1. Oscar Kahan, "Dainty Dodgers at the Dish," *The Sporting News*, February 12, 1966, 20.

2. Chris Gutierrez, "1965 Dodgers Built on Pitching," *MLBwww*, June 25, 2005, http://m.mlb.com/news/article/1084072.

3. Maury Wills, *On the Run: The Never Dull and Often Shocking Life of Maury Wills* (New York: Carroll & Graff, 1991), 37.

Interlude

1. United Press International, "It's Unanimous! Koufax the Best," *New York Times*, November 4, 1965.

2. United Press International, "Mays Is Chosen Over Koufax as Most Valuable," *New York Times*, November 11, 1965.

3. Jim Enright, "Eckert, Baseball's New Boss, has a Standout Military Record," *The Sporting News*, November 27, 1965, 13.

4. Max Frankel, "Thousands Walk in Capital to Protest War in Vietnam," *New York Times*, November 28, 1965.

5. Earl Lawson, "Reds Swap Robby—Get Hurler Pappas," *The Sporting News*, December 18, 1965, 9.

6. Charles P. Korr, *The End of Baseball as We Knew It: The Players Union, 1960–81* (Urbana: University of Illinois Press, 2002), 15.

7. Marvin Miller, *A Whole Different Ball Game* (New York: A Birch Lane Press Book, 1991), 3.

8. *Ibid.*, 4.

9. Staff Writer, "Johnson Pledges Domestic Gains," *New York Times*, January 1, 1966.

10. Sam Pope Brewer, "That Asks Bombing Halt as Peace Initiative by U.S.," *New York Times*, January 1, 1966.

11. John Hess, "De Gaulle Urges U.S. to Quit War," *New York Times*, January 1, 1966.

12. "Vietnam—Escalation of the War," http://www.globalsecurity.org/military/ops/vietnam2-escalation.htm.

Chapter 11

1. Koufax and Linn, *Koufax*, 289.

2. Don Drysdale and Bob Verdi, *Once a Bum, Always a Dodger* (New York: St. Martin's Press, 1990) 132.

3. Buzzie Bavasi with Jack Olsen, "The Great Holdout," *Sports Illustrated*, May 15, 1967, 81.

4. Bob Hunter, "Dodger Road Show Lays Egg with Top Bananas Missing," *The Sporting News*, March 12, 1966, 12.

5. Koufax and Linn, *Koufax*, 285.

6. United Press International, "Dodgers Reject Demands of Koufax, Drysdale," *Washington Post*, February 28, 1966.

7. Bob Addie, "Collective Bargaining," *Washington Post*, March 2, 1966.

8. Sid Ziff, "Bavasi Digs In," *Los Angeles Times*, February 28, 1966.

9. Staff Writer, "Bavasi Digs In," *Los Angeles Times*, March 3, 1966.

10. Frank Finch, "Drysdale Keeping in Touch with Dodgertown Activities," *Los Angeles Times*, March 6, 1966.

11. Staff Writer, "Osteen Being Groomed as Starter in Opener," *Los Angeles Times*, March 9, 1966.

12. Charles Maher, "Wills Expects No Signing Trouble," *Los Angeles Times*, March 9, 1966.

13. Al Wolf, "Wills Spurns $75,000 Offer, Remains in L.A.," *Los Angeles Times*, March 12, 1966.

14. Frank Finch, "Wills Going to Camp, Will Talk with Bavasi," *Los Angeles Times*, March 14, 1966.

15. Frank Finch, "Wills Ends Holdout, Signs with Dodgers for $75,000," *Los Angeles Times*, March 16, 1966.

16. Jim Murray, "Sandy Eager to Play, Waits for Buzzie's Call," *Los Angeles Times*, March 17, 1966.

17. Staff Writer, "Koufax and Drysdale Sign Pacts—as Movie Actors," *Los Angeles Times*, March 19, 1966.

18. Staff Writer, "Koufax Peddles His Biography for Tidy Advance of $110,000," *Los Angeles Times*, March 19, 1966.

19. Frank Finch, "Year's Layoff Could End Careers for K&D," *Los Angeles Times*, March 19, 1966.

20. Charles Maher, "Big D Implies Duo Ready to Come to Terms," *Los Angeles Times*, March 22, 1966.

21. Charles Maher and Frank Finch, "Big D Implies Duo Ready to Come to Terms," *Los Angeles Times*, March 22, 1966.

22. Peter Bart, "Koufax-Drysdale Pitch: A Fight Against 'Slavery,'" *New York Times*, March 27, 1966.

23. Charles Maher, "L'Affaire Drysdale-Koufax: Villains or Heroes?" *Los Angeles Times*, March 27, 1966.

24. *Ibid.*

25. *Ibid.*

26. United Press International, "Koufax and Drysdale Warm Up for the Opening Scene," *New York Times*, March 29, 1966.

27. Staff Writer, "Twins-Dodgers," *The Sporting News*, April 16, 1966, 54.

28. Drysdale and Verdi, *Once a Bum, Always a Dodger*, 129–30.

29. Charles Maher, "Peace at Last! K&D Return to Fold," *Los Angeles Times*, March 31, 1966.

30. Buzzie Bavasi with Jack Olsen, "The Great Holdout," *Sports Illustrated*, May 15, 1967, 81.

31. Frank Finch, "Club Jubilant, Alston Expects Aces to Pitch During Season's First Week," *Los Angeles Times*, March 31, 1966.

32. Dick Kaegel, "Miller Confident Despite Players' Noisy Opposition," *The Sporting News*, March 26, 1966, 27.

33. United Press International, "Judge Cannon Quits as Player Representative," *Washington Post*, February 5, 1966.

34. Jerome Holtzman, "Miller Suggests Hike in Majors' $7,000 Minimum Player Salary," *The Sporting News*, April 16, 1966, 42.

35. Richard Goldstein, "Marvin Miller, Union Leader Who Changed Baseball, Dies at 95," *New York Times*, November 27, 2012.

36. United Press International, "DODGER STARS GIVE SIX RUNS IN DEBUT," *New York Times*, April 6, 1966.

37. Frank Finch, "It's a 'No-Hitter' for Sandy—and 9 Whiffs, Too!" *Los Angeles Times*, April 10, 1966.

Chapter 12

1. Associated Press, "ASTROS WIN, 7–6, ROUTING KOUFAX," *New York Times*, April 14, 1966.

2. Frank Finch, "Drysdale Goof Hastens Dodgers' Downfall, 8–5," *Los Angeles Times*, April 20, 1966.

3. Associated Press, "Writers Predict Reds and Twins Will Win Pennants," *Chicago Tribune*, April 9, 1966.

4. Joseph Durso, "JOHNSON TO MISS WASHINGTON GAME: Humphrey to Throw First Ball," *New York Times*, April 11, 1966.

5. Edwin L. Dale, Jr., "Humphrey Sees Cleveland Wipe Out Lead Created by Howard's Home Run," *New York Times*, April 12, 1966.

6. Staff Writer, "Ballplayers Pick Miller to Direct Association," *New York Times*, April 13, 1966.

7. United Press International, "OSTEEN, DODGERS, BEATS ASTROS, 3–2," *New York Times*, April 13, 1966.

8. Frank Finch, "Good Grief! Sandy Shelled," *Los Angeles Times*, April 14, 1966.

9. Charles Maher, "Sandy Began Slowly and Then Got Worse," *Los Angeles Times*, April 14, 1966.

10. Bob Hunter, "Regan 'Mr. Regal' of L.A. Blue Berets," *The Sporting News*, September 3, 1966, 3.

11. *Ibid.*

12. Jim Murray, "Phil Regan—The Man Who Came to Dinner," *The Sporting News*, September 17, 1966, 2.

13. Bob Hunter, "L.A.'s New Big D Sutton Death to Foes," *The Sporting News*, May 14, 1966, 3.

14. *Ibid.*

15. Frank Finch, "Scouts' Sales Talk Landed Don Sutton," *Los Angeles Times*, July 7, 1966.

16. Bob Hunter, "L.A.'s New Big D Sutton Death to Foes," *The Sporting News*, May 14, 1966, 6.

17. Staff Writer, "Don Sutton Celebrated His Twenty-First Birthday," *The Sporting News*, April 16, 1966, 51.

18. Staff Writer, "Don Sutton Completed the 6–0 Victory," *The Sporting News*, April 23, 1966, 32.

19. Bob Hunter, "L.A.'s New Big D Sutton Death to Foes," *The Sporting News*, May 14, 1966, 3, 6.

20. Frank Finch, "Astros' Staub Nips Dodgers Again, 4–2," *Los Angeles Times*, April 15, 1966.

21. Staff Writer, "Durocher Signs Three-Year Contract as Manager of Cubs," *New York Times*, October 26, 1965.

22. Frank Finch, "Dodgers Win on Lefebvre Homer," *Los Angeles Times*, April 16, 1966.

23. Edward Prell, "Lefebvre's 4th Home Run Beats Cubs, 4–2," *Chicago Tribune*, April 16, 1966.

24. Richard Dozer, "DODGERS WIN BEHIND OSTEEN," *Chicago Tribune*, April 17, 1966.

25. Frank Finch, "Claude Shows He's Dodgers' Top Banana," *Los Angeles Times*, April 17, 1966.

26. Frank Finch, "Sandy and Friends Make Cubs' Visit Complete Bust, 5–0," *Los Angeles Times*, April 18, 1966.

27. Associated Press, "Astros Lose to Dodgers on Nylon!" *Chicago Tribune*, April 19, 1966.

28. Frank Finch, "Dodgers Belt Roberts, Win One for Sutton," *Los Angeles Times*, April 19, 1966.

29. Frank Finch, "Drysdale Goof Hastens Dodgers' Downfall, 8–5," *Los Angeles Times*, April 20, 1966.

30. Associated Press, "OSTEEN WINS 3RD, DOWNING ASTROS," *New York Times*, April 21, 1966.

31. Frank Finch, "Dodgers' Bull Runs Wild in Dome," *Los Angeles Times*, April 21, 1966.

32. Richard Dozer, "DODGERS WHIP CUBS: KOUFAX FANS 11: ELLSWORTH BEATEN. 2 TO 1," *Chicago Tribune*, April 23, 1966.

33. Frank Finch, "Koufax Slipping, Gives up Run to Cubs in 2–1 Win," *Los Angeles Times*, April 23, 1966.

34. Richard Dozer, "JENKINS WAS HOCKEY STAR: But Found Baseball Paid Better," *Chicago Tribune*, April 24, 1966.

35. Frank Finch, "Dodger Short-Circuit Leaves 14 Stranded in 2–0 Defeat," *Los Angeles Times*, April 24, 1966.

36. Richard Dozer, "CUBS WIN WITH JENKINS, 2–0," *Chicago Tribune*, April 24, 1966.

37. Richard Dozer, "HOLTZMAN TAKES 1ST START WITH LIFT FROM KESSINGER," *Chicago Tribune*, April 25, 1966.

38. Frank Finch, "Ferrara Fumble Penalizes Dodgers," *Los Angeles Times*, April 25, 1966.

39. David E. Skelton, "Larry Jaster," SABR Baseball Biography Project, http://sabr.org/bioproj/person/5delbd44.

40. Frank Finch, "Dodgers Have a Blank Looo-ooo-oook Again," *Los Angeles Times*, April 26, 1966.

41. United Press International, "Jaster, Cardinals, Sets Back Dodgers on Seven Hits, 2–0," *New York Times*, April 26, 1966.

42. Jeff Angus, "Jim Gilliam," SABR Baseball Biography Project, http://sabr.org/bioproj/person/3c15c318.

43. United Press International, "Dodgers Return Jim Gilliam to Playing Roster," *Washington Post*, April 27, 1966.

44. Frank Finch, "Run-Drought Over as Dodgers Score Early," *Los Angeles Times*, April 27, 1966.

45. Associated Press, "Koufax Far Off Form but Keeps on Winning," *Washington Post*, April 27, 1966.

46. Frank Finch, "It's Sutton Death for Braves, 4–1," *Los Angeles Times*, April 28, 1966.

47. Associated Press, "Parker Drives in 3 Runs as Sutton Hurls 5-Hitter," *New York Times*, April 28, 1966.

48. Frank Finch, "All's Well; Dodgers' Big D Notches First Win," *Los Angeles Times*, April 29, 1966.

49. Frank Finch, "Dodgers Barely Win It with Fairly," *Los Angeles Times*, April 30, 1966.

50. Associated Press, "RALLY BY DODGERS DEFEATS REDS, 3–2," *New York Times*, April 30, 1966.

51. United Press International, "DODGERS' KOUFAX BOWS TO REDS, 3–1," *New York Times*, April 30, 1966.

52. Frank Finch, "SANDY SLIPS A LITTLE ... AND CINCY SLIDES ON BY," *Los Angeles Times*, May 1, 1966.

53. Charles Maher, "Sandy Loses His Concentration and the Game on a Single Pitch," *Los Angeles Times*, May 1, 1966.

54. Frank Finch, "Dodger 'Kid' Stifles Cincy," *Los Angeles Times*, May 2, 1966.

55. Associated Press, "SUTTON, DODGERS, DEFEATS REDS, 3–0," *New York Times*, May 2, 1966.

56. Charles Maher, "Drysdale Blitzed Because of .077 Hitter," *Los Angeles Times*, May 4, 1966.

57. Frank Finch, "Marichal's Magic Works on Dodgers Again, 8–1," *Los Angeles Times*, May 4, 1966.

58. Associated Press, "Marichal Yields 4 Hits in 8–1 Victory—Drysdale Routed," *New York Times*, May 4, 1966.

59. Associated Press, "Mays Wallops Record No. 512 As Giants Subdue Dodgers, 6–1," *New York Times*, May 5, 1966.

60. Hirsch, *Willie Mays*, 460.

61. Frank Finch, "Mays Hits 512th Homer; Dodgers Hit the Skids," *Los Angeles Times*, May 5, 1966.

62. Frank Finch, "Koufax Routed as Giants Win Third Straight, 9–8," *Los Angeles Times*, May 6, 1966.

63. Sid Ziff, "We Want Wills!" *Los Angeles Times*, May 6, 1966.

64. Charles Maher, "Dodgers Paying Stiff Price Now for Big Holdout," *Los Angeles Times*, May 6, 1966.

65. *Ibid.*

66. United Press International, "REDS, WITH PAPPAS, DOWN DODGERS, 7–1," *New York Times*, May 7, 1966.

67. Frank Finch, "Skidding Dodgers Bombed Again," *Los Angeles Times*, May 7, 1966.

68. United Press International, "Lefebvre Blasts 2 Homers as Dodgers Rout Reds, 14–2," *Washington Post*, May 8, 1966.

69. Frank Finch, "Dodger Bombers Blast Five Homers, Humble Cincy, 14–2," *Los Angeles Times*, May 8, 1966.

70. Frank Finch, "Dodgers Can't Get Show on the Road; Lose to Reds, 2–1," *Los Angeles Times*, May 9, 1966.

71. United Press International, "Giants Trade Cepeda, a Hitter, To Cards for Sadecki, a Pitcher," *New York Times*, May 9, 1966.

72. Associated Press, "Dodgers Trade Podres to Tigers," *Washington Post*, May 10, 1966.

73. Charles Maher, "DODGER DEAL TURNS PODRES INTO TIGER," *Los Angeles Times*, May 10, 1966.

74. Frank Finch, "Dodgers 'Steal' One, 6–1," *Los Angeles Times*, May 11, 1966.

75. United Press International, "Dodgers Steal 6 Bases," *New York Times*, May 11, 1966.

76. Associated Press, "Dodgers Top Phils, 5–0," *New York Times*, May 12, 1966.

77. Frank Finch, "SUTTON SLINGS, SWATS DODGERS TO 5–0 ROMP," *Los Angeles Times*, May 12, 1966.

78. United Press International, "DODGERS LOSE TO BUNNING, PHILLIES, 5 TO 1," *Chicago Tribune*, May 12, 1966.

79. Frank Finch, "PHIL 'SLUGGERS' GROAT, BUNNING BOMB DRYSDALE," *Los Angeles Times*, May 13, 1966.

80. Frank Finch, "Another Famous Flinger, Fryman of Bucs, Tops Dodgers," *Los Angeles Times*, May 14, 1966.

81. Associated Press, "Triple by Clemente Helps Fryman Gain Triumph," *New York Times*, May 14, 1966.

82. Bob Hunter, "Lineup Card Biz Booms as L.A. Injuries Rocket," *The Sporting News*, May 28, 1966, 12.

83. Frank Finch, "Pirates Play Long Ball, but Koufax Achieves 5th Win," *Los Angeles Times*, May 15, 1966.

84. Associated Press, "KOUFAX TOPS PIRATES, 4–1," *New York Times*, May 15, 1966.

85. Associated Press, "DODGERS' 6-HITTER TOPS PIRATES, 3–1," *New York Times*, May 16, 1966.

86. Frank Finch, "Sutton Feasts on Bucs with Regan's Help, 3–1," *Los Angeles Times*, May 16, 1966.

Chapter 13

1. Maury Wills, "No Club Can Stop Dodgers," *Los Angeles Times*, June 12, 1966.

2. Frank Finch, "Dodgers Take Chances—and Giants—in 13th," *Los Angeles Times*, May 18, 1966.

3. Associated Press, "Parker Scores in 13th on Wild Throw by Brown," *New York Times*, May 18, 1966.

4. Frank Finch, "Bumbling Dodgers (4 Errors) Boot One," *Los Angeles Times*, May 19, 1966.

5. Associated Press, "Bad Fielding Plagues Dodgers," *Washington Post*, May 20, 1966.

6. Associated Press, "LOS ANGELES ACE FANS 10, WALKS 2," *New York Times*, May 20, 1966.

7. Bob Hunter, "Sandy Is Stepping on Gas—Curve Is Razor Sharp," *The Sporting News*, June 4, 1966, 8.

8. Frank Finch, "Sandy Blanks Giants, 4–0, on 3 Singles," *Los Angeles Times*, May 20, 1966.

9. United Press International, "Pirates Score 5 Runs in First to Turn Back Dodgers, 7–3," *New York Times*, May 21, 1966.

10. Frank Finch, "Pirates Knock Out Sutton in Hurry, Drub Dodgers, 7–3," *Los Angeles Times*, May 21, 1966.

11. Frank Finch, "Bumbling Dodgers (4 Errors) Boot One," *Los Angeles Times*, May 21, 1966.

12. Frank Finch, "Wills' Single in 12th Gives Perranoski First Win of Year," *Los Angeles Times*, May 22, 1966.

13. Frank Finch, "Veale Too Tough on Dodger Batters," *Los Angeles Times*, May 23, 1966.

14. Frank Finch, "No, It's Fair—Dodgers Win, 3–2," *Los Angeles Times*, May 24, 1966.

15. Associated Press, "'Weirdest Play' Helps Dodgers Nudge Pirates," *Washington Post*, May 25, 1966.

16. Bob Hunter, "Plans Completed for Dodger Post-Season Tour of Japan," *The Sporting News*, June 4, 1966, 8.

17. Walter O'Malley—The Official Website, http://www.walteromalley.com/docu_detail.php?gallery=1&set=19&docuID=224&pageNum=1.

18. Associated Press, "Fairly's Homer Decisive," *New York Times*, May 25, 1966.

19. Frank Finch, "Dodgers Accelerate in the Clutch, 3–2," *Los Angeles Times*, May 25, 1966.

20. Frank Finch, "Mets Just What Osteen Needed," *Los Angeles Times*, May 28, 1966.

21. Joseph Durso, "KOUFAX IS VICTOR: Gains 8th Triumph on 3-Hitter," *New York Times*, May 29, 1966.

22. Frank Finch, "Koufax Toys with Mets, Snares 5th in Row, 7–1," *Los Angeles Times*, May 29, 1966.

23. Frank Finch, "Dodgers Lose to (and Like) Mets," *Los Angeles Times*, May 30, 1966.

24. Joseph Durso, "Mets Get 3 Runs in 9th to Top Dodgers, 7–6," *New York Times*, May 30, 1966.

25. Frank Finch, "Wills Homers as Slugging Dodgers Maul Braves, 10–6," *Los Angeles Times*, May 31, 1966.

26. Associated Press, "Drysdale Leads Way," *New York Times*, May 31, 1966.

27. Frank Finch, "'What's Wrong?' Cries Bragan as L.A. Wins Again," *Los Angeles Times*, June 1, 1966.

28. Associated Press, "Koufax of Dodgers Wins Ninth with 1–0 Triumph Over Cards," *New York Times*, June 2, 1966.

29. Frank Finch, "Sandy, Willie D. Combine to Beat Cards," *Los Angeles Times*, June 2, 1966.

30. Frank Finch, "Sutton, Perranoski Combine for Another Dodger Shutout," *Los Angeles Times*, June 3, 1966.

31. Associated Press, "DODGERS WIN 9th OF LAST 10 GAMES, 2–0," *Chicago Tribune*, June 3, 1966.

32. Frank Finch, "Mets Slip 6–2 Loss to Dodgers and Big D," *Los Angeles Times*, June 4, 1966.

33. Joseph Durso, "WILLIE DAVIS HURT—Dodgers' Johnson Is Also Injured," *New York Times*, June 5, 1966.

34. Frank Finch, "Johnson, W. Davis Hurt; L.A. Wins," *Los Angeles Times*, June 5, 1966.

35. Joseph Durso, "LOS ANGELES ACE TAKES 7TH IN ROW," *New York Times*, June 6, 1966.

36. Frank Finch, "Dodgers Can't Win 2 with 18 Runs," *Los Angeles Times*, June 6, 1966.

37. Frank Finch, "Dodgers Act Like Giants, Club Cubs," *Los Angeles Times*, June 8, 1966.

38. Richard Dozer, "CUBS BEATEN, 8–6, IN 10TH," *Chicago Tribune*, June 8, 1966.

39. Frank Finch, "Cub 'Gopher' Drysdale in a Big Way, 8–1s," *Los Angeles Times*, June 9, 1966.

40. Richard Dozer, "Cubs Rout Dodgers, 8 to 1," *Chicago Tribune*, June 9, 1966.

41. Frank Finch, "KOUFAX LIFTS DODGERS INTO 1ST PLACE," *Los Angeles Times*, June 11, 1966.

42. Associated Press, "KOUFAX 4-HITTER BEATS GIANTS, 6–1," *New York Times*, June 11, 1966.

43. Frank Finch, "Hot Dodgers Have Too Much Wills-Power for Giants," *Los Angeles Times*, June 12, 1966.

44. Associated Press, "TWO RUNS IN NINTH DOWN GIANTS, 4–2," *New York Times*, June 12, 1966.

45. Charles Maher, "Dodger-Giant Game Dull ... Just Like Park," *Los Angeles Times*, June 13, 1966.

46. Fred P. Graham, "High Court Puts New Curb on Powers of the Police to Interrogate Suspects, 4–2," *New York Times*, June 14, 1966.

47. Tony Mauro, *Landmark Cases: 12 Historic Supreme Court Decisions* (Washington: CQ Press, 2015), 93.

Chapter 14

1. Associated Press, "Koufax Not Satisfied with Form Despite Winning 11 of 13 Games," *Washington Post*, June 16, 1966.

2. Associated Press, "GIANTS SET BACK DODGERS, 4 TO 1," *New York Times*, June 18, 1966.

3. Charles Maher, "KOUFAX RIGHTS DODGERS' SINKING SHIP," *Los Angeles Times*, June 19, 1966.

4. Associated Press, "KOUFAX TRIUMPHS OVER GIANTS, 3–2," *New York Times*, June 19, 1966.

5. Associated Press, "DODGER RUN IN 8TH BEATS GIANTS, 2–1," *New York Times*, June 20, 1966.

6. Charles Maher, "DRYSDALE LENDS HAND—BUT AS BATTER, 2–1," *Los Angeles Times*, June 20, 1966.

7. Frank Finch, "Shannon (The Cannon) Shoots Down Koufax," *Los Angeles Times*, July 2, 1966.

8. Frank Finch, "Osteen Wins 10th—with Help of Regan and Fumbling Cards," *Los Angeles Times*, July 3, 1966.

9. Frank Finch, "Jaster Tosses Sparkler and Dodgers Burned," *Los Angeles Times*, July 4, 1966.

10. United Press International, "JASTER OF CARDS TOPS DODGERS, 2–0," *New York Times*, July 4, 1966.

11. Wayne Minshew, "Hats Off! Tony Cloninger," *The Sporting News*, July 16, 1966, 41.

12. Associated Press, "Dodgers Turn Back Reds, 2–1, on Single by Roseboro in Sixth," *New York Times*, July 5, 1966.

13. Frank Finch, "SHELL-SHOCKED SUTTON STAVES OFF REDS," *Los Angeles Times*, July 5, 1966.

14. Frank Finch, "SANDY HITS 15, AHEAD OF DIZZY'S PACE," *Los Angeles Times*, July 6, 1966.

15. Paul Zimmerman, "Sandy Winner the Hard Way," *Los Angeles Times*, July 6, 1966.

16. United Press International, "DODGERS' OSTEEN DEFEATS REDS, 1–0," *New York Times*, July 7, 1966.

17. Frank Finch, "OSTEEN ZEROES IN (1–0) ON REDS," *Los Angeles Times*, July 7, 1966.

18. Associated Press, "Dodger Run in 8th Beats Braves, 3–2," *New York Times*, July 8, 1966.

19. Associated Press, "Lemaster Hurls 5-Hitter to Gain Seventh Victory," *New York Times*, July 11, 1966.

20. Richard Dozer, "MELE'S GLAD ROBINSON IS HIS FOR ONCE," *Chicago Tribune*, July 11, 1966.

21. James Enright, "Owners Again Reject Player Fund Proposal," *The Sporting News*, July 23, 1966, 7.

22. Bob Addie, "Wills' Hit in 10th Beats AL All-Stars," *Washington Post*, July 13, 1966.

23. Leonard Koppett, "M'CARVER SCORES TO TOP AMERICANS," *New York Times*, July 13, 1966.

24. Frank Finch, "WHERE THERE'S A WILLS THERE'S A WIN," *Los Angeles Times*, July 13, 1966.

25. Richard Dozer, "Santo Calls B. Robinson 'The Greatest,'" *Chicago Tribune*, July 13, 1966.

26. Joseph Durso, "JOHNSON BELTS HOMER OFF SHAW," *New York Times*, July 14, 1966.

27. Frank Finch, "Mets' Reject Stuart Returns to Spark Dodgers' 4–3 Win," *Los Angeles Times*, July 16, 1966.

28. Associated Press, "Wills Flies to LA for Knee X-Rays," *Washington Post*, July 17, 1966.

29. Frank Finch, "Single by Roseboro Gives Dodgers

Split with Philadelphia," *Los Angeles Times*, July 18, 1966.

30. Associated Press, "Short Wins on 2-Hitter, 3–0; Dodgers Top Phils in Second," *Washington Post*, July 18, 1966.

31. Associated Press, "Jackson of Phils Hurls 5-Hitter To Beat Koufax of Dodgers, 4–0," *New York Times*, July 19, 1966.

32. Frank Finch, "KOUFAX ON THE OTHER END, 0–4," *Los Angeles Times*, July 19, 1966.

33. Bob Hunter, "Bandaged Like a Mummy, Wills Lifts Dodgers," *The Sporting News*, August 6, 1966, 7.

34. Frank Finch, "Bucs Explode for 6 Runs, Rip Dodgers," *Los Angeles Times*, July 21, 1966.

35. Associated Press, "DODGERS WIN, 4–3, WITH 2-RUN 10TH," *New York Times*, July 22, 1966.

36. Frank Finch, "Kennedy's Hit (by Pitcher) Gives Dodgers 4–3 Victory," *Los Angeles Times*, July 22, 1966.

37. Joseph Durso, "FRIEND'S 8-HITTER FIRST '66 SHUTOUT," *New York Times*, July 23, 1966.

38. Frank Finch, "Sandy Not Sharp But Still Wins, 6–2," *Los Angeles Times*, July 24, 1966.

39. Joseph Durso, "MOELLER VICTOR IN SECOND GAME," *New York Times*, July 25, 1966.

40. Frank Finch, "Dodgers Give Mets Plenty o' Nothin'," *Los Angeles Times*, July 25, 1966.

41. Leonard Koppett, "MOELLER VICTOR IN SECOND GAME," *New York Times*, July 25, 1966.

42. Associated Press, "Dodger Rally Tops Phils, 6–3," *New York Times*, July 26, 1966.

43. Frank Finch, "SANDY FANS 16 PHILLIES, BUT ONLY DODGERS WIN," *Los Angeles Times*, July 28, 1966.

44. Jane Leavy, *Sandy Koufax: A Lefty's Legacy* (New York: HarperCollins, 2002), 228.

45. Associated Press, "Cardinals Top Dodgers, 3–1, on Jackson's 6-Hitter," *New York Times*, July 31, 1966.

46. Associated Press, "Dodgers Top Cards in 9th, Take First Place," *Washington Post*, August 1, 1966.

Chapter 15

1. Associated Press, "ASTROS WIN, 7–6, ROUTING KOUFAX," *New York Times*, April 14, 1966.

2. Associated Press, "Regan Wins as Koufax Goes Out for Pinch-Hitter in 8th," *New York Times*, August 2, 1966.

3. Frank Finch, "Mota Knocks L.A. Out of Lead, 6–5," *Los Angeles Times*, August 3, 1966.

4. Leonard Koppett, "Pittsburgh Ends Loss Streak at 4," *New York Times*, August 3, 1966.

5. Leonard Koppett, "Veale Strikes Out 11 as Pirates Take 2nd Place From Dodgers," *New York Times*, August 4, 1966.

6. Frank Finch, "Clemente's Homer Rips Dodgers, 3–1," *Los Angeles Times*, August 4, 1966.

7. Leonard Koppett, "PIRATES' 16 HITS SINK DODGERS, 8–1," *New York Times*, August 5, 1966.

8. Associated Press, "Koufax Hurls 6 Innings and Posts His 18th Victory," *New York Times*, August 6, 1966.

9. Bob Hunter, "Wills Cools Short Stop at Hot Sack," *The Sporting News*, August 20, 1966, 9.

10. Frank Finch, "Johnson, Kennedy Stars of Show in Dodgers' 4–3 Win," *Los Angeles Times*, August 7, 1966.

11. Associated Press, "LOS ANGELES WINS THIRD IN ROW, 14–3," *New York Times*, August 8, 1966.

12. Frank Finch, "Dodgers Blow 9–6 Lead in 9th, Fall to Third Place," *Los Angeles Times*, August 9, 1966.

13. Associated Press, "ATLANTA VICTOR ON 4 RUNS IN 9TH," *New York Times*, August 9, 1966.

14. United Press International, "Braves Jolt Koufax," *Chicago Tribune*, August 10, 1966.

15. Frank Finch, "Mathews' Homer Beats Koufax in 9th Inning, 2–1," *Los Angeles Times*, August 10, 1966.

16. Associated Press, "Koufax Loses, 2–1, on Homer in the Ninth," *New York Times*, August 10, 1966.

17. Frank Finch, "Atlanta Hands Dodgers Third Straight Loss, 3–1," *Los Angeles Times*, August 11, 1966.

18. Associated Press, "GILLIAMS ERROR LEADS TO DEFEAT," *New York Times*, August 11, 1966.

19. Robert Markus, "Cubs Score 2 in 9th to Beat Dodgers, 2–1," *Chicago Tribune*, August 13, 1966.

20. Frank Finch, "CUBS 'BOUNCE' BACK TO BEAT DODGERS," *Los Angeles Times*, August 13, 1966.

21. Frank Finch, "TOMMY D. UPSTAGES SANDY IN 6–1 WIN," *Los Angeles Times*, August 14, 1966.

22. Robert Markus, "CUBS SPLIT; MARATHON LASTS 8 HOURS!" *Chicago Tribune*, August 15, 1966.

23. Frank Finch, "L.A. Loses Finale in 10th after 14-Inning Victory," *Los Angeles Times*, August 15, 1966.

24. Robert Markus, "Cubs Score 2 in 9th to Beat Dodgers, 2–1," *Chicago Tribune*, August 13, 1966.

25. Associated Press, "Johnson's 2-Run Homer Helps Dodgers Turn Back Reds, 4–3," *New York Times*, August 16, 1966.

26. Frank Finch, "Sutton's 2-Hitter Stymies Cincy, 2–0," *Los Angeles Times*, August 17, 1966.

27. Frank Finch, "SANDY'S ELBOWS FLARES UP IN 5–1 LOSS," *Los Angeles Times*, August 18, 1966.

28. Associated Press, "Koufax Leaves Game in 5th After Injuring Elbow," *New York Times*, August 18, 1966.

29. Associated Press, "Koufax Hopes to Take Regular Turn Sunday," *Washington Post*, August 19, 1966.

30. *Ibid.*

31. Frank Finch, "Big D Comes Up with Big Win," *Los Angeles Times*, August 19, 1966.

32. United Press International, "Jaster of Cardinals Shuts Out Dodgers for 4th Time, 4–0," *New York Times*, August 20, 1966.

33. Frank Finch, "Cepeda Lends Bat—and Dodgers Pay," *Los Angeles Times*, August 21, 1966.

34. Associated Press, "CARDS WIN IN 13TH FROM DODGERS, 3–2," *New York Times*, August 21, 1966.

35. Associated Press, "Pain Severe; Koufax Thinks of Retirement," *Chicago Tribune*, August 21, 1966.

36. United Press International, "Sandy Throws; Aims to Start Tomorrow," *Chicago Tribune*, August 20, 1966.

37. Frank Finch, "KOUFAX OK, KO'S CARDINALS FOR NO. 20," *Los Angeles Times*, August 22, 1966.

38. United Press International, "Dodgers Set Back Giants, 4–0," *New York Times*, August 27, 1966.

39. Frank Finch, "KOUFAX SUBDUES GIANT SLUGGERS, 4–0," *Los Angeles Times*, August 27, 1966.

40. Frank Finch, "GIANTS HALT DODGERS, TAKE OVER FIRST," *Los Angeles Times*, August 28, 1966.

41. Bill Becker, "Mays, Hart Connect as Right-Hander Wins His 19th," *New York Times*, August 28, 1966.

42. Bill Becker, "PERRY IS BELTED FOR 3 HOME RUNS," *New York Times*, August 29, 1966.

43. Associated Press, "Beatles' Closing Concert on Coast Attracts 25,000," *New York Times*, August 31, 1966.

44. Frank Finch, "Lowly Mets Spoil Dodgers' Bid for Lead, 5–3," *Los Angeles Times*, August 30, 1966.

45. Joseph Durso, "SHAW GOES ROUTE WITH A 7-HITTER," *New York Times*, August 30, 1966.

46. Frank Finch, "Koufax Cooled, Dodgers Drop 2 Behind," *Los Angeles Times*, August 31, 1966.

47. Joseph Durso, "FRIEND'S PITCHING IN RELIEF EXCELS," *New York Times*, August 31, 1966.

48. Dick Kaegel, "King of the Jester—That's Bob Prince," *The Sporting News*, September 3, 1966, 12.

49. Frank Finch, "L.A. Blows Chances, Game to Bucs," *Los Angeles Times*, September 1, 1966.

50. Associated Press, "PITTSBURGH WINS WITH 4-RUN FIFTH," *New York Times*, September 1, 1966.

51. Jerry Hopkins and Danny Sugerman, *No One Here Gets Out Alive* (New York: Grand Central, 1980), 90.

Chapter 16

1. Joseph Durso, "Dodgers Fly High on Injured Wings," *New York Times*, September 15, 1966.

2. Joseph Durso, "Dodgers Fly High on Injured Wings," *New York Times*, September 15, 1966.

3. Frank Finch, "Fairly Paces Dodgers Again, 6–1," *Los Angeles Times*, September 3, 1966.

4. Frank Finch, "Sandy Spins No. 22, Dodgers Shoot into 2nd," *Los Angeles Times*, September 4, 1966.

5. Associated Press, "Dodgers Top Reds, 7–3, Behind Koufax and Take 2nd Place," *New York Times*, September 4, 1966.

6. Frank Finch, "'Fever' Fells Reds for Dodger Sweep," *Los Angeles Times*, September 5, 1966.

7. Frank Finch, "SUTTON HURT AS DODGERS WHIP GIANTS," *Los Angeles Times*, September 6, 1966.

8. Associated Press, "Injury Jinx Hits Dodgers' Pitching Staff," *Washington Post*, September 6, 1966.

9. Frank Finch, "Giants Batter Crippled Dodgers, 6–0," *Los Angeles Times*, September 7, 1966.

10. Leonard Koppett, "DASH FROM FIRST ON SINGLE DECIDES," *New York Times*, September 8, 1966.

11. Frank Finch, "DODGERS 'KICKED' OUT OF SECOND," *Los Angeles Times*, September 8, 1966.

12. Frank Finch, "OSTEEN SHOOTS 7–0 BLANK AT HOUSTON," *Los Angeles Times*, September 10, 1966.

13. Frank Finch, "DODGERS CLOSE IN ON FIRST, 1–0," *Los Angeles Times*, September 11, 1966.

14. Associated Press, "Dodgers Win, 1–0, in 10th," *New York Times*, September 11, 1966.

15. Edward Prell, "CUBS' 17-HIT SPREE ROUTS PERRY," *Chicago Tribune*, September 11, 1966.

16. Associated Press, "CARDS' RALLY TOPS PITTSBURGH, 6 TO 5," *New York Times*, September 11, 1966.

17. Frank Finch, "BLANK, BLANK—DODGERS LEAD LOOP," *Los Angeles Times*, September 12, 1966.

18. Associated Press, "Plunging Pirates Lose to Cards, 4–3," *Los Angeles Times*, September 12, 1966.

19. Edward Prell, "Bolin's 2–0 Triumph Halts Skid; Cubs Take First Game, 4 to 3," *Chicago Tribune*, September 12, 1966.

20. Joseph Durso, "Dodgers Rally to Turn Back Mets, 3–2, at L.A.," *New York Times*, September 13, 1966.

21. Charles Maher, "Sutton Reinjures Arm, May Be Out for Season," *Los Angeles Times*, September 14, 1966.

22. Joseph Durso, "Dodgers Rout Mets, 8–3, on 5-Run 5th," *New York Times*, September 14, 1966.

23. Frank Finch, "JOHNSON'S TWO HOMERS HELP DODGERS ROUT METS," *Los Angeles Times*, September 14, 1966.

24. Joseph Durso, "Dodgers Fly High on Injured Wings," *New York Times*, September 15, 1966.

25. Frank Finch, "PIRATES CALL ON LAW TO HANDCUFF DODGERS," *Los Angeles Times*, September 15, 1966.

26. Associated Press, "DODGERS EXPLODE EARLY, WHIP BUCS, 5–3," *New York Times*, September 16, 1966.

27. Frank Finch, "KOUFAX, JOHNSON KEEP DODGERS FLYING!" *Los Angeles Times*, September 17, 1966.

28. Edward Prell, "Dodgers, Koufax Trip Pirates, 5 to 1," *Chicago Tribune*, September 17, 1966.

29. Frank Finch, "Jackson Dampens L.A. Bid," *Los Angeles Times*, September 19, 1966.

30. Bill Becker, "Pirates Beat Giants, 3–1," *New York Times*, September 19, 1966.

31. Edward Prell, "PIRATES WIN; DODGERS BEAT PHILS," *Chicago Tribune*, September 20, 1966.

32. Joseph Durso, "MAYS'S PINCH HIT TIES GAME IN 9TH," *New York Times*, September 20, 1966.

33. Bill Becker, "KOUFAX WINS 25TH WITH FIVE-HITTE," *New York Times*, September 21, 1966.

34. Bob Hunter, "Dodgers Swoon-Proof with Sandy on the Hill," *The Sporting News*, September 8, 1966, 11.

35. Joseph Durso, "LAW HOLDS LOSERS TO EIGHT SINGLES," *New York Times*, September 21, 1966.

36. Frank Finch, "DODGERS SADDER BUT 'WISER' TEAM, 3–2," *Los Angeles Times*, September 22, 1966.

37. Jon Hall, "Marichal Strikes Blow for Dodgers in 6–5 Triumph," *Los Angeles Times*, September 22, 1966.

38. Associated Press, "Baltimore Tops Athletics by 6–1," *New York Times*, September 23, 1966.

39. Frank Finch, "DODGERS FLYING HIGH, WHIP CUBS TWICE," *Los Angeles Times*, September 24, 1966.

40. Charles Maher, "Pirates Come Back Slugging—Veale Wins, 3–0," *Los Angeles Times*, September 24, 1966.

41. Richard Dozer, "CUBS' ROOKIE TRIUMPHS, 4–0," *Chicago Tribune*, September 25, 1966.

42. Charles Maher, "DODGERS' LOSS (4–0) IS PIRATES' GAIN," *Los Angeles Times*, September 25, 1966.

43. Associated Press, "Giants Beat Astros with 5-Run 13th," *Washington Post*, September 25, 1966.

44. Richard Dozer, "HOLTZMAN'S 2-HITTER BEATS DODGERS," *Chicago Tribune*, September 26, 1966.

45. Frank Finch, "Cub Rookie's Two-Hitter Nips Koufax," *Los Angeles Times*, September 26, 1966.

46. Joseph Durso, "Dodgers Down Cards, 6–3, and Lead by 2½ Games," *New York Times*, September 27, 1966.

47. Charles Maher, "Phils Edge Bucs in 11th," *Los Angeles Times*, September 27, 1966.

48. Joseph Durso, "Dodgers Bow, 2–0, and Lead Is Cut to Game and a Half as Pirates Take Two," *New York Times*, September 29, 1966.

49. Frank Finch, "JASTER DERAILS DODGER PENNANT PUSH," *Los Angeles Times*, September 29, 1966.

50. Leonard Koppett, "PITTSBURGH BEATS PHILS, 2–1 AND 4–2," *New York Times*, September 29, 1966.

51. Joseph Durso, "Left-Hander Sets Strikeout Mark," *New York Times*, September 30, 1966.

52. Frank Finch, "Koufax Lifts Dodgers 2 Games Ahead," *Los Angeles Times*, September 30, 1966.

53. Richard Dozer, "Koufax Wins, Dodgers Lead by Two," *Chicago Tribune*, September 30, 1966.

Chapter 17

1. Charles Maher, "LIFELESS CLUB—Dodgers Unable to Get Interested in World Series," *Los Angeles Times*, October 8, 1966.

2. Richard Dozer, "PHILS BEAT DODGERS 5–3; LEAD CUT TO 1½," *Chicago Tribune*, October 1, 1966.

3. Joseph Durso, "HOMER BY WHITE IS DECISIVE BLOW," *New York Times*, October 1, 1966.

4. Frank Finch, "PHILLIES SHORTEN DODGERS' LEAD TO 1½," *Los Angeles Times*, October 1, 1966.

5. Frank Finch, "Idle Dodgers 'Sleep-In' to Gain Tie," *Los Angeles Times*, October 2, 1966.

6. Charles Maher, "GIANTS WIN 2, KNOCK BUCS OUT OF RACE," *Los Angeles Times*, October 2, 1966.

7. Joseph Durso, "Long Watch on TV—DODGERS CLINCH TIE ON RAIN-OUT," *New York Times*, October 2, 1966.

8. Leonard Koppett, "Bolin Hurls One-Hitter; GIANTS TAKE PAIR AND OUST PIRATES," *New York Times*, October 2, 1966.

9. Richard Dozer, "KOUFAX PITCHES DODGERS TO PENNANT!" *Chicago Tribune*, October 3, 1966.

10. Shirley Povich, "Koufax Pitches Dodgers to Pennant, Wins 27th," *Washington Post*, October 3, 1966.

11. Bob Addie, "Koufax Is Human," *Washington Post*, October 4, 1966.

12. Associated Press, "Koufax Hurts Shoulder, but Will Hurl in Series," *New York Times*, October 3, 1966.

13. Dick Young, "Young Ideas by Dick Young," *The Sporting News*, October 15, 1966, 14.

14. Joseph Durso, "KOUFAX'S VICTORY IN FINALE DECIDES," *New York Times*, October 3, 1966.

15. Frank Finch, "SANDY ENDS THE AGONY—DODGERS DO IT!" *Los Angeles Times*, October 3, 1966.

16. Charles Maher, "LIFELESS CLUB—Dodgers Unable to Get Interested in World Series," *Los Angeles Times*, October 8, 1966.

17. Jane Leavy, *Sandy Koufax: A Lefty's Legacy* (New York: HarperCollins, 2002), 229.

18. Ibid., 16.

Chapter 18

1. Charles Maher, "Willie D: 'If I Can See Them, I Can Catch Them,'" *Los Angeles Times*, October 7, 1966.

2. Jim Murray, "The Dodger Story: A Classic Case of Ineptitude," *Los Angeles Times*, October 10, 1966.

3. Frank Finch, "Alston Agrees—Dodgers Have Edge," *Los Angeles Times*, October 4, 1966.

4. Warren Corbett, "Hank Bauer," *Society for Baseball Research*, http://www.baseball-reference.com/players/b/bauerha01.shtml.

5. Joseph Durso, "Orioles Beat Dodgers, 5–2, as the World Series Opens," *New York Times*, October 6, 1966.

6. Mark Armour, "Dave McNally," *Society for Baseball Research*, http://sabr.org/bioproj/person/11d59b62.

7. Paul Zimmerman, "How Will Dodgers Pitch to Robbie—Carefully!" *Los Angeles Times*, October 5, 1966.

8. Frank Finch, "BIG D (BUT IT'S DRABOWSKY) WINS, 5–2," *Los Angeles Times*, October 6, 1966.

9. Shirley Povich, "Drabowsky Strikes Out Six in Row," *Washington Post*, October 6, 1966.

10. Jon Hall, "Stunned Drabowsky Modest in Series Victory," *Los Angeles Times*, October 6, 1966.

11. Dick Kaegel, "Birds Sing Praises of Notes Written by Veteran Scouts," *The Sporting News*, October 29, 1966, 25.

12. Bob Burnes, "Moe Mows Down Dodgers," *The Sporting News*, October 22, 1966, 10.

13. Frank Finch, "Sandy Meets an 'Old' Fan—Palmer," *Los Angeles Times*, October 6, 1966.

14. Robert Lipsyte, "Palmer Thought of Shutout Before Game—Only Way to Beat Koufax," *New York Times*, October 7, 1966.

15. Joseph Durso, "Willie Davis, World Series Goat," *New York Times*, October 7, 1966.

16. Bob Burnes, "Davis' Three Boots Help Palmer Put Birds Two Up," *The Sporting News*, October 22, 1966, 9.

17. Jack Mann, "Those Happy Birds!" *Sports Illustrated*, October 17, 1966, 34.

18. Frank Finch, "A TRAGIC COMEDY—DODGERS LOSE, 6–0," *Los Angeles Times*, October 7, 1966.

19. Bob Addie, "Sun's Glare Blamed for Errors by Willie Davis," *Washington Post*, October 7, 1966.

20. Bob Burnes, "Davis' Three Boots Help Palmer Put Birds Two Up," *The Sporting News*, October 22, 1966, 11.

21. Charles Maher, "LIFELESS CLUB—Dodgers Unable to Get Interested in World Series," *Los Angeles Times*, October 8, 1966.

22. Don Gulbrandsen, ed., *Ballparks Yesterday and Today* (New York: Chartwell Books, 2007), 104.

23. Bob Burnes, "Bunker, Blair Boost Birds Nearer to Topmost Branch," *The Sporting News*, October 22, 1966.

24. *Ibid.*

25. Mike Huber, "Paul Blair," *Society for Baseball Research*, http://sabr.org/bioproj/person/f7f74810.

26. Shirley Povich, "Blair's Homer Gives Orioles 1–0 Victory, 3–0 Lead in Series," *Washington Post*, October 9, 1966.

27. Tom Adelman, *Black and Blue: Sandy Koufax, the Robinson Boys, and the World Series That Stunned America* (New York: Little, Brown, 2006), 177.

28. Joseph Durso, "Dodgers, Scoreless in 24 Straight Innings, Insist They Can Win 4 in Row," *New York Times*, October 9, 1966.

29. Bob Burnes, "Banners Rib the Dodgers," *The Sporting News*, October 22, 1966, 12.

30. Bob Burnes, "Orioles End Dodger Reign with Third Shutout in Row," *The Sporting News*, October 22, 1966, 12.

31. Bob Burnes, "Robby Sees Series Homers as His 'Greatest Thrills,'" *The Sporting News*, October 22, 1966, 12.

32. Frank Finch, "Robinson's Homer Puts Dodgers Out of Their Misery, 1–0," *Los Angeles Times*, October 10, 1966.

33. Leonard Koppett, "ORIOLES TRIUMPH OVER DODGERS, 1-0, TO SWEEP SERIES," *New York Times*, October 10, 1966.

34. Shirley Povich, "Orioles Sweep Series, Blank Dodgers Again," *Washington Post*, October 10, 1966.

35. Bob Burnes, "Orioles End Dodger Reign with Third Shutout in Row," *The Sporting News*, October 22, 1966, 12.

36. Bob Burnes, "Lou Went for Distance," *The Sporting News*, October 22, 1966, 13.

37. Bob Burnes, "Wrapping It Up," *The Sporting News*, October 22, 1966, 13.

38. Joseph Durso, "Humphrey Helps Cheer Up Dodgers in Dressing Room," *New York Times*, October 10, 1966.

39. Associated Press, "Joy in Baltimore Is Nearly a Riot," *New York Times*, October 10, 1966.

40. Associated Press, "Baltimore Wild for Orioles," *Chicago Tribune*, October 10, 1966.

Chapter 19

1. Frank Finch, "Wills 'Jumps' Tour to get Knee Treated," *Los Angeles Times*, October 28, 1966.

2. Charles Maher, "Wills Regrets Jumping Tour but Feels Career Imperiled," *Los Angeles Times*, November 12, 1966.

3. Associated Press, "Sutton Scratched From Dodgers' Trip," *Washington Post*, October 12, 1966.

4. Associated Press, "Alston Named Best in NL for 4th Time," *Washington Post*, October 13, 1966.

5. Charles Maher, "Wills Regrets Jumping Tour but Feels Career Imperiled," *Los Angeles Times*, November 12, 1966.

6. *Ibid.*

7. Frank Finch, "Wills 'Jumps' Tour to get Knee Treated," *Los Angeles Times*, October 28, 1966.

8. Charles Maher, "O'Malley Charges Wills 'Embarrassed' U.S.," *Los Angeles Times*, November 3, 1966.

9. Charles Maher, "Sportscaster 'Finds' Wills in Hawaii," *Los Angeles Times*, November 4, 1966.

10. Charles Maher, "Wills Regrets Jumping Tour but Feels Career Imperiled," *Los Angeles Times*, November 12, 1966.

11. Robert Trumbull, "Dodgers Drop 'Real' Series in Japan," *New York Times*, November 17, 1966.

Chapter 20

1. Sandy Koufax Press Conference video, https://www.youtube.com/watch?v=DD8vIBKof2k, November 18, 1966.

2. Charles Maher, "Koufax Quits Because of Ailing Arm," *Los Angeles Times*, November 19, 1966.

3. Bob Hunter, "One Bombshell After Another," *The Sporting News*, December 3, 1966, 41.

4. *Ibid.*

5. Sandy Koufax Press Conference video, https://www.youtube.com/watch?v=DD8vIBKof2k, November 18, 1966.

6. *Ibid.*

7. Associated Press, "Koufax, Dodger Pitching Star, Retires Because of Ailing Arm," *New York Times*, November 19, 1966.

8. Charles Maher, "Koufax Quits Because of Ailing Arm," *Los Angeles Times*, November 19, 1966.

9. *Ibid.*

10. Alston Alston with Jack Tobin, *A Year at a Time* (Waco: Word Books, 1976), 194.

11. Charles Maher, "Koufax Quits Because of Ailing Arm," *Los Angeles Times*, November 19, 1966.

12. Bob Hunter, "One Bombshell after Another," *The Sporting News*, December 3, 1966, 41.

13. Associated Press, "GAME'S LEADERS BEMOAN ITS LOSS," *New York Times*, November 19, 1966.

14. Jerome Holtzman, "Koufax Tagged by Holland as 'Greatest of Our Age,'" *The Sporting News*, December 3, 1966, 55.

Epilogue

1. Associated Press, "Koufax, Dodger Pitching Star, Retires Because of Ailing Arm," *New York Times*, November 19, 1966.

2. Joseph Durso, "Mets Trade Hunt, Hickman to Dodgers for Tommy Davis," *New York Times*, November 30, 1966.

3. Joseph Durso, "Dodgers Trade Wills to Pirates

for Bailey and Michael," *New York Times*, December 3, 1966.

4. Sid Ziff, "Wills' Mistake," *Los Angeles Times*, December 11, 1966.

5. Deane McGowen, "Retired Pitcher Gets Radio-TV Job," *New York Times*, December 30, 1966.

6. Frank Finch, "Koufax Signs $1 Million Pact as Commentator," *Los Angeles Times*, December 30, 1966.

7. Bill Becker, "Drysdale, Plagued by Shoulder Injury, Retires," *New York Times*, August 12, 1969.

8. Richard Lyons "Don Drysdale Is Dead at Age 56," *New York Times*, July 4, 1993.

9. Deane McGowen, "People in Sports," *New York Times*, February 23, 1973.

Bibliography

Books

Adelman, Tom. *Black and Blue: Sandy Koufax, the Robinson Boys, and the World Series That Stunned America.* New York: Little, Brown, 2006.

Alston, Alston, with Jack Tobin. *A Year at a Time.* Waco: Word Books, 1976.

Bavasi, Buzzie, and John Strege. *Off the Record.* Chicago: Contemporary Books, 1987.

Branch, Taylor. *The King Years: Historic Moment in the Civil Rights Movement.* New York: Simon & Schuster, 2013.

Branch, Taylor. *Parting the Waters: America in the King Years 1954–63.* New York: Simon & Schuster, 1988.

Dallek, Robert. *An Unfinished Life: John F. Kennedy 1917–1963.* New York: Little, Brown, 2003.

Daniel, Clifton, ed. *The 20th Century Day by Day.* New York: DK, 1999.

Delsohn, Steve. *True Blue: The Dramatic History of the Los Angeles Dodgers, Told by the Men Who Lived It.* New York: HarperCollins, 2001.

Drysdale, Don, and Bob Verdi. *Once a Bum, Always a Dodger.* New York: St. Martin's Press, 1990.

Endsley, Brian M. *Bums No More: The 1959 Los Angeles Dodgers, World Champions of Baseball.* Jefferson, NC: McFarland, 2009.

_____. *Finding the Left Arm of God: Sandy Koufax and the Los Angeles Dodgers, 1960–1963.* Jefferson, NC: McFarland, 2015.

Finch, Frank. *The Los Angeles Dodgers: The First Twenty Years.* Virginia Beach: Jordan & Company, 1977.

Gibson, Bob, and Pepe, Phil. *From Ghetto to Glory: The Story of Bob Gibson.* Englewood Cliffs, NJ: Prentice-Hall, 1968.

Goldblatt, Andrew. *The Giants and the Dodgers: Four Cities, Two Teams, One Rivalry.* Jefferson, NC: McFarland, 2003.

Gruver, Edward. *Koufax.* Dallas: Taylor, 2000.

Hirsch, James S. *Willie Mays: The Life, The Legend.* New York: Scribner's, 2010.

Gulbrandsen, Don, ed. *Ballparks Yesterday and Today.* New York: Chartwell Books, 2007.

Hopkins, Jerry, and Danny Sugarman. *No One Here Gets Out Alive.* New York: Grand Central, 1980.

Jacobson, Steve. *Carrying Jackie's Torch: The Players Who Integrated Baseball—and America.* Chicago: Lawrence Hill Books, 2007.

Kahn, Roger. *The Boys of Summer.* New York: Harper & Row, 1972.

Korr, Charles P. *The End of Baseball as We Knew It: The Players Union, 1960–81.* Urbana: University of Illinois Press, 2002.

Koufax, Sandy, and Ed Linn. *Koufax.* New York: Viking, 1966.

Leavy, Jane. *Sandy Koufax: A Lefty's Legacy.* New York: HarperCollins, 2002.

Leahy, Michael. *The Last Innocents.* New York: HarperCollins, 2016.

Mathews, Chris. *Jack Kennedy: Elusive Hero.* New York: Simon & Schuster, 2011.

Mauro, Tony. *Landmark Cases: 12 Historic Supreme Court Decisions.* Washington: CQ Press, 2015.

McCue, Andy. *Mover and Shaker: Walter O'Malley, the Dodgers, & Baseball's Westward Expansion.* Lincoln: University of Nebraska Press, 2014.

Miller, Marvin. *A Whole Different Ball Game.* New York: A Birch Lane Press Book, 1991.

Robinson, Frank and Al Silverman. *My Life is Baseball.* Garden City: Doubleday, 1968.

Rosenbaum, Robert A. *The Penguin Encyclopedia of American History.* New York: Penguin Reference, 2003.

Rosengren, John. *The Fight of Their Lives.* Guilford, CT: Lyons Press, 2014.

Schlesinger, Arthur M., Jr. *A Thousand Days.* Boston: Houghton Mifflin, 1965.

Shelton, Robert. *No Direction Home: The Life and Music of Bob Dylan.* Milwaukee: Backbeat Books, 2011.

Smith, Ron, ed. *Heroes of the Hall: Baseball's All-Time Best.* St. Louis: The Sporting News, 2002.

Snider, Duke, and Phil Pepe. *Few and Chosen: Defining Dodgers Greatness Across the Eras.* Chicago: Triumph Books, 2006.

Snyder, John. *Dodgers Journal: Year by Year & Day*

by Day with the Brooklyn & Los Angeles Dodgers Since 1984. Cincinnati: Clerisy Press, 2009.

Stout, Glenn, and Richard A. Johnson. *The Dodgers: 120 Years of Dodgers Baseball*. New York: Houghton Mifflin, 2004.

Travers, Steven. *Dodgers Past & Present*. Minneapolis: MVP Books, 2009.

Whittington, Richard. *Illustrated History of the Dodgers*. Chicago: Triumph Books, 2005.

Wills, Maury. *On the Run: The Never Dull and Often Shocking Life of Maury Wills*. New York: Carroll & Graff, 1991.

Newspapers

Chicago Daily Tribune
Los Angeles Times
New York Times
Washington Post

Index

Numbers in **_bold italics_** indicate pages with illustrations